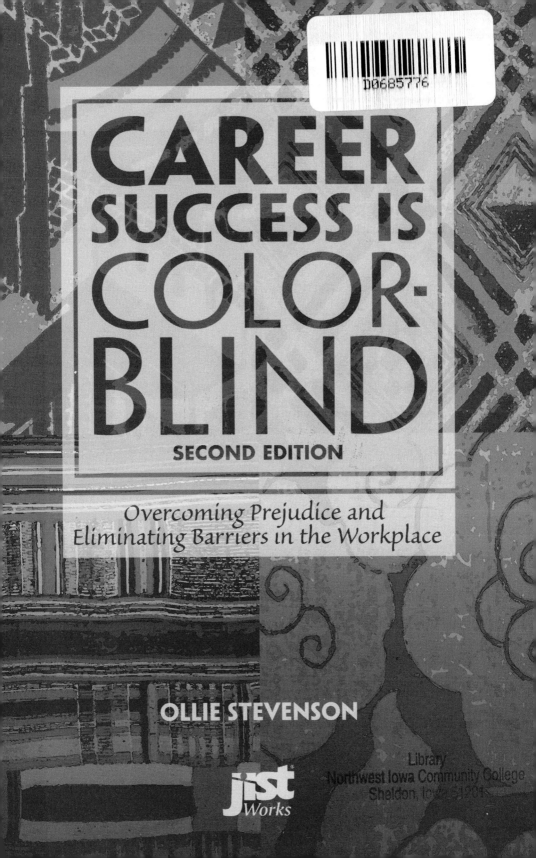

CAREER SUCCESS IS COLOR-BLIND

SECOND EDITION

Overcoming Prejudice and
Eliminating Barriers in the Workplace

OLLIE STEVENSON

jist Works

Library
Northwest Iowa Community College
Sheldon, Iowa 51201

Career Success Is Color-Blind

Overcoming Prejudice and Eliminating Barriers in the Workplace

© 2000 by Ollie Stevenson

Published by JIST Works, an imprint of JIST Publishing, Inc.
8902 Otis Avenue
Indianapolis, IN 46216-1033

Phone: 800-648-JIST   Fax: 800-JIST-FAX   E-mail: editorial@jist.com

Visit our Web site at http://www.jist.com for more information on JIST, free job search information and book chapters, and ordering information on our many products!

Also written by Ollie Stevenson:
101 Answers to the Toughest Job Search Problems

Quantity discounts are available for JIST books. Please call our Sales Department at 1-800-648-5478 for a free catalog and more information.

Acquisitions Editor: Michael Cunningham
Development Editor: Lorna Gentry
Editor: Kris Simmons
Cover & Interior Designer: Katy Bodenmiller

Printed in the United States of America.

03 02 01 00   9 8 7 6 5 4 3 2 1

All rights reserved. No part of this book may be reproduced in any form or by any means, or stored in a database or retrieval system, without prior permission of the publisher except in case of brief quotations embodied in articles or reviews. Making copies of any part of this book for any purpose other than your own personal use is a violation of United States copyright laws.

We have been careful to provide accurate information throughout this book, but it is possible that errors and omissions have been introduced. Please consider this in making any important decisions. Trust your own judgment above all else and in all things.

Trademarks: All brand names and product names used in this book are trade names, service marks, trademarks, or registered trademarks of their respective owners.

ISBN: 1-56370-733-0

You're Busy...
I'll Get to the Point

If you've picked up this book instead of the many, many résumé, job-hunting, and career development books that no doubt surround it, it is because you are interested in more than just a job. You want a career and you want to know how to obtain it and how to be a success at it. You've picked the right book. *Career Success Is Color-Blind* will provide you with the support to start a career and progress until you accomplish your goal and then move on to whatever level you choose.

In addition to providing a frank and informed look at the concepts of career success, this is a "how to" book: how to get a job. How to get out of a dilemma. How to fix a poor work reputation. How to maneuver around a situation. How to advance with as little risk as possible. How to make a career change. How to change companies. How to interview. How to know what to expect as you move from level to level. Here, you're encouraged to think about where you're going and how you want to get there; then, you get the tools, advice, and practical techniques you need to accomplish the journey.

Good Luck!

CONTENTS

Part Three: Make Your Career a Work in Progress   165

INTRODUCTION

Anybody in America Can Succeed

Familiar with the expression "It's easy if you know how?" *Career Success Is Color-Blind* provides the "how" for you to reach your goal. There are rules for succeeding in America, and the rules are not exclusive to white Americans. I categorize these rules as "the business mindset," and they will help any of us—no matter what our race, culture, or gender—to succeed in our chosen career. *Career Success* outlines and explains the business mindset, which has been used effectively by hundreds of thousands of successful people in America. As you learn in Chapter 1, the business mindset isn't a magic formula; it's a sound, practical set of guidelines that you can use to enter and succeed within the American workplace.

How This Book Is Organized

As a career-minded person, you're busy. If you're like me, you' re not going to spend a lot of time reading, so I don't want to waste your time. Therefore, I've set this book up so that the material you need will be easily accessible to you at any given point as your career unfolds. *Career Success* is set up as follows:

Part One, "Clear the Path," is about clearing out negative thoughts and adopting the right attitude for success. It's designed to encourage you to have confidence in your ability to build a career on the talents and gifts you've been given. It also challenges you to make sure your choice is grounded in reality and you are willing to commit to the choice. In other words, you learn to clear your pathway to success of negative or wrong precepts.

In **Part Two, "Forge Your Path to Success,"** you learn about the importance of choosing your first "career" job and how to go after it. You learn about conducting job research, constructing a resume, doing your best in interviews, and developing a full set of job-seeking skills. Next, you learn how to "play the game" and succeed in the workplace, as you discover that there's more to success than just landing a great job.

Careers plateau, or stall, or sometimes get off track. Sometimes the success we sought stops feeling like the success we need. In **Part Three, "Make Your Career a Work in Progress,"** you learn how to assess your career and determine whether you're ready to move on, move up, or move out and into another career path. You explore different options for re-energizing your career: a change in careers within your current workplace, a move to a new company, or a complete redirection of your career and work environment.

Part Four, "What Next, After Success?" is all about matching late-phase career goals to changing life goals. As you move into the mature phases of your career, you find yourself taking on the role of mentor, discovering new ways to use your skills, and finding new avenues that appeal to the realities of this part of your life. Here you can explore new ways to think about gaining maximum satisfaction and meaning from your work life when you've moved beyond the "struggling years" of your career.

In **Part Five, "Food for Thought,"** you'll find helpful resources—both online and in print—for every phase of your career development. Finally, I ask you to take a moment to reflect on some final thoughts regarding your pursuit of career success.

Making the Most of the Format

As you can see by its organization, *Career Success Is Color-Blind* starts at the beginning of career planning, moves to the first job that will support your goal, provides guidance in ways to expand your career, and then offers support as you redefine your career goals and your life goals mature. If you are interested in gathering information about the whole process of developing a career, you'll want to read the entire book from beginning to end. But if you're looking for help with a specific issue or during a specific phase in your career development, you can go directly to that information in the book:

- If you're doubtful about your ability to have a career and succeed at what you *really* want to do, read Chapter 1 first.

- If you are just beginning your career, and you haven't yet defined your specific career goals, read Part One.

- If you know what you want to do, go right to Part Two and work on getting your first career job.

- If you are already on a career track and want to know how to expand your current career horizon, deal with the politics in your organization, and move to the next career level, go straight to Part Three.

- If you've already succeeded in your career but can't help but ask yourself "What's next?" Part Four is for you. If you're preparing to enter a new career area or re-enter the job market after a long absence, this part gives you the "update" you'll need on job-hunting and interviewing techniques for mature career professionals.

Some Special Elements of This Book

As you read through *Career Success Is Color-Blind*, you'll notice some recurring elements that I use throughout the book to help you absorb and retain the information you're reading. Use these special elements to make the most of your time spent reading these pages.

Case Studies

In most chapters of the book, you'll find one or more Case Studies. These "frontline" experiences of real people whom I've known and worked with over the years provide valuable illustrations of the successes—and potential pitfalls—that await all of us in the pursuit of a career.

The Interviews

Successful people, no matter what their age, culture, race, gender, or profession, have shared common experiences in reaching their goals and generally share much in the way of a common philosophy about what it takes to succeed. *Career Success Is Color-Blind* includes interviews with some of these people—real men and women who are just like you and me—who have achieved real success within the American business system. These interviews will inspire you to succeed, and they'll add a new dimension to the advice and information you receive in the book.

MY BOTTOM LINE | In critical points throughout each chapter, and always at each chapter's close, you'll find short pieces called My Bottom Line. In these short statements, I summarize the critical point of the information that precedes them. If you're not sure whether you need to read a chapter, read its My Bottom Line statements; you'll get the essence of the chapter's information and can use it to determine whether you want or need to read the chapter or should just move on.

Résumés

This is not a résumé book. I give you solid information about how to put together your résumé, and I include three sets of résumés for three phases within your career: a set for getting your first job, a set for advancing when you have a lot of experience, and a set for making a career change. Within these sets you'll find examples of chronological, functional, and scannable resume formats. That's all you need. If you want to see more examples of résumés, there are a lot of really good résumé books on the market, and I've suggested a few of them in the "Resources" chapter of Part Five.

Finally, Help Me Succeed

No one person or book has all the answers to achieving career success. Mainly because no book can include the most important element of your journey to a successful career—*you* and your gut instincts about the road you should travel. As you read this material, remember that your instincts are your most important tool for finding career success. Trust yourself, stay positive, and use the material in this book as your personal "career success" coach. If you do this, I will feel I have succeeded.

ACKNOWLEDGMENTS

I believe that the material for books is given by divine inspiration, so I feel blessed to be the person to author this book. This book and its message is written for anyone who wants to succeed within American business. It has come to me through my own experience and those of all the interviewees and others who have helped to develop this material. I thank all of you for your contributions.

A special thanks to a caring publisher, Michael Cunningham, whose dedication to the cause of helping people achieve their career goals came through loud and clear to me from the very first time we talked. A special thanks to my editor, Lorna Gentry, whose excellent editing skill has made this material focused and easy to read. She, too, has been dedicated to making sure that you, the reader, have the best possible information to support your career development.

Finally, my most heartfelt thanks to all the people whose careers I've had an opportunity to be involved with in my years as a career counselor. It is those experiences that have provided the essence of the material in this book.

Dedication

To Tina Turner,
who has inspired me greatly with her spirit, will, and courage.

PART ONE
Clear the Path

What does it take to have a successful career in mainstream America? Why do some people seem to have all the luck and others can't make anything work? Is there a path to success that only a few fortunate people can travel? Is it mostly based on who you know, or are there other things that are key?

Part One of the book will help you find the answers to these questions and more. It is for those of you who question why you're not advancing or those of you who are just starting out—whether you just finished school, you finally decided to commit to a career after a period of working simply to pay the bills, or you are re-entering the workforce after an extended absence.

The information in Part One will help you get in touch with and eliminate negative programming that might be getting in the way of your progress. It will show you how to adopt a business mindset for success and how to have the confidence to build a realistic career based on your talents.

CHAPTER 1

Learn the Ground Rules for a Successful Career in America!

What does a 30-something black male, born a prince in Lagos, Nigeria, have in common with a 20-something white male, born to upper-middle class parents in Wichita, Kansas? In the American business system, a lot. Both are open, focused, and positive. Both are unhampered by barriers in the work-place and refuse to let them diminish their focus. Both accept that the color of the economic system in America is green—the color of money. Both have accomplished tremendous success within the American corporate system because they believed they could.

Quite simply, Kingsley Oluwagbemi (see the section "Let Go of Your Hang-Ups") and Clint Everton (see the section "Success Is Amoral") have learned the rules and how to apply them to achieve success in America. They don't allow issues of color, gender, age, or culture to hamper them in their career quest. They know that, like it or not, to reach success, they have to adapt to a standard of behavior that fits their business environment. For the most part, this standard is formed by the business mindset of the white male. And this business mindset forms the "ground rules" for achieving success in America's business arena.

The simplest way to accept this business mindset is to understand that in any free-market system, the majority of people in the system set the standards. Their ideas and values become the mainstream. Currently, the majority of people at the top levels of American "big business" are white, so they set the standards for behavior within the American business system.

As more people of color and various cultures enter the business arena and move to higher levels of influence, the mindset underlying American business will change to incorporate a greater diversity of values. Consider that we are part a global economy and that only 8 percent of the people in the world are white. (See the section "They Can't Stop You From Succeeding" later in this chapter.) As Clint Everton points out, being white doesn't guarantee success or prevent you from having to deal with obstacles. American workers with disabilities face many barriers, both physical and psychological, and American women are still battling to break the glass ceiling. Increasingly, older Americans are remaining in or re-entering the workforce and struggling to gain recognition for the contributions made possible by their experience and strong work ethic. At the same time, white businessmen are learning to abandon the stereotypes of the past to benefit from the new multicultural and multi-generational workforce. No matter what your color, culture, sex, age, or special circumstance, today's workplace demands that you meet the challenge of succeeding in a diverse workplace.

Whatever your individual circumstance, you can be part of the thinking that influences the business mindset if you're on the inside. But first, you've got to eliminate any internal barriers that might get in your way as you move forward in your career. An important step toward eliminating those barriers is to learn and follow the ground rules of "standard operating procedures" in today's American business environment.

The Wrong Mindset Can Be a Business Barrier

Some people approach a job with a negative mindset or one based on their individual cultural or racial influences. This mindset is not conducive to either the growth or well-being of their career. Statements such as these indicate a lack of business savvy and project the image of a person who doesn't really want a successful career:

- ■ "I just want to be left alone to do my job, and as long as I do that, no one should have anything to say."

- ■ "I'm an educated, qualified person. I shouldn't have to tell anybody this; it's obvious."

- ■ "What I wear doesn't matter. I'm just here to do the work."

- ■ "All they're getting out of me is my 8 hours; then I'm outta here."

- ■ "I don't care…what they think…who they are…what they say…about this job."

Any statement that begins with "I don't care" surely suggests a negative attitude. My father used to say, "I don't care don't have no home" (meaning that such an attitude is not appropriate anywhere). And that's exactly where a person can end up with these kind of attitudes—without a home or, in this case, without a job (or without a job that is challenging and rewarding).

Let Go of Your Hang-Ups

Nigerian born Kingsley has worked in London, Germany, Poland, Australia, and now the United States. One could easily wonder how he has managed all these transitions. For him it has not been as difficult as one might imagine. "I am basically a very flexible person. My mind is free. The person who keeps a lot of negative thoughts in his mind is very much in pain and worse than a dead person. People should loosen up and not let their business lives be ruled by the bad things of the past. They need to believe this is a country of free opportunity and equality."

In his business, Kingsley interacts with people of all races and cultures, but 70 percent of the people he interacts with are white males. "Most of them say 'It seems I find a connection between me and you, and I am surprised.' I say it is because I am African. I know that it is because I do not have feelings of segregation and discrimination that I have to deal with when talking with them. They connect with me because my mind is open to everyone."

Even with a flexible attitude, working in America is not a piece of cake. Most people of other cultures who have overcome obstacles to immigrate to America run headlong into another barrier— mastering the English language with all its slang expressions and subtle twists and turns. Language even can be a barrier for those immigrating from West Africa, where they were taught to speak perfect British English rather than American English. Because of this difficulty with the language, a lot of immigrants prefer to seek success in technical jobs where they can show their skill through their handiwork, rather than struggle with the nuances of the English language.

"I had to work very hard from the time I was a small lad. I was forced to learn discipline early. I learned first from my father and followed his example. He was tough. Even when I was in high school I had a 7 p.m. curfew. He would enforce his rules, but he always did it with love. I never had a feeling of entitlement. I have observed that some American people who have not had to acquire the discipline so early are not accustomed to working hard. I think this can be a barrier to success when they reach adulthood because they are soft. But even with all of this, for a person in American who already knows the language, has the desire to succeed, and is willing to put forth the effort, the sky is the limit."

Kingsley Oluwagbemi
African immigrant
Entrepreneur/Electronic Engineer, Houston, Texas
Business: Transportation, PC electronics

Three Stories of Lost Opportunity

In my years as a career counselor, I have seen many people lose out on opportunities because they haven't learned enough about the culture and values of the business world and have, as a result, incorrectly applied their own individual cultural or racial values to their business dealings.

Three young women I've counseled are good examples: Gina, a young law school graduate; June, a secretary with an advanced degree; and Amy, a factory worker. Each of these women, mostly without knowing it, let her cultural values and background get in the way of achieving success.

(When only a first name is used in an anecdote in this book, the anecdote represents an amalgam of various experiences.)

 You cannot fill a bag that is already full, nor is it good to put something new into an old, worn bag. If you have never experienced success, or you want to succeed again, you must change. You must empty the old bag (you) of its contents (outdated thinking, hang-ups, past pain, and so on) to make room for new success.

Case 1: Who Is Responsible for Gina's Career?

I met Gina during a book tour. She approached me in an intense, serious manner with questions about how to succeed with her newly acquired law degree. We talked about her career goals and I soon discovered that she had unrealistic expectations about what a company could offer her. She was frustrated in her career because she mistakenly believed that her education had already fully prepared her to handle a position in her chosen field, and in spite of this qualification, she was not advancing at her place of business.

A college degree is something to be proud of, but getting a degree is only part of anyone's preparation for achieving success. After the degree, finding a job and moving forward is the real challenge. Things change quickly in almost every business, and to stay at the top of your profession and move up the career ladder, you have to continue to learn and grow professionally. Gina expected that once she found a position and established herself, the company would assume the responsibility of training her and helping her to advance. She expected the same nurturing support she received in her cultural environment to be present in her job. The other people listening to our conversation nodded in agreement, indicating that they expected the same thing. Unfortunately, they were all applying the wrong set of values to the job; in other words, they had the wrong mindset.

Like so many others, Gina had not been taught how to succeed. School gave her the technical skills needed for her work, and her family and culture gave her the necessary emotional support. But her home and school had not prepared her to assert herself and get the help she needed. Instead, they had prepared her to be quiet and respectful and to wait for guidance.

To succeed in business, she needed to apply one of the values of the business mindset, which is to be assertive and take responsibility for your own career. Bottom line: Gina needed to seek out training, get mentors, join professional groups; in essence, she needed to develop her own training program. Because her cultural training had not prepared her to be assertive in this way or to understand the benefits of these types of activities, she was floundering.

Case 2: June Can't Win if She Won't Compete

June, a secretary who was married and had a child, approached me at a conference. She had obtained an advanced degree in marketing but was unsure what step to take to start using her degree—or even whether she should launch her career right away. I offered her suggestions for how she could apply her degree, but to each of my suggestions she offered no response. Finally, June told me she'd probably be better off if she could just make herself content with the job she had and with taking care of her family. Taking care of a family is truly an honorable thing to do; the problem is that this alone was not giving June the satisfaction she needed. Her career dreams were not being fulfilled.

June's culture was supportive of her obtaining an advanced degree, but it didn't give her the drive to go out and get a job using that degree. Instead, her cultural values taught her to emphasize peace and harmony over "getting ahead." When she stated to me in conversation that maybe she "should just stay home and be satisfied," I knew her values were in conflict with the culture of business, which rewards people for going out and actively competing for what they want.

Thanks to her educational pursuit, June's career prospects were promising—if she could overcome the barriers of her cultural limitation.

Case 3: Amy's Career Sinks Without a Network "Lifeline"

Amy's career derailed before it even got started. When she finished high school, Amy knew that she wanted to pursue a degree in engineering. However, she delayed her education and, following the example of most of her friends, started working temporarily in a factory. The temporary job turned into a two-year stint.

Amy explained her situation to me at a workshop I was conducting at her company for employees who were being laid off. She had been working to prepare herself financially to quit working and return to school. When I told her about the options of using scholarships and grants to attend school while she was still working, she was dismayed that she had wasted so much time. She may have found out all I shared with her much earlier if she had known about and exercised another element of the business culture and mindset, which is networking with people (of any race or culture) to find mentors.

They Can't Stop You from Succeeding

"The other day my wife and I were looking at homes in a nice area of Los Angeles when she commented that the area would be a fine place to own a home but that 'they' don't want us living there. I've heard people use that term before, and even though I know what it means, I don't give any thought to it; I certainly don't let it rule my life."

Keith sees this attitude—that "they" (white people) can hold blacks back—as a result of the negative brainwashing that is an outgrowth of centuries of discrimination. He believes that blacks that allow themselves to be held hostage by the invisible "they" are giving white people the power of approval over them.

"Sure, there is hate and discrimination—on both sides—because there are radical whites as well as radical blacks, but these types are on the fringe of society and do not represent the norm," Keith says.

"Most white people are concerned about their own needs—not about us. And we should likewise be concerned about our needs."

According to Keith, blacks and whites would be better off following the Japanese approach to handling problems, which is to just solve the problem and forget about whose fault it is. "Once the problem is solved," he says, "the Japanese then set mechanisms in place to prevent it from happening again. The way we solve problems in America is not as productive because it focuses more on finding fault and placing blame than on problem resolution."

For Keith, the force behind a person's success is his or her belief system, which is based on one's spiritual and mental wisdom. "My grandfathers achieved their goals in the face of all obstacles because of their belief systems: It was the only thing they had. They inspired my father and me to start our own businesses." Keith followed his grandfathers' example and started his own business when his consulting position lost its challenge.

Although Keith says he has never been discriminated against because of his race, he does point to an unpleasant experience that occurred when he worked in the aerospace industry under a manager who was abusive to all his subordinates. When he became the target of one of this manager's attacks, Keith challenged the man's behavior—behind closed doors—and was never singled out again. "I didn't make a big deal out of what had happened, but it was important for me to have the respect that I deserved, so I got it.

"I believe that I am able to influence a situation based solely on the dollars I can generate for a company. And since the American system rests on economics, not race, I believe anyone can accomplish his or her dreams just by being an important team player and being good at what they do."

Keith Webster
African-American entrepreneur
President, Champion Technical Services, Los Angeles, California
Business: Facilities support, temporary services, manufacturing

We All Make Mistakes—
and You Can Learn from Mine

I identified easily with the dilemmas that Gina, June, and Amy faced. Like them, my culture gave me emotional support, but it did not provide me with the mindset, knowledge, or tools to succeed in mainstream American business.

I remember some of the lessons and adjustments I had to make when I first started in my career:

- I refused an opportunity to work as director of a community services agency because I felt it was a man's job. Even though I had been handling the responsibilities of the position all along, I didn't have the official title so I considered what I was doing as only "helping out"—a position with which I was more comfortable.

- Another time, I missed an opportunity to join the staff of a Fortune 100 company as a public relations consultant to one of its senior executives. I passed over this opportunity because I had no clearly defined career goal and, as a result, no sense of how the position could help my career.

- Later in my career, I failed with a project because I had not realized I needed to gather a consensus. After designing a process to revamp a national system within the company, I got input from all the relevant people, but I didn't revisit them to confirm their support before I presented my recommendations to a team of executives. That was a mistake. They were caught off guard when the executives approached them for feedback on my idea.

- Finally, I missed out on a promotion because of my naiveté regarding company politics. I was the logical candidate (in my mind) for a position at the next level above mine, so it did not occur to me that I would have to campaign for it. I was quite shocked, then, when the position went to someone who did campaign for it. Take this lesson to heart and remember: If you ask, you may receive. If you don't ask, don't be surprised if you don't get anything.

I had no mentors or support system during that time, nor did I know that I needed any. I mistakenly thought that all that was necessary for success was knowing how to do a job and then working hard and proving my skills. My ignorance was compounded by my belief that there was *men's* work and there was *women's* work (and that men's work was the kind that required decision making and authority over others), which, of course, stopped me from pursuing certain career opportunities.

Some elements of my cultural programming actually limited my business growth. The professional associations I joined at that time (must I mention how long ago?) were made up mainly of other African-Americans like myself and focused mostly on issues of discrimination. As a result, I didn't gain much in terms of professional growth and knowledge. Plus the groups generally had an attitude of "them" against "us," making it seem as if I'd be a traitor to ask one of "them" for help (see "They Can't Stop You from Succeeding"). So like June, Amy, and Gina, I, without knowing it, applied the standards of my cultural programming—rather than those of a business mindset—to my career. By making this critical mistake, I delayed my success unnecessarily. I spent a long time following the wrong patterns of business behavior before I learned the values and culture of the business world and adjusted my path accordingly.

MY BOTTOM LINE	In the quest to reach your goal, if along the way you feel discriminated against, you're not alone. All people, all races, all cultures, have been discriminated against at some time for some reason or other. Deal with an injustice legally if you choose, or forget it and move on to accomplish your goals. Either way, let go of the pain connected with it.

Make the Business Mindset a Working Reality

The business mindset is reflected in an attitude that is geared toward achieving success in the business arena. Now when I step into a corporate business role in America, I do so with the mental attitude that I am prepared to make the adjustments necessary to accomplish my goal. I adopt the attitude, behavior, and dress that are most effective for accomplishing my goals in that environment.

You're about to read a list of 12 methods for making the business mindset a part of your own working reality. These methods help you apply the standards of the culture of business to your own job and daily work routine. Where appropriate, I have included examples of situations in which I've observed people unintentionally applying inappropriate standards. I hope these examples will help you avoid making similar mistakes in your own career.

Although this is hardly an all-inclusive list, it contains what I believe to be the best ways to address some of the "universal" values and principles of the culture of business—those that I have found apply in most situations. When you get into a specific industry and then a particular company, you'll want to pay attention to the unique culture you find there and adjust your business mindset to incorporate its standards.

Ollie's Advice for Developing Your Own Business Mindset

Keep your cultural distinctiveness in the workplace, but adapt it to the mainstream corporate culture.

I am not suggesting you give up the values, pride, and dignity that make up your cultural identity—because I certainly do not intend to give up mine. I am a black woman and I love all that identifies me as a black woman. Whether you are Asian, Native-American, African-American, Hispanic, white, or a member of any other group, I certainly hope that you feel the same way about your culture—that you wear your cultural identity proudly. However, if your long-term goals include developing a successful career within the American corporate system, you must learn to align with the dominant mindset of your company while in that business arena. While you are in your business environment, your values, attitudes, and behavior must be in alignment with those of your workplace—as long as that business mindset doesn't conflict with what you believe to be morally correct.

Be assertive and take responsibility for developing and advancing your career.
Some people are passive about developing a career; they enter the business world with the expectation that they are going to be led and guided up the

ladder of success. It is possible to get step-by-step guidance in doing that, but you have to seek out that guidance yourself. This book, and all the books mentioned in it, will help you learn how to find that kind of guidance and mentoring. But you cannot stop there. You'll have to read more books, talk to people, and watch and model behavior that works. The important point is that if there is something you want, you have to research the ways to get it; choose the best strategy for your personality and the company culture, and then go for it. You must also be willing to accept *all* of the consequences of your action (or non-action), including any rewards. That's the essence of taking responsibility for your career.

Accept that networking is an essential component of the business mindset.
This is one of the basics of the business mindset: Network with everyone. A simple example of how to network is what I do for lunch. When I can, I make a point of having lunch with any one of my peers—male, female, older, younger, white, black, Hispanic, Asian, or whatever. And guess what? It is actually very enjoyable, because my peers and I have a lot in common. Lunch is a great time to network. While casually enjoying each other's company, we discuss our common goal, which is how to improve our process so that our company can maintain its competitive edge in the marketplace (and so we can receive our reward for helping to bring this about).

In his best-selling book *Success Runs in Our Race*, George Fraser shares a vision of networking that's worth aspiring to: "It is the brand of networking that calls upon you to give (information) until it hurts, and then give until it feels good. It is the kind of networking that over time delivers to your doorstep your every dream and every hope." I've found this approach to networking to be absolutely true for me, and it can be for you as well—if you apply the principles. But don't limit yourself to a few select people and your own limited social circle; otherwise, you'll narrow your opportunities.

I've actually had clients who refused to network to get a new job. They perceived it as asking for a favor and, thus, did not want to feel obligated or beholden to anyone. What an unfortunate attitude! Statistics show that more than 70 percent of people seeking a job get it through networking. The statistics are even higher for prime jobs because these are often only accessed through a network.

Be brave: Take the initiative to introduce yourself in new situations.

Remember when you were in school and a new person joined your class? You and your classmates probably stared at the person with curiosity and maybe wondered what he was about, until finally something happened to break the ice. Eventually the newcomer found his way into a group of kids and that was that. Things haven't changed much. When you join a company, you're the new kid. And you'll probably stand out even more than the new kid in school. Most likely, your fellow employees won't stare at you outright, but they will be just as curious. In spite of their curiosity, some of them may hesitate to approach you because they don't know what to say. In some environments, there will be people who have had limited exposure to people other than their own race or culture, so why not be the brave person? Take the initiative to introduce yourself and say how you're looking forward to learning the job. Tell people that you'd welcome any help they can give you in learning the ropes.

Use social gatherings as an opportunity to be visible and advance your causes.

Being committed to a profession means more than going to work from 9 to 5. Socializing is part of the mix. You have to let people get to know you, and you need to take the time to get to know them. When you are working on projects that will involve others, it is helpful to have already developed a friendly relationship with the other individuals. This will not only enhance your chances for advancement, but it will also make you more comfortable with the people that you'll be working with as you move forward in your career. Consider social gatherings an extension of your workweek.

Be willing to tell others about your skills and abilities: In other words, toot your own horn.

Learn the strategies appropriate in your environment for letting decision makers know what you do. Too much humility can be a real barrier in the business world! And hoping to get recognized for your accomplishments without letting others know about them will probably get you nowhere. If you want to advance, you need to subtly and strategically feed information upward to the decision makers. They need to know about your interests and abilities so that when they are considering which employee has what it takes to assume certain responsibilities (usually this means who is ready for advancement), your name will come up.

I've worked with clients who've made me pull information out of them about their qualifications because they didn't want to sound like they were bragging. "Tooting your own horn" may feel awkward—especially at first—because it is a different behavior from what you're accustomed to. But refusing to communicate accomplishments can interfere with your ability to be competitive in an environment in which accomplishments are valued. Often your efforts to let others know about your positive contributions to the company can be your ticket for advancement.

This isn't to say that you need to constantly tell your supervisor and colleagues that you're doing a great job or update them about your successes on a daily basis. Consider these ways of communicating your accomplishments to the people who matter: preparing status reports, writing articles for the company newsletter, communicating through co-workers, participating on committees, gathering letters of commendation from clients, and so on. And I would encourage you to spread the word about the success of your colleagues, as well. By recognizing the accomplishments of those around you, you contribute to an atmosphere in which this kind of recognition is standard. Above all, watch how others communicate their successes in your company. Then apply those methods to your situation.

Wear the right clothes for the environment, geographic location, and your body type.

Just as you wear different outfits to attend a formal dinner or to walk on the beach, the clothes you wear to work should be right for that environment. They should be similar to the attire worn by the greatest number of people within your industry, company, and job type. Never call attention to yourself with your clothes (unless you're in a job where you need to stand out, such as a sales clerk in a trendy clothing boutique). All people of color that I've known from all races have colorful wardrobes. And rightly so, because bright colors look better with our skin tones. Even so, our wardrobes need to be tempered for the workplace. With a little creativity, we can strike a reasonable balance. Think of it this way: Your clothing is your "professional uniform." It communicates to customers and co-workers who you are and what you do. Your business uniform helps you look, act, and feel like the career-minded professional you are.

Take rejection in stride: Maintain pride in your accomplishments, analyze the situation, regroup, and persevere.

No matter how good you are, how talented, or how exceptional, you will not get every single job you go after. Accept this fact and it will reduce your chances of feeling frustrated when you don't get a coveted position. Even when you are the most technically qualified for a position, don't expect that it will automatically go to you.

A number of factors go into any hiring decision. First there's what I call "the mix." If a company already has a person on board with a similar background and qualifications to yours, managers may want to add someone else with a different background to round out the team.

Your "chemistry" can also be an important factor. Chemistry cannot be learned or manufactured; you're just going to hit it off better with some people than with others. Other factors an employer might consider include perceived motivational level, potential for adding value based on previous experience, outside business contacts, and potential for growth and advancement.

If you don't get a position, feel honored that you were part of the group selected for consideration. If you were involved in a selection process within your company, you might be able to network (or observe) and find out why the other person was chosen. If you discover that it was because of office politics, forget it. That's life, and one day you'll be the chosen one. If, on the other hand, you learn that the person who got the job had qualifications that you're lacking, then get busy and get qualified for the next opening.

Seek out mentors.

Ask for advice from people working in jobs like the one you want. Ask about skills that are rewarded and how to acquire them so that you can advance. A mentor serves as a guide and teacher to help you move forward in your career. You do not choose your mentors; they choose you. But they cannot choose you unless they know you need to be chosen. And how will they know unless you ask them for advice?

People love to give advice, to share their knowledge; it's a wonderfully uplifting thing to do. I look at it this way: Allow someone to experience the joy of helping guide your career. And don't limit yourself; be willing to accept whomever the universe provides to you as a mentor. Seek out a mentor of power. It is good if the person is someone of your race and ethnicity who has made it through the system. If not, look for two mentors—one of any race who can help guide your career and one of your race who can identify and help you overcome the obstacles facing people from your background.

Ask for feedback on your performance so that you can continually improve and grow.

No matter how significant your last accomplishment was, today it's old news. As long as you live, you need to be striving to accomplish goals and be the best you can possibly be. Make feedback a part of your education. Mentors can be very helpful here because part of their role is to provide valuable feedback. But don't limit your search for feedback to the mentor relationship. Ask people in your peer group for feedback on ideas and activities—and be willing to take time to give it to them as well. Then, take the information you gather from your friends and colleagues and incorporate it into your objectives for growth.

If you are totally comfortable in your profession and everyone says that you're just great—just perfect at what you do—then I don't think you're being truly challenged. And if you're not really challenged, you're not growing. If you don't grow, you can't make the contribution you're capable of making. So find out what you can do better and then do it, or initiate your plan to expand the scope of what you do or to move up a rung on the ladder.

Learn to team with others to accomplish objectives.

The latest management model in progressive companies is cross-functional, multi-level teaming. This is a significant step up from the individual contributor model. This process involves teaming with people who are in different departments and roles, people who are at a higher level than you, and those at lower levels as well. Added to this mix is the multicultural aspect of most workplaces today. Quite simply, the new working style is becoming more fluid; it doesn't fit the traditional boxes and roles. To work effectively within this type of model, you must be open to the ideas of others and willing to have your ideas challenged. The more you understand other cultures, the easier it will be to work in this model.

Establish a positive pattern for success.

As my career progressed, I learned that an important part of taking responsibility for it was establishing early on the right pattern for developing and advancing. You, too, will see this pattern emerging, and you'll find yourself repeating it over and over as you advance level by level up the ladder of success. The pattern very simply is

- Set a goal based on your own desires or dreams.

- Assess your talent and ability to accomplish the goal.

- Develop a plan to get the experience, education, and training you need.

- Develop a strategy to get to the goal.

- Be committed to attaining the goal, despite possible detours and setbacks.

 If your cultural ideas get in the way in the business arena, put them aside from 9–5. No company hires you to be part of a racial or cultural group. They hire you to be a good employee and do it their way.

In the Global Melting Pot, All People Have a Greater Challenge

The global melting pot where people of all races and cultures are coming together in the workplace will prove to be very challenging for everyone. My experience has taught me that adopting the business mindset can be especially difficult when some of your key cultural values are different from the majority of those in your business environment. For instance, if your cultural norms center on an ingrained respect for authority based on age and title, you might have to struggle to learn to supervise someone who is older than you. At the same time you may, at first, have trouble taking orders from someone your age or who shares your rank or title. Depending upon the values and traditions you've learned, you may have trouble standing out and taking credit for accomplishments, being assertive in the workplace, working in groups, or adhering to an established standard for advancement. You also may have trouble overcoming the natural tendency to project your cultural values—and your stereotypes about the values and beliefs of other cultures—on your co-workers. Remember, the culture and value of business are the only givens in any workplace. We all are challenged to let go of our prejudices and work together toward a common goal of personal and professional success.

All of that being said, even those of us who have already adopted the business mindset will at some point be faced with the challenge of dealing with discrimination, racism, and prejudice. These problems exist—and, in view of human nature, probably always will. Some of this ignorance will be overcome as people of color advance in the workforce and the cultures blend and assimilate each other's values. In the meantime, it is important to know that you are likely to encounter discrimination at various points in your career. Sometimes you will have to confront it, and other times you will choose to ignore it. I've included two books in the chapter called "Resources" that can help in dealing with issues of discrimination.

Finally, we are challenged daily to make the switch in thinking from our cultural views to the business mindset as we travel from home to work and then back home again. To do this we must always remember our roots and involve ourselves in activities that will help us maintain our mental health and emotional balance. If you get too caught up in the business culture, you run the risk of allowing your cultural values to slowly fade or disappear altogether.

In fact, one of the downsides of the culture of business is that it is not nurturing. Because of this, we need to be involved in activities outside of work that help us stay in touch with the essence of *our* culture. As a black person, my spiritual nurturing (church and prayer) and getting together with family and a few friends to gab and make fun of ourselves totally revives me. Some of my friends from other cultures tell me they value the get-togethers for big family meals, with all the babies and the laughter and hugs and kisses. And of course, men of all cultures seem to get reinforcement from watching or participating in a sporting event together.

Whatever is a normal part of your culture that rejuvenates you and keeps you in touch with core aspects of your being, do it on a regular basis. We need to maintain our base of emotional support because we will need to rely on it often during our career journey. As individuals, our ultimate career challenge is to learn to handle the realities of the work world while maintaining our own cultural values.

Success Is Amoral

"I'm confused by the extreme behavior that I sometimes see in the media coming from some of the civil rights leaders. I was not born during the times they are referring to, so I guess I just don't understand. But it seems to me that the behavior is divisive. Why can't people just sit down and talk out the issues and come to some resolution? The name of the game is money, and if you have a good product or service to sell, you can make money and be successful at it. Success has no race or religion attached to it; actually success is amoral.

"I personally don't have a problem with any race, and I actually think blacks and whites are pretty much aligned in their thinking. The cultural issue for me and a lot of people my age who I work with is older people. Most of them have a top-down mindset, which represents a traditional business structure as opposed to the fluid dynamic organization I'm accustomed to. But I'm passionate about what I do and I believe in it, so I've learned to adjust. Basically, if the issue is about business in America, the driving force is performance that translates to money."

Experience has been Clint's best teacher, and it taught him early in his life that the American economic system is driven by the bottom line. At the age of six, he had a lawnmowing business going and loved it. This gave him the idea that he would be a politician, a lawyer, or an entrepreneur. He laughingly states his parents would have killed him if he had opted for politics or law, so being an entrepreneur was his choice. He started his software technology business in 1995. It sprang from an idea he had while playing video games at the fraternity house. The games were fun, and he wondered why learning couldn't be that much fun. So he and a couple of friends started developing software around a class business assignment. One step lead to another, and with some networking support and help from his family, he was able to gain the investors he needed to start the business and make it profitable. Three years later he sold the business for millions and retained the role of president, and he is now jazzed about the possibility of another startup.

Success was not a slam-dunk for Clint. "I had to work hard to make my business a success. Sure, I had some advantages. In the beginning my father helped me with some networking contacts. But I still had to sell the concept—and myself. Raising money was difficult. I had to learn to remove myself from the rejection. It's not me personally; they just don't want the idea. They're (investors) looking at how much money they want to make. I had to suck up some of my pride and go along with some of the ideas of investors to accomplish my goal. I had to learn to talk the language of investors, board members, programmers, employees, customers, whoever had an influence on the business. I had to learn about accounting, finance, and marketing. Along the way, I learned you can't be this young Turk with all the answers. I had to pay my dues, get my hands dirty, and work my way up.

"It's the golden rule: He who has the gold makes the rules. I had to make many adjustments to make my vision a reality. You can be yourself when you're making the rules. But even then you'll usually have someone to be accountable to, even if it's your customers. Making adjustments does not mean you have to compromise your values. It's about approaching your audience the right way and speaking their language. You can do this and still maintain your integrity and be honest. Ultimately, though, for me the journey is the reward. Taking a concept that was nothing and making it happen; I can hardly wait to do it again."

Clint Everton
White-American entrepreneur
President, Knowledge Communication Library (KCL),
Dallas, Texas
Business: Software technology

Knowledge Is Power

Understanding the problem is halfway to the solution. I believe that no matter what your color, sex, or physical disability, you can equip yourself to meet the challenge of adopting a business mindset. With the information you learned in this chapter, you're ready to start on your journey toward a satisfying career. Here are a few tools and techniques that will come in handy while you're on that journey:

- **Educate yourself on how to handle discrimination.** There may be times when you need to deal with an issue that violates your civil rights. In those instances, you should contact the U.S. Equal Employment Opportunity Commission, 2401 E Street NW, Washington, D.C. 20507, or call 800-USA-EEOC to contact an EEOC field office. (For the hearing impaired, EEOC's TDD number is 202-634-7057.) Also, read books focusing on work and people of color. (See "Resources" at the end of the book for some examples.)

- **Educate yourself about the business mindset by reading.** Books such as those listed in the "Resources" section of this book are examples of ones that provide excellent advice for all people on a career journey.

- **Educate yourself by socializing.** Join groups—professional associations as well as some that are just for fun—that includes people from more than one culture. Take the initiative to say "hello" first when you join a new group. Get to know others and be open to letting them know you. Look for the things you have in common and build relationships based on those things. These same people may be helpful to you later in your career when you need advice or support.

- **Educate yourself by getting involved.** Volunteer for activities in some of the groups you join. Learning to work together with people of another culture within the low-risk environment of a volunteer activity will prepare you well for working with others in the workplace. Volunteer for a responsible position on at least one committee a year.

MY BOTTOM LINE

To succeed…or not…is your individual responsibility. If you reach out to attain success, the universe will support you. If you choose not to succeed, the universe will support that decision as well. Either way, it's your choice.

CHAPTER 2

Follow Your Vision and Find Your Dream

Many who've dreamed of success have turned their dreams into realities, not because these individuals were more unique or talented than others, but simply because they were persistent. They really wanted it. That's part of the beauty of living in America: All people have the opportunity to make their career dream a reality if they are hungry enough for it and willing to adopt a business mindset to accomplish it. (See the section "Living the American Dream" later in this chapter.)

In his book *Live Your Dreams*, Les Brown describes this determination as an absolutely compelling, deeply rooted, and powerful motivation. Paul and Sarah Edwards, in their book *Finding Your Perfect Work*, describe the motivation this way: "For some people, there is no crisis that catalyzes them to pursue their dreams. Quite the contrary, they simply decide they're no longer willing to compromise, delay, or forego what's in their hearts and souls. So they summon up their courage to make a specific choice that will change their lives."

Your dream may be fired by a compelling force that burns in your heart—driving you, inspiring you, and providing a constant source of motivation. Or it may be kindled by a subtler, but equally powerful, force—a quiet, abiding commitment that comes from a deeply rooted sense of inner purpose. Whether it's a fiery passion or a steady inner light, the important thing is that you have a dream that you can be passionate about and committed to achieving.

In every walk of life, you can find numerous examples of people who have been drawn to a dream and then unwaveringly followed a path to success: the finely tuned, completely disciplined athlete who competes on a field of champions and wins by a breath, a split second, a last perfectly executed step; the musician whose musical rendition captures our souls with a sound so exquisite that we dare not breathe for fear of marring its perfection; or the scientist who, after years of painstaking analysis and self-sacrifice, suddenly finds the solution to a problem that changes the world in some way.

These feats of greatness are not the exclusive right of superstar sports figures, larger-than-life entertainers, or exceptionally brilliant scientists. Success is possible for all people who will not settle for less.

A Look Down the Road Ahead

We can be proud of the talented men and women who throughout this country's history—and especially in the past four decades—have made significant strides and won tremendous achievements. Role models of every culture exist at every level and within virtually every arena of American enterprise. In today's workplace, there are more and better career opportunities than ever before; we're now in a position to achieve some of the biggest career successes of all time and to make outstanding contributions to American history.

This isn't to say that the road to success will be easy. Even though increased opportunity exists, the workplace of this century will be more challenging than ever, for all people.

Following are some of the business-world realities you can expect on the road ahead.

Instead of being supported by programs or implied promises of cradle-to-grave employment, everyone will have to compete and achieve individually by setting high goals and taking responsibility for turning their dreams into realities.

Job security as we used to know it is quickly disappearing. The days have passed when you could expect to get a "good job" with a company and never have to do much to maintain your employment. Lifetime employment with any one company will be rare in the new millennium. Corporations are constantly changing, and they're changing their staffs along with their goals. To maintain employment you need to be able to add skills, grow in capability and responsibility, and be willing to constantly compete with internal and external applicants for positions.

No matter what your color, age, gender, culture, or disability, you will likely face some form of racism or discrimination.

Even in a global workplace, prejudice and intolerance are alive and well; no one can deny that. As no one can truthfully deny, we all have our prejudices. Still, thanks to the men and women who fought those battles for all people—and to those who continue to fight the battles—these are obstacles that can be overcome legally if necessary. We have rules to keep us all honest. With that path cleared, the best way to overcome these obstacles on the job is with superior performance. This performance translates to money on the bottom line and supports the reasons business exists in the first place.

You will be challenged to break free of any cultural programming or stereotypes that limit your professional growth.

When you pursue a career that was not planned for you or isn't the norm for your gender or culture, you face additional obstacles—perhaps lack of support from family and peers, friction on the job, or, possibly, slower upward mobility. You have to be courageous to move past programming that says that success is limited for you because of your race, culture, or physical limitations. It simply is not true.

If Oprah Winfrey, a black woman, can make more than $45 million a year, I would say there is no limitation to the success a black woman can achieve. If Connie Chung, an Asian-American anchorperson for national news, or Tiger Woods, a young biracial (Asian and black) golfer, can rise to the top of fields dominated by white men, then there is no limitation to the potential success of biracial men and women in any field. And if Colin

Powell, a black man, can be encouraged by millions of Americans to run for the presidency of the United States, I would definitely say there is no limitation to the potential political success of any person of color.

Some of you will have to refuse to be pushed into a stereotypical job. Refuse to be a basketball player just because you're 6'5" if it doesn't fulfill your soul and make you happy. Refuse to pursue a degree in the sciences just because you're supposed to be good in math; do it only if you feel you will be operating at your highest level by doing so. Refuse to be a gardener or a cook just because you know others in your culture who are doing this work; do it only if it satisfies the creative urge within your spirit. Follow only the profession that is a calling—that work about which you can truly be passionate.

MY BOTTOM LINE | When you have been given a vision and a passion about something, then you are truly blessed because all that went before and all that comes after will help you to make that dream a reality.

Seeing Beyond the Challenges of Internal Fear and Community Opposition

No one can argue that overcoming barriers created by cultural tradition or racism in the workplace are significant challenges; however, they are external factors that are pretty easy to recognize. The biggest challenges you will face may be internal ones—beliefs and ways of thinking that are blocking you from achieving your potential. You may also be challenged to overcome opposition to change within your own family and cultural community. Actually, you might not even be aware of these internal obstacles because they are so deeply ingrained in your psyche.

Try to identify these potential internal barriers by asking yourself some hard questions about what might be holding you back. Or brainstorm with a friend you trust to give you honest feedback. Ask these types of questions:

- Are you afraid to pursue your goal because it means making changes or venturing into something unknown?

■ Are you being held back by inner voices telling you "You don't have what it takes to do that," "You'll never be anything," or "You're not smart (talented, aggressive) enough?"

■ Are you afraid that if you achieve success in your chosen career, you may face rejection in your personal life or your community because you no longer fit in?

Being aware of these internal fears is half the battle. Once you can identify the fears that may be holding you back, you can take steps to overcome them. Realize that everyone is afraid at some point in life. Everyone is confronted by some kind of programming they have to deal with—whether it was developed in the home, by the media, in school, or whatever. This "programming" of internal fears happens to us all, no matter how rich or poor our families may be. Such fears are a fact of life. But if you want to make your dreams a reality, you have to be willing to proceed in spite of the fear. Sometimes resisting that fear will actually propel you forward toward accomplishing your goal.

Overcoming this kind of negative programming may be difficult, but you'll need to do it before you can achieve your goals. Here are some practical steps for conquering your own internal fears about stepping into a non-traditional career:

■ Start by examining any negative reactions you have to your career dreams.

■ Try to identify the motivation for the negative feeling.

■ Discuss your conflict with someone you trust and respect to help you see the reasons behind your choices.

■ Determine whether it truly makes sense for these negative feelings to influence your career decision.

Latino Success by Augusto Failde and William Doyle can help you learn to deal with this negative programming and have the courage to take on a role that is not traditional for your culture. Although the book highlights Latino people and focuses on issues specific to their perspective, it can be helpful for anyone trying to work through negative programming.

As hard as it is to overcome your own internal barriers, it also takes courage and a great deal of mental fortitude to break from cultural tradition and pursue something that your family might not support. If you find yourself feeling drawn to such a calling, and you want to gain the support you need to follow your dream, the following steps may help:

- Make the effort to get your family's commitment and support by slowly involving them in the process.

- Discuss your plans with the parent or sibling whom you expect to be the most receptive to your endeavor. Expect to provide a lot of information and a systematic plan for achieving your goal with the lowest amount of risk. Show how you will be able to support yourself and develop the foundation for a solid financial future.

- When you've gained the backing of that individual, ask for his or her help in anticipating the arguments of the more difficult family members and in developing a plan for how you will respond to their arguments.

The right career does not have to be a lofty ideal that will impact thousands; it simply needs to be based on what you want to do. (See the section "Just Do What Makes You Happy.") Whether it comes from a need for creativity or practicality, it must bring psychological fulfillment based on your own dreams and unique personal talents. With a clear vision and true aptitude as your foundation, you can achieve success in any profession, as long as you are committed and willing to take the steps necessary to bring that talent to fruition.

MY BOTTOM LINE | I am totally convinced that all people know exactly what they would like to do. I am also convinced that when they don't follow their hearts, it's because they don't know how or they're afraid to try.

Where Do You Want to Go? Bringing Your Dream into Focus

Of course, knowing about potential obstacles won't help if you haven't yet identified a definite career goal—or if you don't believe that you can come up with one. If you're in this situation, don't think you're alone or that your case is hopeless. You just need some tools and guidance to help you determine your career goal and gather the confidence to achieve it.

The ideas and advice that follow should help you focus lifelong dreams into realistic career goals. Keep an open mind and find honest answers for the questions you'll need to ask yourself. But don't dream small because you're afraid you can't make big dreams come true. If you choose the right career for your life, one that comes from your heart, you will know it because the universe will respond by providing you the support you need to accomplish the goal. Be open to receiving support from wherever or whomever it comes. Working to accomplish a goal is the essence of being truly alive; without it, you are just existing. When you pursue your dreams, you fit perfectly into the universal plan; you enhance your life as well as the lives of others and ultimately help make the world a better place for everyone.

What Did You Want to Be When You Grew Up?

When I look at the steps that led to my current profession as a career consultant, speaker, and writer, I truly believe I was guided subconsciously along this path by my childhood aspirations. As a little girl, I wanted to be a missionary. And a teacher. And a philanthropist. (at the time, I didn't actually know the title; I just knew I wanted to have enough money to help others achieve their dreams.) Even though I didn't go into any of these professions, my career incorporates activities from all of them. The career dreams of children are powerful, because such aspirations are not yet tainted by any "reality" that says they cannot happen. They often reflect strong inner drives and can be indicators of where success will be found in your future.

Think back to when you were a child; can you remember having a clear idea about what you wanted to be when you grew up? The avenue for discovering your dream career may stem from desires you expressed or felt in your early childhood:

> ▨ As a child, what did you tell your parents and friends when they asked what you wanted to be when you grew up?

- When you played with other children, what kind of games did you want to play and what role did you assume—the leader, the organizer, the follower, the helper, or the problem-solver?

- Did adults make comments to you about the kind of work you should do based on their observations of your actions? ("Honey, you're always trying to take care of someone; you'll probably be a doctor or social worker when you grow up.")

Recalling your childhood vision may be your key to finding true career satisfaction.

Does Your Childhood Dream Fit Your Adult Vision?

As you think about the career you dreamed of as a child, be sure to look at the origins of that dream. This way you can determine whether the underlying motivation is a valid one on which to build a career. Will it truly represent the type of profession that will give you satisfaction?

For instance, you may be thinking of becoming a firefighter only because you admired Uncle Pete when you were growing up; you wanted to be just like him. If you pursue a career as a firefighter for this reason, it probably won't provide you with the same satisfaction as it did your role model. On the other hand, if you wanted to become a firefighter because you loved the idea of saving people's lives and homes and working in emergency situations, then your career choice is most likely motivated by the desires of your heart.

Whether you build your career on a childhood dream or simply on some-thing you enjoy doing, the motivation needs to spring from your heart to be truly fulfilling. If you formulate a goal based on the wrong motivation, it won't provide a solid foundation for you to endure the challenges you'll face ahead.

MY BOTTOM LINE If you say there is something that you want to do but have done nothing at all about it or you have no genuine enthu-siasm for it, then you probably have the wrong goal. Look for another one that you can pursue with passion.

Can You Build Your Dream from the Things You Love?

Blanca and Sean clearly remember their childhood dreams, and these dreams led them both to their present careers. As a child, Blanca often told her mother that she wanted to get a job hiring people so that she could give everyone she knew a job. Now, as a human resources professional, her job involves making employment recommendations and hiring people. Sean dreamed of enjoying personal freedom while making a lot of money to help his family. He realized these ambitions by going into sales; working on commission gives him freedom, and by working hard and excelling at his job, he is able to generate the high income he needs.

Obviously, doing work that you love and are good at will provide you with the greatest satisfaction and an ongoing sense of challenge and motivation. Think about the activities you involve yourself in—either through work, for fun, or as a volunteer. Your responses to the following questions will help you determine if the goal you are currently pursing is based on your own motivation, skills and interests, a childhood infatuation, or someone else's expectations:

- What aspects of these activities do you particularly enjoy?

- Can you trace the activities or skill used back to any desires you expressed during childhood?

- Do you love being involved in activities that are aligned with your chosen goal—so much so that you spend much of your leisure time doing them? For instance, if you're planning to be an attorney, do you love going to the courthouse or the law library, following a trial for its points, or analyzing the merits of a case?

- Do you spend some of your leisure time involved in reading information that supports your goal? For example, a person who wants to start his own business might be found reading books on business start-up, finances, or developing a winning marketing plan.

- Do you volunteer your time in any activity associated with your goal? An aspiring photographer who wants to build her portfolio in order to compete on a professional level will be likely to volunteer to photograph a variety of occasions.

■ Would you still pursue your current goal if you could do something else and make more money?

Just Do What Makes You Happy

"I can't say that I've ever really had a dream job in mind; I've just always looked for a job where I would be happy," says Phyllis, who believes that taking risks and doing what you love are the keys to success. "You have to be willing to put your best foot forward, take chances, and not be afraid to try something different. After that, if you're not happy, be willing to move on."

Phyllis acknowledges that most Asian-American women have careers in an analytical field such as finance, accounting, financial analysis or in helping professions such as teaching and human resources. But in spite of these cultural influences, she opted to pursue a career that led to sales. After deciding at age 16 that she wanted to work behind a sales counter, Phyllis applied for a job at a large department store. The person in charge of hiring told her that the company would not hire her to work behind the counter but could offer her a job wrapping gifts. She thanked the person nicely and went across the street to one of that store's competitors, where she got the job she wanted. She chuckles when she says, "I still don't shop at that other store to this day."

After that, Phyllis developed her career by continually seeking out new opportunities that made her happy and that also advanced her career. "I always moved forward and haven't wasted time with a job that did not offer me what I wanted. Her attitude toward people and discrimination has helped her professionally. "I refuse to see the racial attitudes of a few people as a factor that can stop my progress. Also, I don't view people in terms of what group they belong to; I deal with them as individuals. My two best friends in school were a Jewish girl and a black Catholic girl. I was the Asian Protestant, and people referred to us as the three musketeers. We were drawn together because of our ambition. We loved talking about our differences and really learned a lot from each other."

For Phyllis, sharing common values and goals can provide a stronger bond than race. She also believes that cultural diversity within business has the potential to improve relationships among people of different backgrounds. "In the new team environment, we have to be able to count on one another, or we're all going down. We need to be aware of other cultural backgrounds. It's our responsibility as individuals to find out about each other."

Phyllis Miyoshi
Asian-American female
Account Executive, Drake Beam Morin, Inc.,
Los Angeles, California
Business: Global transition consulting firm

Is the Vision Your Own—or Someone Else's?

I've known people who have lost sight of their dreams or pushed them aside to follow career paths based on the hopes, needs, or expectations of others. A young man I knew who grew up with dreams of being an artist entered a profession his parents thought would guarantee him a good living. A young woman who had her heart set on becoming a lawyer struggled instead to become an actress to satisfy her mother's own thwarted ambition for a profession in the arts. Similarly, a young husband set aside his wish to teach and entered a more lucrative profession to accommodate his wife's need for economic security.

Clearly, these people are living someone else's dream. When others insist that you follow a path other than the one you have chosen for yourself, they are usually motivated by their own needs and not by yours. When people offer you career advice or urge you in a specific direction other than one you've chosen, you need to consider their suggestions in light of their biases and values.

Often, we let others control our dreams because we think it's our only option. What if you had a mate, two children, and a job paying $100,000, which you had been encouraged to take because of the security? Would you quit to change professions if the new profession was something you had dreamed of—but paid considerably less? Probably not. You'd probably continue to work in frustration and at half-mast in the current job.

Karen's story is an example of what can happen when you live someone else's dreams. A nursing professional, Karen always wanted a career in the fashion industry but instead followed her mother's advice to enter the nursing profession so that she would have job security. As a nurse, Karen's credentials and knowledge enabled her to move rapidly into a supervisory position. However, as a supervisor, she felt frustrated and often received complaints for being abrupt with the staff. People on the job thought she was angry with them much of the time.

Karen may have been difficult to work with as a nurse, but in her off hours she was a different person. Spending her evenings and weekends working as a freelance fashion coordinator, Karen seemed stimulated and happy. She assembled and maintained wardrobes for a select clientele that she had developed mostly through referrals. When she wasn't working directly with a client, she would spend hours browsing the clothing stores and discount marts, looking for bargains or special items for her clients. In spite of the demands it put on her time, working as a fashion coordinator energized Karen because she loved the work.

Although Karen found some element of satisfaction in both nursing and fashion because both were service-oriented and required attention to detail, her heart was in fashion. Even so, she continued working full-time in nursing and freelancing in fashion until outside circumstances forced her to make a choice. After a 25-year nursing career, the catalyst to change professions came when her hospital changed hands and the new management offered Karen the option to leave her job with a large severance. Realizing that it was now or never, Karen decided to follow her lifelong dream. Now, she earns a modest income as a fashion coordinator and supplements that with the income she gets from the real estate investments she made with her severance money. Although Karen's story has a happy ending, it's important to remember that she postponed that happiness 25 years by choosing a career based on someone else's expectations and advice, rather than pursuing her own interests and aptitudes.

MY BOTTOM LINE | It will be worth the effort to get on the right track early because, in the long run, working hard for something you believe in is actually easier than hardly working for something you don't want to do. In the first instance, you will be motivated because your heart is in your work; in the latter, you will eventually feel as if you've died spiritually—because your creative instinct will perish without the nourishment of a dream.

Have You "Retired" Your Dreams?

Perhaps you have a clear vision of your career goals but have told yourself that you're too old or too far along in your career to pursue them. You convince yourself to stay where you are by talking yourself out of trying to attain new goals. Do these excuses sound familiar?

- "I'm not 20 anymore; it's too late for me."

- "I should be happy to just get a job and try to make the best of it."

- "Pursuing a dream is not for people with responsibilities like me; it's for those who can afford to take a risk."

- "Why should anyone hire me when they can get a younger, more enthusiastic person?"

Are you tempted to use any of these reasons for not allowing yourself to have a dream? A person over 40 who has a vision brings more than passion to the goal; she often brings maturity and wisdom as well. These qualities can make a person more goal-oriented and able to reach her goals, and they can provide added value for potential employers. If you are re-entering the workforce or changing careers, there is no reason to be deterred by age. Dreams are eternal. They have no age connected to them. At any point in time that you are blessed to have a dream, then you have what it takes to make it a reality.

Dare to Challenge Your Vision

Some people abandon their dreams to pursue a career that they think—
or that others think—they "should" follow. But just as often, people allow
their dreams to fall by the wayside for other reasons: lack of confidence in
their ability to achieve the goal, lack of knowledge about what it takes to
succeed, or negative programming that limits their ability to succeed. If you
give in to psychological obstacles such as these, you'll probably never come
close to achieving your goals. If, on the other hand, you work to overcome
these roadblocks while keeping your vision strong, your chances for success
are almost guaranteed.

It's unrealistic to expect that any positive goal won't be challenged by
obstacles; that's a given. Just because you have a vision doesn't mean that
it is going to be easy to bring it to fruition or that glory, fame, and fortune
will come instantaneously. Most often, the road to success involves education and training, followed by hard work and a commitment to slow but
steady progress.

Realizing this, how do you work to overcome any psychological obstacles
that are blocking your progress? Try these methods:

- If your problem is lack of confidence, you can build it up by
  accomplishing small steps related to your goal.

- If your goal seems overwhelming to you, simply think of it in
  terms of one step at a time, moving ahead slowly but steadily in
  the right direction.

- As you grow more confident in your vision, keep your eyes—
  and your mind—open to opportunities and support from wherever or whomever they come.

- Don't abandon the idea of any career that appeals to you just
  because you aren't sure what it takes to succeed in that profession. Instead of being fearful about the unknown, take the steps
  to research your career and find out exactly what you will need
  to achieve success in your profession of choice.

MY BOTTOM LINE | Understand this: The bigger the dream, the more you will be challenged. No one has a free ride through life. No one moves toward their goal without fear. No one knows all the answers before they set off on the journey. Your fear does not make you unique.

Make Sure Your Dream Fits Your Life Goals

The right career plan works in conjunction with your life goals. A truly fulfilling dream will involve career goals that fit well with the goals you have for the noncareer parts of your life. Satisfaction with your career plan may depend upon fulfilling some of your most important life goals.

It's important that you identify what will truly motivate you in choosing the direction for your dream. For instance, you may dream of producing movies, but after you research the profession, you find that it conflicts with your spiritual goal. You may then find that you can gain as much satisfaction in writing the novel and letting someone else get it to the screen. The more you learn about your dream profession, and your nonprofessional goals, the better prepared you are to choose and follow a career path.

The following list represents areas where you may have "life" goals. Although it is not all-inclusive, it should stimulate you to think about important life goals that you need to consider when choosing a career path. Clarify the goals you have in each area, and then prioritize the areas in terms of their importance:

- **Spiritual:** Goals that contribute to moral or spiritual ideals: being involved in a religious community, making a contribution to help humankind, making the environment better, becoming a better person in some way.

- **Physical:** Goals that involve developing overall good health: eating right, exercising, engaging in sports and other group activities.

■ **Financial:** A short-term and long-term dollar or asset goal: How much money do you need to support the lifestyle you want and still have reserves for the future?

■ **Family:** Goals that involve marriage, children, parents, or other family members you have responsibility for and with whom you want to spend time.

■ **Lifestyle:** Goals that lead to a good quality of life: environmental circumstances, such as commuting time between work and home; where you want to live; ability to control work and schedule; balance between work and personal life.

■ **Interests:** Goals that involve personal hobbies, extracurricular activities, community service, a creative endeavor.

Living the American Dream

Omar has achieved his version of the American dream. He did it by placing a strong focus on education and professional growth and by striving to get along with others in his field. His advanced education, which includes a bachelor's degree from California State University, Long Beach, followed by a master's degree in engineering from Stanford University, has enabled him to turn an interest in math and science and a mechanical inclination that he inherited from his father into a career as a mechanical engineer.

His father, who never finished high school, strongly encouraged all three of his children to get a good education. Besides this lifelong support from his family, Omar was also motivated by a strong love of learning. Even so, getting his degrees proved to be a major challenge. He worked his way through school, spending two years in the army to help finance his education and then, while in school, earning extra money tutoring other students. "I liked school and really wanted to go, but it was hard. Sometimes I would ask myself why I was doing it and was it worth it. But you just have to set your goals and not let anything distract you, no matter how hard it is. In the end, it's worth the effort."

Now, with his schooling behind him and firmly established in his chosen career, Omar still does not see his education as complete. "In a sense, I'm just at another stage of training. I expect to learn 90 percent of what I need to know on the job. It takes about five years before you can say that you are an engineer. I'll be glad when I get to that point, but for now I'm satisfied to still be growing in my field."

He attributes part of his career success to his ability to get along well with his co-workers. (His diverse workgroup is 90 percent white.) "We all get along well. We work together, lunch together, and communicate well. I don't have a problem with any racial group. Race is not an issue for me: I don't think any outside forces can prevent me from accomplishing my goals because of my race."

Omar Miramontes
Mexican-American male
Mechanical engineer, TRW, Redondo Beach, California
Business: Aerospace

Evaluate the Strength of Your Dream

Before committing to a goal based on your vision, evaluate your dream against the following statements to help determine whether you have resolved any conflicting issues around it. If you can say yes to each statement, then you're ready to take the next step:

- You have resolved issues about conflicting responsibilities or finances and are ready to proceed.

- You have elected to follow your career dreams, even though some other type of work seems more lucrative.

- Comments from others that your career dream is unrealistic have only served to provide you with more areas to research before setting your goal.

Build a Map to Follow Your Dream

Once you've identified your dream, the next step is to establish a realistic career goal based on it. To do this, you'll need to explore and research your chosen profession as a whole to determine which specific area will best support your goal and what steps you need to take to get there. The next few chapters will help you do just that.

What makes you unique is sucking it up and moving forward in faith—just as everyone who has succeeded before you has done. Blind faith is not required. Research, planning, information, and support will help lessen the fear and give you a practical foundation for building your future.

CHAPTER 3

From Dream to Reality: Build Your Career Roadmap

Allowing your mind to be free of any restrictions so your dream can surface is a wonderful process. It allows you to enter a realm where all things seem possible. But putting that dream into focus and translating it into a career goal can be agonizing. For instance, let's say you want to be a writer (the dream). The next step is to ask yourself what kind of writing you want to do (the goal). Magazine articles? Novels? Poetry? Educational books? Children's books? Finally, and possibly the hardest part: You need to figure out what it will take to get there (the objective).

Hard as it is, when you've determined a career goal based on your dream, you will have taken the next important step to getting where you want to be. Your career goal is the cornerstone of your success—but to build your career, you'll need other crucial building blocks, including the right education, relevant experience, and an action plan. Without these, you might end up taking a flying leap to nowhere or spinning your wheels in frustration at your lack of progress.

Setting your goal and reaching it will be your responsibility—and yours alone. By accepting this responsibility, you set yourself apart from people who take the first jobs offered to them and then passively let their company or manager dictate the progression of their careers. Managing and directing your career will make you feel more in control of your destiny and, ultimately, happier and more secure in your work. To do this, you need to plan to carve out your career path, independent of a particular job or company, and not expect anyone—employer or colleagues—to help you make your dreams a reality.

This chapter will help you begin that process. "The Action Plan" at the end of this chapter provides a guide for analyzing past work experience and gathering additional information needed for developing steps to reach your goal. Once you have completed the plan, you should use it to determine your first job or the next job that will lead to your goal. After deciding on that job, evaluate your decision against "The Reality Check," which is also at the end of the chapter. Your responses to "The Reality Check" will help you confirm whether you have made the right career choice. It's a good idea to continue using these tools to help you stay focused on your goal when making a decision about other jobs and activities.

Look First, Leap Later

The responsibility for accomplishing your goals might seem overwhelming at first. But believe me, if you proceed slowly and learn as much as you can about the career you think you want before really committing to it, you'll develop the insight to make informed choices and move forward in a direction that is right for you. In fact, a clear and practical understanding of what you need to reach your goal and what you can expect once you get there can actually strengthen your commitment and enhance your motivation.

To get a sense of what it means to proceed slowly and build your commitment, consider the different approaches taken by two friends of mine—Kristine and Judy.

Case 1: Passion...and a Plan

Kristine worked in the public relations department of a large manufacturing company, and she dreamed of owning her own company. When she told co-workers of her ambition to own her own public relations firm, they found her passion and determination so forceful that no one dared challenge her plan by expressing a lack of faith in it. Still, some believed she didn't have the ability or experience necessary to realize her dream. In a sense, they were right, but Kristine took the steps necessary to build her skills and get the education and experience she needed to successfully strike out on her own.

She began by assisting with public relations for community functions on a freelance basis. The efforts reinforced her goal but also made her aware of her need for more specific training and education. Instead of stopping her freelance work and enrolling in school full-time, Kristine decided to keep working while attending school. Her commitment steadily grew stronger and helped her to persevere through the long hours and to manage the many demands on her time. Eventually, she accumulated enough experience and know-how to start her own company. (Use "The Reality Check" to determine whether you are on track with your plan.)

Case 2: Scaling Down a Big Dream

Unlike Kristine, Judy jumped headfirst into pursuing her dream of owning her own realty company. She quit her job as a junior accountant, went to school to get her real estate license, and then started marketing single-family dwellings. Just three months into her new career, however, Judy realized she hated the real estate business. She detested wearing a beeper and having to work evenings and weekends, and she could not get used to the insecurity of knowing that any deal could fall through at the last minute.

Judy was trying to drive a BMW dream with a Pinto commitment. The realities of her chosen career forced her to admit that the demands were not worth the rewards. Ultimately, she achieved some aspects of her dream by finding a position that drew on her real estate training. Judy gladly gave up the goal of owning her own company and returned to a more structured and secure position as an office manager with a large real estate development company.

MY BOTTOM LINE	Research can be tedious, but it is necessary to avoid wasting precious time going in the wrong direction. A willingness to do research on your chosen profession is another big test of your seriousness. If you don't want to do the basics, maybe you've chosen the wrong profession.

Ask Questions—and Find Answers

Kristine's and Judy's stories show how important it is to research a major career move before making a full commitment to it. Before you give up your current job or enroll in an educational program, take the time to see whether your dream can be translated into a workable goal for you.

Begin exploring your dream career by making a list of questions you need answers to, and then add to the list as your process of discovery unfolds. Here's a start:

- What are the various professional categories connected with your goal? (For example, if you're exploring the field of engineering, are you interested in mechanical, electrical, structural, civil, or systems engineering?)

- How much money can you expect to make at the beginning and, ultimately, at the height of this career?

- How easy or difficult is it to find work in this field?

- Do you have—and want to invest—the time and money your education will require?

- Do you like the work culture that supports the profession?

- What are the best geographic locations for this field? Do you live in one or would you be willing to relocate to one of them to advance?

After you've listed all the questions that come to mind, start doing the leg-work to find your answers. Here are some good basic techniques for gathering information about a career that interests you:

- Go to your public library or college career-planning center and ask the librarian for help in gathering information about your prospective profession.

- Ask to see trade journals so you can get a sense of the industry or past issues of the Sunday paper so you can look through the classifieds to find out about the job market in your area.

- Talk with as many people as you can about your goals. You might need to step outside of your cultural group and expand your social activities so that you interact with people of other races and cultures. Sharing your ideas, goals, and interests with a diverse group of people can help you—and them—accomplish career goals.

- Speak with professors at local colleges and vocational schools who teach in the subject area where your interest lies.

- One of the very best sources for gathering information is the World Wide Web. In the chapter "Resources" at the end of this book, I have included popular web sites for research as well as for job listings. I've also included a web site that provides a beginner's guide to the Internet, for those of you who are computer novices. If you do not have your own computer, you can access the Internet through a school, public library, or career center.

- Hook up with people who are already doing what you want to do: Contact professional associations that represent your career interest (check the *Encyclopedia of Associations* at your public library, or for similar information online, enter http://search.yahoo.com/search?p=professional+associations), and network with friends who might be able to introduce you to people working in your area of professional interest.

- If you're working now, you might be able to talk with someone in your company's human resources department about new career opportunities in the company and ask for referrals to others who can help you in researching your goal.

Get Prepared

"I didn't have a lot of direction. Neither of my parents went to college, and I didn't have counselors directing me toward career goals and helping me to understand my options. Eventually, however, I fell into a career that matched my skill set." Like many people, Charsetta chose her college because she had friends there and she liked the location. She decided to work toward a degree in speech pathology and, after graduation, to become a teacher. Because she had several relatives who were teachers, this career choice seemed familiar and comfortable to her.

"It wasn't until my senior year that I realized that teaching wasn't for me because it was not stimulating enough. The school atmosphere was not what I wanted." Deciding that business would provide the challenge and stimulation she sought, Charsetta found an entry-level job in a corporation. At the same time, knowing she needed more education if she wanted to advance in a business career, she went back to school part-time and earned an M.B.A.

"My first job was in human resources. I enjoyed the people contact, which matched my skill set of language and verbal competence. I came in at a clerical level and worked my way up. I wouldn't recommend that path for a degreed person, though; it's hard to make the jump to the professional ranks after having been labeled clerical because people don't automatically think of you as a candidate for professional positions. If you have some options, come in as a professional."

After 17 years and 4 companies, Charsetta has progressed from clerk to her present position as manager. Now, positioning herself for a move to a director level, she continues to prepare herself by developing professional breadth and depth. By taking on human resource assignments, both at the plant and the corporate office, Charsetta has mastered all aspects of human resources management, including compensation, staffing, training, benefits, and equal employment opportunity. In the future, she plans to further broaden her skills by seeking assignments in management development, organizational development, and training. Meanwhile, she continues to prepare herself for future career advancement by teaching herself computer skills and taking classes to stay current with new software packages.

For Charsetta, the importance of taking responsibility for one's own professional growth cannot be understated. "Companies are not taking a strong involvement in helping people get ahead, so mentors and networking are becoming increasingly important," she says. "Competing will be difficult. Many of us are still in awe of whites because we have not interacted with them in schools, colleges, and in our social circles, so we hold back. Instead, we need to be more assertive, toot our own horns, and take responsibility for our own careers."

Charsetta Henderson
Black female manager
Kraft Foods, Chicago, Illinois
Business: Human resources management

Questions of Culture: Do You Fit in This "Family?"

While you're reading about your area of interest and talking to those who work in it or know it well, compare everything you learn about the job to the realities of your personality, your interests, and your life goals. Do the people you talk with "in the trade" have a personality similar to yours? Do you like the activities and environment surrounding the profession? As you learn more about the job, is it as appealing to you as it was before you began your research?

To get a sense of how a work culture will suit you, ask yourself:

- Am I comfortable with the people in the culture? Do we share some common interests? Do some of them have personalities similar to mine? Would we be likely to laugh at some of the same things?

- Would I be able to network easily with the people, or would I feel I was "brown-nosing?" Could I be myself?

- Do I feel my race or gender will make a significant difference in my being successful within the culture?

Of course, it can be more of a challenge to feel comfortable in a working environment when you are a different race from that of the majority of the people in your business culture. Understandably, these co-workers will notice the difference as will you. But if the overall culture appeals to you, this might not be a big issue. If you allow yourself to be open and focus on the common work interests you share with your colleagues, you can establish a positive bond and develop strong working relationships.

MY BOTTOM LINE | In addition to technical skills, interpersonal skills are just as important. Develop a style that allows you to get along with everyone.

The Importance of Avoiding a "Culture Clash"

Why is it so important to get a sense of the working culture that you'll be in once you achieve your professional goal? If you feel comfortable in the working environment and share with your colleagues a similar outlook, personal style, and sensibility, you have the greatest chance of being happy in your work. And if you choose an industry that's aligned with your personal values, you're more likely to understand the culture and feel compatible with the people in it. You also have a better chance of getting a job within a culture that matches your personal and life goals. The employer's opinion of how well you'll "fit" in the organization will strongly influence the hiring decision. Generally, if you have common interests with the interviewer or interests that align well with the culture of the organization, you will you make a more positive impression.

One of the greatest benefits of being part of an industry that complements your values and personal style (cultural mindset) is the tremendous psychological advantage of being able to easily network with people you like as opposed to people you're only able to tolerate. In a compatible working culture, networking and finding mentors—both essential for your professional progress—will come naturally. People have a tendency to communicate naturally and work well with others who share their interests and values. When you're working in a comfortable business culture, getting along, supporting the ideas of your fellow workers, working as a team member, and everyday office courtesies don't feel like "politicking"; they feel like just plain considerate behavior.

If, despite your planning, you find yourself stuck in a work environment that goes against your grain, there are things you can do about it—as you'll see in the following profiles of Naomi and Claudia. You might be able to simply transfer your skills to a different industry as Naomi did, or you might decide to switch careers altogether as Claudia did. But both Naomi and Claudia might have avoided landing in working cultures that did not suit them if they'd done more research before committing to their careers. Taking the time to do good research will help you better determine whether you'll fit into a particular work environment.

Case 1: Can This Career Be Saved?

Immediately after graduating from college, Naomi took a position with a company in the defense industry. The job was in purchasing, and she considered it an important one. After 18 months, however, she realized that the industry and the attitudes inherent in this male-dominated militaristic arena conflicted with her basic nature. A lighthearted woman who functioned best in an unstructured environment, Naomi felt constricted by the serious personalities, rules, and regulations of the industry.

The experience turned Naomi off in terms of her job and made her want to chuck her whole career, return to school, and start off in a new direction. But with the help of a career counselor, she figured out a way to transfer her skills to an industry that better fit her personality. She found a job in the purchasing department of a toy manufacturer and felt immediately at home in the company's more casual and fun environment.

Case 2: Starting Over

Claudia had a similar experience, although her discomfort with her working environment compelled her to start over on an entirely new career path. After graduating with a Bachelor of Science degree, Claudia found an engineering job with an aerospace company. She thought the new job would give her a sense of accomplishment and that she would be satisfied with her career progress. But she wasn't. Naturally outgoing and sociable, Claudia found the quiet, structured life of the engineer stifling. However, because she had followed the engineering path to satisfy her parents' wish for her to have a career with a good future, she decided to stick it out.

After four years, she almost jumped for joy when the company decided to reduce its staff and presented her with an easy out. The layoff gave her the perfect opportunity to find a new path. Claudia met with a career counselor who pointed out that she would likely find greater satisfaction by combining her ability to handle details and follow through with her outstanding interpersonal skills. After agonizing over how a career change would disappoint her parents, Claudia did some networking with her friends and mentors and eventually elected to pursue a career in hotel management.

Through one of her networking contacts, she found a position as an assistant to the sales and marketing manager for a medium-size hotel. It didn't pay much, but it had the potential to lead to a position of responsibility within hotel management. It took only a few days on the job for Claudia to know that she had made the right decision. She felt absolutely at home in the more social atmosphere, amid the hustle and bustle of organizing conferences and banquets at the hotel. Within a few weeks, she had made the commitment to take a course in hotel management to prepare herself for career advancement.

Match Your Skills, Education, and Training with the Demands of the Job

Once you have a firm sense of the work culture that surrounds the job you're interested in, you'll have to figure out what practical skills you need to get there. Of course, we've all heard of those gifted people who, without the specific education or experience needed for their career goals, manage to soar gracefully and easily to the top of their fields solely on the basis of their talent, energy, and belief in themselves. If you're one of those fortunate few, blessed with a finely tuned talent that's ready-made for the present and future workplace, congratulations! The rest of us have to commit to some level of formal training now, as well as later, to move forward in our professions. (See "Get Prepared.")

Obviously, the ideal time to get formal training is before beginning a serious career trek, when you have fewer commitments and financial pressures. But for any number of reasons, that simply might not be possible. You may have started working before you had clearly identified a goal; you may not have had the money to attend school; or you may have majored in an area that does not support your current career goal. But once you've established your goal, don't let your concern over starting late deter you from getting the proper training and education. With commitment and motivation, you can attain the skills and knowledge you need and still achieve your goal.

I suggest that you use one or all of the following sources for help in pinpointing the specific education and skills needed in your chosen career:

- **Local university, community college, or high school:** All three of these sources have career-planning departments and guidance/career counselors. Make an appointment with one of them, explain your career goal, and ask for guidance on the appropriate training.

- **Your local library:** Speak with the librarian about your career goal and your need to obtain information about the training for the profession. This individual will direct you to the appropriate publications and specific reference materials for learning about the educational requirements for your profession. You can also obtain information on college and certificate programs from the library.

- **Professional associations:** Use the *Encyclopedia of Associations*, the Internet site mentioned earlier in this chapter, or the Yellow Pages to contact local chapters of associations that represent your profession. These organizations will be an excellent resource for the education and skills needed for the profession. Additionally, you might luck out and get a mentor out of this group.

■ **Companies in your local area that hire people from your chosen profession:** Contact the human resources department of companies you are interested in. Let them know that you want to prepare for a career and ask whether you could speak with them for about 30 minutes about the skills and education needed. Try to do this in person, as you might develop a mentor situation here. At the very least, these contacts might prove to be good networking sources for later.

Explore Options for Learning While You're Earning

Maria, a quality control inspector with a major electronics company, had tears in her eyes when she told me how much she wanted to be a software engineer. She had never been interested in the type of work she was currently doing, but with only a liberal arts degree and poor English skills, she was unprepared to pursue her dream. Although she was only 23, Maria thought she was getting a late start in going after the career she truly wanted. Still, being highly intelligent and very motivated, she ignored this worry and began to work to overcome her deficiencies. Although it was tough on her, she went to night school to enhance her English-speaking skills and to get the technical training she needed to become a software engineer.

If you're getting a late start on a career path you are truly driven to pursue, remember that you, like Maria, can work and get paid while gaining the experience and training you need. The only excuse for not doing so is lack of commitment. If you want more education but cannot pursue it in a traditional daytime program or at night school, you still have options:

■ **Work-study programs:** Cooperative education integrates classroom theory with practical experience by enabling a student to combine specific periods of attendance at a college with specific periods of related employment. Programs and courses in all disciplines are available in many colleges and universities all over the country. Check with local colleges to see whether work-study programs are available and in what areas of study they are offered.

■ **Distance learning programs:** There are thousands of telecourses and complete degree programs and certificates offered by two- and four-year colleges and universities, delivered to home or work via television, computer, or audiotape and videotape. Distance learning is a good option for people who need to study when and where they want, around busy schedules.

If your action plan includes working and going to school, you'll want to focus on finding work with employers that will support your education and training needs. The best employers are those who are progressive in all their business practices, including employee education, and who offer tuition-reimbursement programs for classes, seminars, and workshops related to the industry. Some employers will even reimburse your education costs regardless of what type of degree you're pursuing.

MY BOTTOM LINE | All professions these days require additional education and study to remain current with the market. A variety of options for learning do not require quitting your job and going to school full-time.

Do a Communication/Interpersonal Skills "Check-Up"

To compete in the high-tech, multicultural, team-oriented global workplace of this century, you will need not only the experience and training required by your profession but also effective communication skills. Being able to interact with people of all races, cultures, and temperaments and to work well within any environment is just as important as having talent and a goal. In fact, a good part of any hiring decision will likely be based on "chemistry" and how well the employer thinks you'll fit into his team. He must feel confident that you can communicate well with all people, particularly those who are part of the business culture of your profession.

I recently observed an excellent example of very effective communication skills. As my colleague Ann, an Asian-American career counselor, and I walked out of a restaurant, we passed a table of hourly workers employed by one of Ann's client companies. The white, Hispanic, and black men were attending a seminar nearby. Away from their normal workday environment and dining in a somewhat elegant restaurant, they looked a little uncomfortable in their surroundings. Ann stopped at the table and asked how they were doing. Her queries were light and casual, mostly comments about the weather, but her smile and her manner communicated the universal language of warmth and caring. Her friendly, relaxed, and mostly nonverbal communication immediately put the group at ease.

Ann's interpersonal skills came to her naturally, but some of us have to work at building them. A long time ago, I discovered a technique (I'm sure it's not new) that helped me develop good interpersonal skills quickly and easily; it can also work for you. I found that once I stopped worrying about how I was coming across and made a point of just being considerate of others, the communication seemed to flow smoothly and naturally. I've also learned that the best way to understand and reach others is to imagine myself in their shoes.

When you find yourself in a difficult or strained situation with another person (for example, when a new manager comes in to oversee your department), ask yourself how you would feel or react if you were in the other person's shoes. Try to step back and observe the situation without judgment while being sensitive to the discomfort and challenges of the other person.

If you're in a new environment, especially one that is culturally diverse, and the people seem reticent, don't assume they're rejecting you. They might only be unsure about approaching you. Instead of waiting for them to make the first move, open up the lines of communication yourself. A warm smile and a friendly "Hello" might be the only things needed to bridge the gap. Always be willing to extend your hand first—even to someone who holds a job or social position superior to yours. But be careful not to be too forceful or aggressive; it can make people uncomfortable. Overall, the recipe for good interpersonal skills is a balanced blend of warmth, self-confidence, modesty, empathy, and humor.

Take Stock of Your Computer and Technical Skills

As fundamental and essential as strong communication skills are, computer skills will be just as important in advancing your career in the current workplace. Computers are everywhere, doing everything, and being used by everybody. Bosses, secretaries, service people, delivery people—workers at all levels of business use the computer to get the job done: to develop reports; retrieve, track, and organize information; plan functions; diagnose diseases; develop blueprints; balance checkbooks; locate missing persons; and train employees, among other things. Without computers, most modern businesses could not function. Now, the Internet has taken computer technology to a whole new level, linking people around the world on one communication network and offering the ability to communicate easily and instantly, transfer documents and data, and operate businesses from thousands of miles away.

Naturally, the future work environment will depend even more on computers and electronic technology. There's no getting around the fact that we'll all need some level of computer skills, no matter what profession we go into. Don't be surprised when an employer wants to know not only whether you're computer literate but also in what software programs you're proficient.

If you've somehow missed out on the computer revolution and have little to no skills in this area, start learning them now. Before you enroll in a class, find out what software programs and computer systems you'll likely use in your field. Even if you're already computer literate, you might need to learn a new program or computer system to match the requirements of your career. There are a number of ways to brush up on computer skills, learn new programs, and explore the Internet:

- For a nominal fee, adult evening classes at a high school or community college offer basic knowledge of personal computers, common word processing and spreadsheet programs, and navigating the Internet.

- Computer training centers generally charge higher fees and offer more specialized and in-depth training at weekend seminars. (If you're working now, your company might pay for these classes.)

- Some computer stores rent out computers on a weekly or monthly basis. If you don't yet have a computer at home, this might be a good way to practice your skills or keep current with new technology.

Practice, Practice, Practice: Getting Practical Experience

A formal education will supply the necessary theory and technical tools to move you in the right career direction, but it's the application of these skills in a practical setting that will be your truest test and teacher. Not only will this hone your talent, but it will also bring your goal into clearer focus. For instance, if you have a degree in finance, you might serve as an assistant (voluntary or for pay) to the controller of a community-based or nonprofit organization. That experience gives you an opportunity to apply the techniques you've learned in school to authentic situations in a real-world environment. You learn more about working in financial management, and you get an opportunity to see how effective you really can be in that role.

Getting experience before you actually get a job will help you find out whether you have the temperament, along with the talent and skills, to work well in a given business culture and to make the sacrifices that might be required. Most important, it could prevent you from committing to something you later realize is not right for you.

Practical experience will almost certainly help you get a job in your chosen field. In a competitive climate where employers want employees to be productive as soon as possible, it pays to have actual experience to support your technical knowledge. Volunteer work and internships are excellent ways to get this experience. (See "Internships: Learning on the Job.") Often, these experiences turn into real job opportunities—after you've demonstrated your value.

Volunteer to Build Your Career

Bob's first job was as an engineer at TRW, but his vision for himself always included helping others. His passion for volunteering has been instrumental to his professional success. "While at TRW, I volunteered to counsel at-risk high school students by bringing them to the company so they could see actual role models of black engineers and scientists. I also got some fellow peers to do the same thing. This led to the write-up in the Los Angeles Times, which credited TRW for initiating the program. As a result, the company decided to institute a companywide social responsibility program."

Managers offered Bob the job of heading this program. He took it and continued his volunteer efforts while at the corporate office—but in another direction. Volunteering at the Opportunities Industrialization Center, headquartered in Philadelphia, he taught welfare-dependent mothers and at-risk youths job skills for electronic assembly, as well as basic reading and math skills. "The beauty of that program was that we were able to incorporate the basic educational skills these people needed with job skills. The participants were motivated because they knew they'd have a job afterwards."

As part of his corporate responsibility position, he connected with an African-American printer who had a $10 million contract with TRW. This brought Bob to the attention of the Interracial Council for Business Opportunity, which recruited him from TRW to serve as the council's executive director. "My task was to spearhead an all-volunteer operation charged with assisting people of color in packaging their loans and business plans to obtain financial aid from financial institutions. I was also responsible for fund-raising." To meet the challenges of this position, Bob enrolled in night classes at UCLA in an executive program to learn about business and finances.

He went on to become a troubleshooter for the council, traveling to its different chapters and developing several branches around the country to work out financing and fund-raising problems. His activities captured the attention of another group, Opportunities

Funding Corporation, which recruited Bob as its volunteer director and charged him with raising funds, including his own salary, for the organization.

Bob's participation in various volunteer projects throughout his career has culminated in the challenging position he now holds— heading the Los Angeles Community Development Bank. The agency was established to assist people of color in south-central Los Angeles in setting up and developing businesses.

Bob's volunteer efforts are directly in line with his vision of service. Through his efforts, he has developed a career that's enabled him to progress from helping people just survive to helping them grow and expand so they can, in turn, help others.

C. Robert Kemp
Black executive
President & CEO, Los Angeles Community Development Bank
Business: Community development

Volunteer Work: What You Get When You Give

Probably one of the easiest and fastest ways to practical experience to support your career goal is through volunteer work. You should consider a six- to nine-month volunteer project as part of your continuing education, an investment in laying the foundation for your career.

Plenty of nonprofit organizations would be happy to allow you to develop skills within their ranks. Numerous agencies in every community need help in areas such as accounting, public relations, newsletter writing, and managing other volunteers. Serving as a volunteer not only develops your skill and builds your confidence, but it also enhances your marketability. You can include transferable skills gained from volunteer work on your résumé, which you can then use when seeking positions for which you have no direct on-the-job experience.

Don't limit your search for volunteer opportunities to nonprofit agencies. Few people realize, for example, that some corporations consider hiring people to work for them on a volunteer basis. Approach the human resources department of a company you'd like to work for and ask about doing some volunteer work in the area you're interested in. The action alone will certainly show that you are committed to your profession. Even if the company does not hire you, after a while you will have developed transferable skills and gained, most likely, an excellent reference that could help you get a job elsewhere.

Volunteering isn't just for first-time career preparation. If you're considering a change of careers, volunteering is a great way to learn more about your new target career while establishing a "presence" in the business. Maybe you've noticed that new community groups and nonprofit agencies often fill key positions with executives from companies in the community. In fact, many executives use volunteering as a transition to a new career. Volunteering allows them to demonstrate capability in the new area as well as make contacts for the future. (See "Volunteer to Build Your Career.") Some community volunteer projects take on quite a high profile. Your successes in these projects can be very visible to the business community, and they might translate into corporate recruitment.

MY BOTTOM LINE | You should think of volunteering as something you'll do throughout your career to develop new skills and contacts, and contribute your time and talent to good causes. Volunteer work helps make you "visible" to the those in the professional community that surrounds your area of interest. You can develop strong references, establish a reputation, and perhaps even meet potential future employers.

Internships: Learning on the Job

Beyond volunteering, an ideal way to gain on-the-job experience is through an internship. If you have sufficient education and training as well as some contacts, you might be able to get an apprenticeship through a school program or start as an assistant to a senior professional. Generally, companies hire interns to work at minimal pay (or sometimes at no pay) while learning and performing the duties of a particular job.

Although interns generally work in low-level positions—as administrative support or assistants, for example—an internship provides exposure and experience that are recognized by other companies and that often open doors—perhaps right at the intern-sponsoring company.

Stephanie, who visualized herself directing a major community service effort, effectively parlayed her volunteer experience into a job. She had little practical experience in community services, and although she had a college degree, it wasn't related to community work. She had a day job at a bank and started volunteering her services in community efforts after work and sometimes on weekends. After doing this for several months, she wrote a program proposal for one of her community groups and requested funding through a local nonprofit agency. This proposal included a position for herself as project director. When the agency granted funding, Stephanie got the job and was on her way to meeting her goal.

Although you can find internships in every area of business, some industries are particularly well-known for using interns. Peterson's annual guide to internships has detailed information on more than 35,000 paid and unpaid internships in the United States and abroad. Listings are organized by subject areas:

- Creative, performing, and fine arts
- Communications and media
- Human and social services
- Public affairs
- Government and law
- Environment
- Education
- Business and technology

Match Your Skills with Market Needs

"My dream has always been to be an entrepreneur. Most of my male family members are self-employed or professionals with a business on the side, so even though I didn't know what kind of business I wanted, I knew that I wanted one."

When Jerry first started out in business, a combination of coincidence, luck, and timing helped him turn a small photography studio into a lucrative modeling agency. "I opened a storefront and taught myself photography, including darkroom work, and learned by trial and error. The first person who came into the studio was a model. During our photography sessions, she complained she was not getting a lot of work because no agency was really handling blacks. About that time, some guys came around selling services in a black directory, so I listed my business as a modeling agency and started getting calls for black models."

For a while, Jerry did well with his modeling agency. Eventually, however, he established himself in a related but more lucrative and diverse endeavor. He relocated from Chicago to Los Angeles, where he developed a niche market placing safety engineers in executive positions. He has built a successful business by continually meeting the sometimes impossible parameters set by his clients in filling their staffing needs.

Jerry learned quickly to focus on the real goal of his business, which is placing qualified people in executive positions, regardless of their ethnicity. He deals with a diverse candidate pool, including black, Hispanic, Asian-American, and white men and women. Basically, Jerry believes that to succeed, a person must be able to recognize opportunity and be adaptable enough to respond to it quickly.

Jerry Medley
Black entrepreneur
Search Professionals, Los Angeles, California
Business: Executive selection

Putting It All Together

Forward planning, knowledge of your various options, and an analysis of how well your action plan aligns with your life-career plan should be an integral part of determining the best places to seek work. For instance, if you want to work in corporate America, research several industries, not just one. That way, if one industry starts to go into a slump (as aerospace has recently done), you will already have an idea of where you could transfer your skills. In addition, being familiar with several industries will give you a broader perspective for making a good job selection.

To help bring your career planning into even sharper focus, you'll also need a clear sense of your economic responsibilities. You might have to plan on working at a full-time job doing what you want, supplemented by a part-time job to keep you afloat until you get on an even plateau with your career—just as an aspiring artist might work part-time as a clerk in an arts supply store while spending her free time in the studio.

Finally, the bottom line will be the number of jobs available. (See "Match Your Skills With Market Needs.") Resources such as *Workforce 2000,* by Joseph H. Boyett and Henry P. Conn, offer valuable information on what to expect in the new workplace as well as the skills needed and the types of jobs that will be most plentiful as we move into a new century. If there are only a few jobs available in your field, you might have to look at changing your objectives to stay in the professional arena in which you think you'd be most comfortable. If, on the other hand, there are plenty of jobs or opportunities in your field, you need only to develop a strong accomplishment-oriented résumé, hone up on your marketing strategy, and go for it.

You might find, as you do your research, that you really don't want to invest the time or money or make the sacrifices necessary to achieve the goal you've selected. Maybe the effort just seems more than you're willing to make or the work culture does not suit you. But don't let this stop you from continuing toward a goal. It might simply mean that you've discovered that you'll be happier pursuing an alternative goal—one that allows you to follow your interests and use your talent and skills but in a different capacity than you first envisioned. If this is the case, use the research you've already compiled as a starting point to explore alternative ways of using your skills, possibly in a different but related capacity or on a part-time, freelance, or volunteer basis.

MY BOTTOM LINE	I see obtaining the education and skills required for your profession as not only mandatory for a person who is committed to a goal, but actually enjoyable to that person if she is pursuing the right goal. This is another test to determine whether you've chosen the right career. If you have, the journey toward the goal (gaining the education and training) will be as rewarding as the actual goal.

Tools for the Road

The most frightening part of a new trip is the beginning. You have had the courage to speak your dream. And you've put it through a test to determine that it's one you can commit to. You've taken a tremendous confidence-building step down the road to your success. Having passed this initial hurdle, you're ready to proceed with focus and enthusiasm to get that first career job. That's just what you're ready to do: The next section of this book will focus on getting that first career job. Use the following "Action Plan" form to help summarize the information you gather while researching your career goal. Photocopy it and continue revising the information as your process of discovery unfolds. Use your final revision of the "Action Plan" as a guide in deciding what kinds of companies and jobs to pursue and to help you make your final decision about the actual job to accept.

"The Reality Check" can help you really assess how well you've done your research and soul-searching about making your career dream a reality. Use it to evaluate the wisdom of your career choice. As you continue into your job search, use these forms again and again to keep your journey on track.

The Action Plan

Revision No. _____ Date _____

My ultimate career dream is to be a(n) _____.

Attainment of this dream would satisfy my (love/passion) for _____
_____.

It fits my natural ability/abilities in the following area(s): _____
_____.

I expect to reach my goal within _____ months/years.

I have talked with _____ and
_____ about the realities of what
I want to do because they have already achieved success in the field.

I have also talked with _____ and _____
because they know me, and I trust their feedback about my capabilities.

Based on my research, I believe that I need additional education in the form of
_____ and _____.

I have investigated how I can get that education and have enrolled at _____
_____ to secure it.

I know from my research that I need experience that will allow me to develop
skills in _____ and _____.

I have spoken with (my boss/a human resources representative/someone at a
nonprofit organization/other) _____ about doing some
work in the area of _____ to get the experience I need.
Within _____ months of securing some experience, I intend to go after a job
doing _____, which will give me more experience and
move me closer to my goal.

I see the following jobs of _____ or _____
_____ as interim jobs to help me reach the goal. My current job of
_____ helps by _____.

I've joined a professional group, called _____, which is
providing me with an opportunity to develop a professional network as well as to
work on activities that I will be able to include on my résumé.

Reality Check

You stand a better chance of being happy and successful in a career you truly love. The following questions apply to anyone on a career quest, and your responses will let you know whether you have chosen a career that will put you on the track to success. Answer true or false to the following statements or questions:

TRUE	FALSE	
☐	☐	I've decided what I want to do or at least the skills I am most excited about using and am looking forward to starting my career. (If you haven't decided what you want to do, then you're trying to steer a ship without a rudder. Reread Chapter 2, "Follow Your Vision and Find Your Dream," talk with a counselor, and decide at least which skills you enjoy using.)
☐	☐	My friends and family are 100 percent supportive of my career choice. (Don't expect everyone to support your dream, especially if it conflicts with their needs.)
☐	☐	I have already done work in my chosen profession or actually volunteered my services because I enjoy using the skills so much. (If you really love your chosen profession, you can't help but do it—sometimes just for the sheer joy of it.)
☐	☐	I already have a degree relevant to my career path, so I don't have to worry about making education and training part of my development plan. (You might not have to get another degree, but never stop updating your training and skills. Continuing professional growth should always be a part of your plan.)

TRUE	FALSE	
☐	☐	I've identified the technical training I need and am currently enrolled in a program. (Start your technical training as soon as possible. Rearrange your lifestyle to accommodate that need. That's what committed people do.)
☐	☐	I've met people who are involved in my desired profession; I like them and the culture I will work in. (If you don't like the people in your profession, you may have chosen the wrong profession or the wrong application of your skills.)
☐	☐	I pride myself on being able to work with and maintain good interpersonal relationships with all people. I like people and it shows. (The ability to maintain good interpersonal relationships is an essential skill for progress.)
☐	☐	I am computer literate and have my own system at home. (If you don't have a system, make some sacrifices to get one.)
☐	☐	I have developed both a short- and long-range goal and a plan for accomplishing both. (If you're serious, you'll have at least drafted a plan of your short- and long-term goals.)
☐	☐	I have reviewed my development plan with someone who has been there. (Reality-testing your plans with someone who has been there can save you time and add value to your ideas.)

PART TWO

Forge Your Path to Success

You know what you want to do. You're determined to get to the goal. You've got a positive attitude, and you're willing to run the race. What now?

Part Two of this book gives you no-nonsense, systematic methods for laying a solid foundation on which you can build your career. It shows you how to take a strong first step and to continue making informed decisions along the way. It takes the mystery out of the process of getting started in a successful career and provides structure for your journey.

CHAPTER 4

Choosing a First Job: Take the Right Fork in the Road

If you know you're committed to a goal, you might wonder whether it will matter if you take a "little" job outside your chosen professional area just to get by while you're working toward the "real thing." The answer is yes; it can matter a lot. In fact, it can ultimately be the first step on a path that you later might find very difficult, if not impossible, to get off of, especially when the "little" job pays reasonably well.

We've all heard certain people talk wistfully about the career that got away, the one they'd always wanted—and one that's dramatically different from the one they have. Usually, circumstances evolved in such a way that never gave them a chance to realize their dreams. Often these are the people who, 10, 15, or 20 years earlier, took that "little" job just to get by.

Don't make the same mistake; don't let yourself be distracted from your goal before you even start the journey. You only get to start once, so make it a good start. That first step can put into motion a set of circumstances that can place you on an irreversible course—so it's essential to stay focused on your goal. (See "Are You on the Right Track With Your First Job?")

When considering a position, ask yourself:

- How will this job move me closer to my goal?

- Am I being honest with myself about the possibilities I see in the option?

- Do I have other options that might be initially more demanding or less lucrative but that might advance my career to a greater degree than the position I'm considering?

Are You on the Right Track with Your First Job?

Whether you already have a job or you're just starting to look, you will fall into one of the following categories. I explain the significance of where you fall following the categories to confirm that you are headed in the right direction or to indicate a need to get on the right track. Choose the one category that best fits your current status:

- I am looking for a position now, and I realize that I need to choose carefully. I am clear about the skills I want to develop to advance my career and will be seeking a job along those lines.

  (Excellent. You are on the right track.)

- I have already accepted a job and can see that it will be beneficial to my skill development and in advancing my career.

  (Excellent. You are on the right track. Start planning now for your next job move, whether in your company or to another company.)

- I have accepted a job, but I am not sure that it will help my career in the long run. I plan to seek advice from a mentor, a career counselor, or a human resource professional at my company to determine whether I am on the right path to reach my goal.

  (Very good. But don't delay seeking guidance to ensure that you are on track. The longer you wait, the harder it will be to make a change.)

- I accepted a position outside my career goal because it was readily available. I like what I am doing so much now that I want to rethink my career goal.

(It is good that you recognize the need for reevaluation because you always need a plan based on a goal if you want to achieve success. Rethink your goal as soon as possible and set up a new career plan.)

■ I accepted a position because I needed immediate money, but I am still looking for a job that will support my career goal, and I will not stop until I have secured one.

(Do not delay in getting on track. Temporary jobs can turn into permanent delays where you end up feeling frustrated and unfulfilled many years later. If you have to accept another "temporary" job, try for something that will allow you to build skills or get exposure in your chosen profession.)

Advice, Advice, Advice—Filter It

Our decisions are influenced even more than we realize by other people and by society's expectations. When someone you respect or who holds a position superior to yours makes a recommendation about your career, you probably take it very seriously. In fact, your thinking might be strongly influenced by her advice.

Look at where that person is coming from—in terms of background, age, culture, work history, and the like. An older person's recommendation, for example, might be tainted with an outdated cultural belief about gender roles. Someone who's suffered through hard times might make recommendations based on survival issues rather than personal satisfaction. People who claw their way up the ranks, taking any opportunity that comes their way, and who feel lucky to have arrived at their current position, might be motivated merely by a need to secure a job. Those who have not developed their own careers often place little value on choosing the right job—one that fits a career plan. Such people might suggest, for example, that you take a job only because it pays more than another position, when the lesser paying position would, in fact, be more in line with your career aspirations. Or if you're being paid well, they might encourage you to stay in this position rather than accept a position at a company where you'll have the opportunity to advance.

Of course, you should give special consideration to advice from your career mentors. The best mentor for you is someone who is currently in the profession you want to join. Advice from this individual is likely to be most beneficial to your planning. Ultimately, you'll need to carefully evaluate all recommendations to determine how they align with your goal. If you find that the advice does not support the career path you've laid out for yourself, then you'll simply have to challenge it.

Case 1: "Your Perspective" Versus "My Vision"

If Fannie, a black plant manager for a major food company, had listened to one of her managers at the first company where she worked, she might never have set a management position as her goal. (See "I Orchestrated My Career.") Claiming that scientists don't make good managers, the manager advised Fannie, who has a master's degree in chemistry, to stay on the technical side of the business. But Fannie had focused her sights on a quality management position in the food industry, and she believed that to make an impact in the business, she needed to combine her technical skills with working with people. Also, she knew she had the necessary interpersonal skills to work in management. By participating in church groups and community activities, she had gained confidence and experience in this area, not to mention transferable professional skills.

Fortunately, Fannie had the strength of mind to ignore the manager's advice. While working as a chemist, a division head observed her interacting with others and recognized her leadership ability. He recommended her for the first management position that came up—and she was ready to take on the new challenge. Because she remained on her path, she ultimately did combine her technical skills with her talent for managing people.

Case 2: A Quick Cure Leads to a Slow Recovery

Of course, not all of us can carve out so straight a path. Carol's career was sidetracked after a family priority forced her to relocate. After holding progressively responsible management positions, she found herself faced with starting over in a new city. Unable to find a position in her field, she accepted a temporary secretarial position on the recommendation of a family friend. She needed quick money and this was an easy solution.

The move proved to be a bad one, however, because it negatively impacted Carol's career in several ways. She did not seem credible as a manager to the people who knew her as a secretary, so they were not comfortable recommending her for managerial positions. Also, she could not establish viable networking contacts at the company where she worked because all her colleagues perceived her as a secretary, not a professional. Finally, making no reference on her résumé to the secretarial position (which lasted for 18 months), she had a hard time explaining to prospective employees what she had been doing for that long stretch of time. It took her a long time to find another position on her career track. Because of the delay getting back on track, she had to start at a lower salary than she expected.

 MY BOTTOM LINE Forging ahead is about evaluating options every step of the way and staying focused by keeping your goal in sight.

Choosing Your First Priority: Money or Career Track

There is a popular saying (and a book of the same title by Marsha Sinetar) that if you do what you love, the money will follow. In an ideal world, we'd all be able to follow our bliss, unencumbered by any real concerns about money. We'd be free to go after our first job, with no other thought than how that job would help us reach our goal.

Well, this is not an ideal world. Sometimes circumstances will throw you off track, forcing you to make a detour in your plans. You might have to take a position for which you are overqualified, but, even then, you should make the most of this detour. Seek out a position that will develop your skills and enhance your career—rather than get stuck in a role that could set you up for future stereotyping. If your circumstances dictate that money be your top priority, then find the best way to earn the money you need while still working toward your ultimate career goal. Although that might sound like difficult advice to follow, here are a couple of suggestions for how you can manage a compromise:

■ Choose a job that will provide networking contacts to support your career goal or a job that will allow you to build skills that can be transferred into your ultimate career job. For instance, a person wanting a position in sales might start off doing market research. The skills and knowledge learned in this role will really help this person later when he or she is building a sales territory. If your ultimate goal is a career in nursing administration, you might benefit from an initial clerical position in a hospital or care facility. You are likely to learn things in that role that will prove helpful later in setting up administrative systems and understanding the needs of the culture. Similarly, a person desiring to pursue a career as a psychologist might benefit from a clerical position in a social services agencies, which would provide some exposure to the types of problems she would encounter later in her work.

■ Choose a job that brings in the money you need but leaves you the time and mental energy to work at something in your chosen field—whether that work is a second-income producing job or a volunteer, internship, or work-study opportunity. Such a compromise or a second job will allow you to build skills that will support your career goal. (See "Pursuing the Right Job for Your Needs.")

Whichever initial job choice you make, it's important to get off to a strong start with your career, even if the job pays a little less than another position that is off your career track. As difficult as it might be, do not be lured in the wrong direction by big money. A big money job off your career track might provide temporary joy, but it can later lead to a lot of disappointment and frustration when you realize that it's very difficult to leave a career track after you've developed a lifestyle around it. Earning less initially in a job that promotes your career goals will ultimately pay higher dividends, such as when you're making big money and supporting the lifestyle you've always wanted in a career that brings you fulfillment.

Planning a Career Path That Leads to the Future

An important factor in your criteria for evaluating job options is knowing what jobs and career fields are likely to be available in the future. It is pointless to plan a career around an occupation that is going the way of the dinosaur.

Statistical trends show that in the future, opportunities will be plentiful in areas relating to computer technology, care-giving, and services that depend primarily on free-flowing interactions with other people. Examples of these type of jobs in corporations might be those that deal with training, consultative selling, public relations, marketing, or advertising. Of course, we can't all be human resource specialists, systems analysts, home healthcare providers, or daycare workers; but being aware of industry trends will help us in evaluating our job options.

How can you keep up on industry trends as an ongoing part of your job search? Read books—such as *Workforce 2000,* by Joseph H. Boyett and Henry P. Conn—that offer insightful information about how growing trends will shape future jobs—and what the future might hold for the career you have in mind. Browse through periodicals, news reports, and magazines for general information and to stay current on changes that could impact your profession. Review national magazines such as *Hispanic Business, Black Enterprise,* and *Fortune.* If you're in a technical field, the *Journal of the NTA* (National Technical Association) will help you stay current on trends in technical professions.

Also, make it a daily practice to scan the front page and business section of your local newspaper. If you live in a major city, that paper will provide you with timely and relevant information on your professional focus. If you live in a small town, consider subscribing to a paper from a large city (especially from a city you might be interested in relocating to someday). Read the newspaper and trade journals not only to stay current on what's happening, but also to keep an eye out for names of people you might contact for informational interviews. If you're ready to assert yourself, make a cold call; if not, write letters to those contacts and request informational interviews. (You learn more about informational interviewing later in this chapter.)

If you have a computer and a modem, go online to gather up-to-the-minute information from a host of excellent sources. Subscribe to relevant newsgroups on the Internet to find out what others in your field have to say about the industry or current trends.

And—always—network with other professionals. Join professional groups or participate in association activities to enhance your knowledge about trends and get real-world information about activities in which companies in your area are involved. The chapter "Resources" at the back of the book will also provide some sources for following job projections and industry trends.

I know this might sound overwhelming. You're probably thinking that participating in all these activities would be so terribly time-consuming that you wouldn't even have time to look for a job—let alone work at your present one. But, I assure you, it's not that difficult to stay current—as long as you set aside some time to do it. For instance, read the newspaper every day, go to the library a couple of times a month to update yourself, and attend a professional group meeting at least once a month. Successful professionals are always looking for work—either within their company or somewhere else. Staying current on trends should be an integral part of your ongoing research and planning effort to establish and advance your career.

Pursuing the Right Job for Your Needs: A Reality Check(list)

Your career is part of your life-career plan; therefore, you need to consider the goals and circumstances surrounding that plan as you decide which jobs to pursue. The process of working through the questions outlined here will help you analyze your options, sort out issues that are important to you at this time, and make the best decision to meet your overall needs. To work through this process, fill in the blanks, honestly and completely.

My career goal (where I am trying to get to) is:_____

_____

Responsibilities or factors that I have to consider at this time that will affect which option I choose (such as no car, sick relative, past-due debt, children): _____

_____

_____

_____

_____

_____

_____

Job options I am considering and their ability to advance my career goal and satisfy factors listed here:

	Pros	Cons
Option 1 _____	_____	_____
	_____	_____
	_____	_____
Option 2 _____	_____	_____
	_____	_____
	_____	_____
Option 3 _____	_____	_____
	_____	_____
	_____	_____

The job option that best satisfies my priorities: _____

_____

The job option that best satisfies my career goal: _____

_____

The job option that will provide the best compromise (if different) to meet my priorities and advance my career: _____

_____

Regardless of the circumstances that will ultimately influence your job choice, it's important to develop and implement an effective job search campaign that will help you meet your goals. First, establish a criteria you can use for evaluating all job options; write down all the factors that you can think of that would influence your decision. Then systematically evaluate all job options against your criteria and select the option that will best enable you to meet your responsibilities and life-career goals.

I Orchestrated My Career

Fannie started her career with a clear vision. "After doing some research at Louisiana State University in the food industry and receiving my master's in chemistry at Southern University in Baton Rouge, I left school with the goal of being a corporate quality manager. I didn't just fall into my current position; I orchestrated it."

Fannie began by doing some research, talking with people and professors who had worked in the industry. This helped her take a realistic inventory of her talents, get a strong sense of the industry, and then successfully land a job. "When I first entered the workforce with Quaker Oats, it was on a trial basis. My alternate plan was to continue my education and to teach. With my first job, I was eager for the experience; it just so happened that the money was good, so I got a great two-in-one deal." Fannie remained with Quaker Oats for 14 years, until the company started downsizing. At this point, she decided to leave rather than move into an area that did not interest her.

After relocating to California, she responded to an ad for a quality supervisor with Kraft. Within a month, she had the job. With her vision still intact, Fannie set out to develop the additional people skills she needed to move closer to her managerial goal. "I took on leadership roles in the church and in community activities wherever I could, and I continue to do so. I still like to teach, so I always find a way to use that skill. Currently, I'm involved in the Adopt-A-School Program, as the principal."

As she continued to develop her leadership and interpersonal skills, Fannie wanted more opportunity to work with people, to guide and motivate them. Fortunately, her company recognized her abilities and offered her just such an opportunity. "I have always been interested in helping people grow and reach their highest potential—to perform to their full capacity. My job as plant manager came about because my boss saw in me that potential to lead and influence others to achieve. After handling a management position in an unfamiliar area, I was asked to interview for the job as plant manager."

> Fannie's advice for people setting out on a career path is simple and to the point: "Take advantage of every opportunity there is to learn. Find a role model. Seek help wherever you can get it."
>
> **Fannie Picou**
> Black manager
> Kraft Foods, California
> Business: Plant manager

Choosing a Geographic Location for Work

In addition to professional or marketplace trends, you'll have to consider the locations of the economic centers of your profession. (See the table called "Business Power Seats.") For instance, if your career goal involves medical research, your action plan might include relocation to a city such as Austin, Texas, that houses many teaching hospitals and research institutes that specialize in medical research. When evaluating location, consider the aspects of your lifestyle that you'd rather not change. If factors such as climate, culture, nightlife, and the nearness of family and friends are important to your happiness, you'll need to determine how they would be affected by the geographic location in which you choose to develop your career. If there are several locations to choose from, it would be a good idea to evaluate the choices against the lifestyle factors to help you make the final decision.

A couple of years ago, a fellow consultant woke up to the realities of her lifestyle preferences when she relocated from California to the East Coast. After six months, she returned home with the firm realization that she could never live anywhere but Los Angeles. She admitted that she had taken her lifestyle for granted and had not considered the dramatic changes that would be involved in such a move. You can avoid making a similar mistake by making a checklist of the aspects of your lifestyle that you consider necessary for your well-being. Then, look them over and determine whether relocating would force you to give them up.

The Chamber of Commerce in the city you're interested in is an excellent source for information about the location. A postcard or call requesting information will get you what you need. Establishing contacts with educators or professionals in the area is another great way to find out about the local *and* professional culture of the area. Area colleges, universities, vocational schools, career centers, professional organizations—any of these is a great resource for finding out more about living and starting a career in a specific location.

BUSINESS POWER SEATS	
City	**Industries**
Atlanta	Financial services, telecommunications
Austin	Medical research, computer software and hardware
Boston	Computer software and hardware, financial services, medical research
Branson	Tourism
Charlotte	Financial services
Chicago	Financial services, medical research, telecommunications
Denver	Computer software and hardware, telecommunications
Houston	Computer hardware, medical research
Las Vegas	Tourism
Los Angeles	Film and TV production, tourism
Miami	Tourism
Minneapolis	Computer software and hardware
New York	Film and TV production, financial services, medical research, telecommunications, tourism
Orlando	Computer hardware, film and TV production, tourism
Philadelphia	Telecommunications
Provo	Computer software
Portland	Computer software
Raleigh/Durham	Computer hardware and software, medical research
San Francisco	Computer software, film and TV production, financial services, telecommunications, tourism
San Jose	Computer hardware and software
Seattle	Computer software, medical research

*Compiled from *Fortune* magazine articles.

Targeting a Specific Industry

As I mentioned in the last chapter, working in the right industry can be very important to starting your career off right. If you've followed the advice in the previous chapters of this book, you've asked yourself serious questions about which industries really fit within your life and career goals. Now, it's time to do some in-depth and specific research to pinpoint a target industry for your job search.

Again, you can use your public library or the Internet for help in getting key information on various industries. For guidance in selecting the right industry on which to focus your search, look at these publications to get answers to the following questions (they are all listed in the reference section of your library):

What are the high-growth industries?

- *Directory of Industry Data Sources* (also lists company names, addresses, and phone numbers)

What are the salary levels in specific industries?

- *The American Almanac of Jobs and Salaries*

- American Management Association surveys (These might not be available at the library; if not, contact the American Management Association directly.)

Who are the competitors in an industry?

- *Dun & Bradstreet's Million Dollar Directory*

What industries use specific types of professionals?

- *Encyclopedia of Associations*

- *The Career Guide: Dun's Employment Opportunities Directory*

- *Encyclopedia of Career and Vocational Guidance*

- *Occupational Outlook Handbook*

- *National Trade and Professional Associations of the United States*

- *Directory of U.S. Labor Organizations*

Selecting Companies

Once you've chosen the industries where you will market your skills, you'll want to make sure that you target companies within those industries that have practices supporting growth and advancement for its employees. I find companies that have such practices for people of color are the best companies for all people.

It's also important to know about the history of a company, its key players (especially if you decide to direct a letter to one of them), and its background. This will give you a sense of the company's philosophy and, possibly, an idea of the corporate culture. Such information will help you not only determine whether you'd fit into that culture and have the opportunity to advance within the environment but would also give you some ideas for how to focus your résumé and for questions you might ask if you're interviewed by the company. You can obtain information about any publicly held company by contacting their public relations department and requesting a brochure and annual report.

You should plan to use the Internet as part of your research. If you're not online yourself, you might be able to use a computer at your college or local public library to find out information about companies. You can use any of the major search engines (Alta Vista, Yahoo, Northern Light, and so on) to do searches for specific company names or business topics. You'll turn up recent articles, industry happenings, press releases, and much more. Many large companies have their own web sites, as do most companies whose business is technology. Usually, all you need to do to find a particular web site is to type http://www. followed by the company name or acronym and finally by .com, leaving out any apostrophes and spaces (for example, http://www.jist.com). It's worth looking at the home pages of companies that interest you; you'll find plenty of information about the company (and sometimes even job listings—we talk about that more in the section that follows). Keep in mind that because companies put together their own web sites, you won't find anything other than a rosy picture there. Another option is to do a key-word search (of the company or industry you're looking into) in the business news section of newspapers featured in commercial online services.

To round out your research, get information from other sources as well. Check out the following reference sources in your library for information on specific aspects of the companies you have in mind:

Products the company offers:

- *Moody's Manuals*
- *Thomas Register*
- *U.S. Industrial Directory*
- *Dun & Bradstreet's Million Dollar Directory*
- *Standard and Poor's Register of Corporations, Directors, and Executives*
- Individual company annual reports—contact the company's public affairs department directly and ask the person there to send you a copy

Key people in the company and their backgrounds:

- *Dun & Bradstreet's Reference Book of Corporate Managements*

Finding the Jobs: It's a Whole New Game!

After you've established a job goal and made a commitment to it, the next step is to develop ways to find the jobs that fit that goal. In the past, the business culture valued people who could be trained and cultivated for long-term employment. Today, however, downsizing and restructuring have created a very fast-paced work environment where there is high turnover and a focus on short-term projects that demand immediate skill sets and experiences.

Because this environment does not allow for a long learning curve, employers want to hire people who can be quickly brought up to speed with minimal training. They therefore meet their staffing needs in a variety of ways, some quite different from those they used in the past. For instance, more employers than ever use outside contractors, consultants, and temporary workers. Some companies also outsource to service groups to meet, for example, their graphics and printing needs rather than have their own in-house groups. All this makes it very important for you to use a variety of search strategies when you're job hunting.

MY BOTTOM LINE Use all roads that lead to your goal—networking, Internet, agencies, ads, and especially the all-important first job.

The Internet

The Internet is the newest way to find out about job openings. It does not replace interacting with people (yet), but it is proving to be a very valid way to find out about a large number of positions across the country and even around the world. Many companies have their own web sites, where they provide information on their corporation and sometimes post job openings and human resource contacts. Many companies have a staff listing or carry information about their departmental heads or chief executives, giving you an opportunity to read up on the major players in the organization. When you go to a company's web site, make sure to visit each of their pages and check out press releases, product lines, and new organizational developments; anything you can learn will help you evaluate the company and its business.

Some web sites are designed especially for job hunters, offering job search advice and lists of positions available in many companies, often sorted by field and by region. Also, trade publications and newspapers from around the country list their classified ads on-line.

The Internet is the worldwide network of computer networks, and the web is only one of the networks on the Internet. An excellent source for using the Internet is *Hook Up, Get Hired!* by Joyce Lain Kennedy.

If you have a computer (or access to one) with a modem, you can easily go online to access jobs on the Net—as long as you know the right sites to go to. Otherwise, you can spend hours searching, with no real results. I suggest you begin your search with some of these sites that focus solely on job search:

■ The Riley Guide—directory of employment resources: http://www.dbm.com/jobguide/

- A meta-list of online job services: http://www.careers.org

- Job search and employment opportunities—Best bets from the Net: gopher://na.hh.lib.umich.edu:70/00/inetdirsstacks/

- The Black Collegian Job Assistance Selection Service: http://www.black-collegian.com

- Career Mosaic: http://www.careermosaic.com

- Career Path: http://www.careerpath.com/

- The Monster Board: http://www.monster.com/

- America's job bank (maintained by the U.S. Department of Labor): http://www.ajb.dni.us/

- Yahoo's listing of employment: http://www.yahoo.com/business/employment

These are just some of the important job-search sites you'll find listed in the chapter called "Resources" at the end of this book.

Networking

Networking simply means using word of mouth to find out about jobs and let jobs find out about you! It means letting people in your life—friends, family members, neighbors, professional contacts, and anyone else you think might now or at some other time know or hear about a job—know that you're looking.

Networking is a key way of meeting as many people as possible face-to-face and letting them know who you are and the skills you have to offer. These people then become agents for you and can lead you to contacts who might provide the link to a wonderful job opportunity. Talk to people—everyone you know—about your goals. And follow these six steps to effective networking:

1. Decide what kind of information you need from industry insiders to help with your job search: salary range, expected responsibilities, key things recruiters will look for on your résumé, questions most likely to be asked in interviews and examples you can give to demonstrate your skills, and contacts for getting into a particular industry or company.

2. Make a list of all the people you know. Decide what kind of information you will seek from each one. One person might provide better contacts than another; a different person might have a better focus on the market. Don't expect everyone to be able to provide the same information. If you restrict your contacts only to people in your own ethnic group, you'll sorely limit your opportunities. I have personally found that when I've networked with people of other races, I've been received very positively and felt that the other individual was very pleased that I would contact him or her for advice.

3. Have your résumé ready to show your contacts when discussing your job goals. Ask for feedback on your résumé. Don't worry about identifying a particular job in your conversations, but do be clear about the industry and companies you're interested in and the skills that you will be marketing.

4. Contact people on the list (try to make personal contact) and ask them for names of others they recommend you contact. If you're not comfortable cold-calling a new contact to whom you've been referred, ask your original contact whether he or she would mind making the initial call for you.

5. Get information and guidance from contacts. If they have a job or know of one, they will tell you about it. Because your purpose for the networking session is to get information and contacts, do not discuss specific job openings—unless the contact brings it up first. If they do, then the networking meeting has turned into an interview, and you should respond in an interview format.

6. When you get your job, call the people you've networked with and thank them all for their help.

Some people believe that the concept of networking has worn thin because so many people are doing it and because the contacts you make through networking are not fooled when you say you're doing research and you just want an informational interview. They know you want a job. That is probably true, but it's also true that if you're networking with people you know and people they introduce you to, then you'll probably be the person to get the recommendation for any open positions they hear about.

Informational Interviews

Your job search should also include informational interviews. You've heard me mention informational interviewing several times throughout this book. It's a great method for gathering the facts about potential careers as you bring your dreams into focus. But when you've pinpointed the career that's right for you and you're ready to land your first job, the informational interview becomes more than a good idea; it's a necessity.

Informational interviews are not interviews for a specific job; rather, they are less formal meetings, phone conversations, or even email exchanges with people to find out about a type of job, a field, or a company that you might be interested in. Ask people you know whether they have contacts you can interview for more information about your chosen profession. Getting and conducting an informational interview takes some thought and practice, if you want to make the most of this important opportunity.

Sonya, a marketing graduate looking for a job in the competitive retail environment, needed help meeting prospective employers for informational interviews. She didn't know anyone in retail but did have a strong network of friends working in good jobs in other industries. She asked them for help in making contact with people who could give her an insider's point of view and tips on how to get into the retail business.

A friend put Sonya in touch with his mother, an attorney who had a good friend working as a marketing director for a major retail store in town. Sonya met with the woman, who was happy to help; she was impressed that Sonya was doing her homework by researching the market before officially approaching an employer about a job. In the interview, Sonya learned what to expect in developing a marketing career in retail and what salary range would be reasonable for her. The marketing director also supplied her with three contacts in the industry, one of which led to an assistant marketing position with a medium-size store.

Classified Ads

Contrary to what you may have heard—that no decent jobs are advertised—companies still use ads as a method of filling their positions. Many companies resist paying agency fees because they know they can access a pool of qualified people by advertising their positions.

Of course, the fact that so many qualified people respond to a single ad can be a problem for you, the job seeker. Ads typically generate a large number of responses, so it's not unusual to be in competition with hundreds of applicants for a published opening, especially if it's a desirable position in a tight market—and it's advertised in the newspaper as well as on the Internet.

To get a leg up on the competition, keep these important strategies in mind when responding to ads:

- Don't be intimidated by the job requirements advertised if you honestly believe that you can do the job. An employer's hiring decision is not just based on how well an applicant meets the job requirements; one's motivation and personality are often just as important. That's why it's essential to indicate in some way in your résumé your motivational level as well as your positive character traits.

- Remember that the primary purpose of the résumé is to stimulate the curiosity of the hiring manager so that he wants to set up an interview. The résumé alone cannot get you the job, so don't try to include so much information you cheat yourself out of an interview. The résumé should target specific skills that were advertised in the ad. Use the language in the ad as much as possible in describing your skills and experience.

- In responding to ads, always include a cover letter. The purpose of the cover letter is to stimulate the screener to read your résumé. To the greatest extent possible, the cover letter should parrot back the advertised requirements of the job. In reading your cover letter, the human resources representative should experience an "Aha. This person has exactly what we are looking for" reaction. The human resource representative (who might have to quickly scan hundreds of résumés) should then be compelled to pass your résumé to the hiring manager instead of putting it in the "later" pile.

- Be careful how you respond to a request for salary requirements. I would suggest you indicate that you are seeking a salary commensurate with your skills and experience for the position. Of, if you've done a lot of research into salaries within the industry for those with your skills, background, and experience, indicate a range that really represents what you will accept. But be prepared to walk away from opportunities that fall outside that range because the employer might disqualify you if your request is out of line with the company's offering. A final, and perhaps best, option is to just ignore the request. Most companies do not expect to get the information, and your résumé and letter won't be rejected because you don't list an expected salary, especially if your experience seems to line up well for the position.

- Do not provide information in the résumé or cover letter that was not requested. Have someone critique your résumé (preferably a human resources professional) to make sure that you are not dating yourself with the information you include. For instance, "33 years experience" in a summary statement means you're probably at least 55 years old. The rule of thumb is that experience older than 10 years is probably not relevant. Examples in the next chapter shows how to address this issue.

- Follow up within a week if you can. Some ads say no phone calls; do yourself a favor and respect this request. After a week, send another letter, indicating you are still very interested in being considered for the position. If the name of the company was indicated in the ad (some are blind ads), do some research about the company so that you can mention something about the company in your follow-up letter. This shows initiative and a true desire to get the job.

The next chapter in this book talks in more detail about what first-time job-hunters should—and shouldn't—include in their résumé; for those of you starting over or dramatically altering your career track, see Chapter 10, "The Grass May be Greener on the Other Side of the Fence," for advice on reworking the mid- or late-career resume. Finally, the chapter called "Resources" at the end of this book includes resume guides that will provide examples of ways to list and describe skills to better align them with a published position.

Permanent and Temporary Staffing Agencies

Don't overlook agencies as an avenue to jobs. Signing up with a permanent or temporary employment agency or contacting a headhunter (or staffing consultant, as they now prefer to be called) can open up opportunities you may not have found on your own. The trick is understanding the different types of agencies out there and what they have to offer:

- A *retainer firm* gets exclusive contracts with companies to fill specific positions. When a company retains an agency to handle a placement, it accepts applications for new openings only through that agency.

- A *contingency agency* does the same thing as a retainer agency, only without exclusivity or a contract; because of this, contingency agencies must compete with other agencies, as well as applicants, for the attention of the employer.

Some agencies maintain retainer contracts with one or more companies while working on a contingency basis with others. When choosing an agency, always ask whether it is a retainer or contingency firm. The biggest advantage of working with a retainer agency is that it is more selective in terms of the applicants it recommends for interviews. This means that if the agency gets you an interview with a firm, you won't have to compete with a herd of people from the same agency for the job. Also, a retainer agency can better prepare you for an interview by providing more comprehensive information on the background of the employer.

Don't limit yourself to permanent placement agencies, however, even if you are looking for a full-time permanent position. Temporary agencies can place people in professional as well as clerical and administrative jobs and, amazingly, are among the nation's top employers. Taking a temporary position is an excellent way to sample a company before seeking permanent employment with it. Similarly, companies often try out employees in temporary positions before extending a permanent offer. In fact, many companies regularly fill a certain percentage of their openings with short-term employees and sometimes will even advertise the position through an agency as "temp to perm."

Here are some guidelines to remember when working with agencies:

- Deal only with agencies that are employer-fee paid. The best agencies are paid by employers to fill their positions, so you gain no advantage by paying an agency fee. Always ask the agency who pays the fee before dealing with it.

■ Don't let yourself be pushed into a permanent or temporary situation unless it is a good fit for your career.

■ Always maintain control of your own job search by telling the representative what you want to do and where you're willing to work.

■ Tell permanent placement agencies in writing that you want to know in advance when they plan to forward your résumé for an opening. That way, if you've already contacted the company on your own, you'll avoid any conflict over the agency's fee. You could incur a similar problem by having a company receive your résumé from more than one agency.

■ Agencies only get paid when they make a placement. Keep in mind that no matter how nice and helpful the representatives are, they are working for themselves and not for you.

Unsolicited Approach

It can sometimes be advantageous to approach a company with an unsolicited résumé—if you do some research and make sure your résumé and cover letter are tailored to the needs of the company. Address your résumé to the head of the department you want to work for, not the human resources department. Find out that person's name by networking, checking the company's web site, or calling the company and asking the receptionist for the name and address of the head of, for example, the editorial, office services, or data processing department.

Be sure to target your unsolicited communication to a select number of appropriate companies. In most cases, you'll be wasting your time and money sending out a mass mailing. You'll find it more effective to send a few letters at a time and then follow up within a week with a phone call to determine whether your résumé met with any interest. You can't expect the companies to contact you.

Job Fairs

Job fairs are common, particularly in highly populated areas, because they offer a very efficient way for employers to connect with a large pool of applicants. A variety of groups host job fairs—colleges and college alumni associations, career planning units of special interest groups (such as the *Los Angeles Times* in Los Angeles), urban social services centers—and typically announce them through newsletters, the media, the Employment Development Department, posted notices, and so on. Job fairs can be geared to college graduates, experienced workers, and sometimes teenagers.

Going to a job fair can be a very effective way to make contact with representatives from many companies. Go to the fair dressed to impress, with an attitude to match. Wear the same type of clothes you'd wear to an interview, pass out your résumés, collect business cards, be pleasant to everyone, and follow up with phone calls. Job fairs give you an excellent opportunity to practice your interviewing skills, beef up your professional network, and gather ideas about the types of jobs available, salaries offered, and other important information for job-hunters. Don't miss these important opportunities!

Professional Associations

As I've mentioned before, professional associations are an excellent source for networking, salary information, and making contacts. The members of these groups often know of openings, and some associations put out a regular publication that lists job openings. Check the *Encyclopedia of Associations* for chapters of appropriate professional groups in your area.

Before making a decision to join an association, attend one of its meetings. Some of these groups charge high membership fees, but you can probably attend one meeting or function for an affordable fee. Paying the fee and going to one or two meetings might be all you need to make some good contacts and get information that will help you later with your job search. Most major associations have their own web sites, where you can get valuable information on dues, meeting schedules, and local chapters.

College Placement Centers

College placement centers are obviously an excellent source for the recent college graduate. Even after you've graduated, you can usually still use these placement centers; most are available to alumni. They have directories and other information similar to what you might find in a public library, and they also post available positions that they receive from employers. Look at the postings carefully; if you see a position that's not in your field, take down the name of the contact person. Even if there are no immediate openings that match your skills, you can contact the companies and submit your résumé for consideration for future openings.

Government Placement Centers

The Employment Development Department (unemployment office) can be a resource for locating companies that are hiring and contact people at those companies. Although most of the positions offered through the EDD are entry-level positions, most EDD agencies have job clubs run by experienced people seeking work, and these people can sometimes be good contacts.

For Federal government employment opportunities, contact The U.S. Office of Personnel Management (1900 E Street NW, Washington, D.C.), which is responsible for nationwide recruiting for civil service positions at GS levels 1–15. As the Federal government's human resource agency, the OPM maintains a network of Federal job information centers in major metropolitan areas. The telephone numbers are listed in the White Pages under U.S. Government, Office of Personnel Management; you can learn more about the OPM and review current job postings from around the country by visiting the web site at www.usajobs.opm.gov.

Organizing Your Research

You can avoid confusion and assess your industry, company, and agency research information quickly if you keep it organized in a standard format. Keeping your research material in order and up-to-date will make your job search a lot easier because you'll have pertinent information at your fingertips to help target your résumés and letters as well as prepare for interviews. The following forms will help you with this process. I suggest you duplicate the forms or use 5×8 cards for all of the information so you can easily file it for later reference. The information I've suggested you gather is a guideline. You might want more or less, but it's a good idea to keep it consistent so you can use like data when making a comparison between companies or industries.

Industry Checklist

This form provides a guideline for gathering information to help determine the stability and potential of an industry. Professional associations are one of the best sources for data here. They could provide forecast information and a significant amount of information listed in the form. The Chamber of Commerce in your preferred geographic location is also a good source of information. Remember that these are only suggested pieces of information to consider. Essentially, you want to determine whether there is room for growth in the industry you're interested in or whether you should consider putting your skills in another industry with more potential.

Industry: _____

Standing: High, medium, low growth (circle one)

Forecasts: _____

Factors contributing to potential changes in the industry (might include pending or current legislation): _____

_____

_____

Growing trends (might include changes in processes, automation, recent downsizing, or mergers): _____

_____

_____

_____

_____

Other pertinent information: _____

_____

_____

_____

_____

Company Checklist

You can use the following form during an informational interview or when collecting data from print and online sources. Complete as much of this information as possible before having the informational interview and use it to guide the conversation. You can later use this information to help structure letters and resumes so they are geared to the needs of the company. Some of this information will be provided in an annual report if it's a publicly held company. If not, the Chamber of Commerce can be a great source of information. You can learn some of this information during the informational interview.

Company name and address: _____

_____

_____

Contact name and phone number: _____

_____

_____

Company history: _____

_____

_____

_____

_____

Current size, growth rate: _____

Profitability: _____

Product/services: _____

_____

_____

_____

_____

Major players:_____

     Names: _____

     Background: _____

     Average age: _____

     Philosophy: _____

Recent changes in company structure: _____

_____

_____

Changes in product lines or services: _____

_____

_____

Sources for Finding Work

Permanent placement agencies (contact name, phone number, and areas of specialty): _____

_____

_____

_____

_____

_____

Temporary agencies: _____

_____

_____

_____

_____

_____

Networking contacts (prepare a separate card for each, including all of the following information, and file the cards according to company or industry):

Name: _____

Address:_____

Title: _____

Phone number:_____

Industry/company: _____

Potential for providing information and other contacts:

_____

Newspapers, industry-related periodicals: _____

_____

_____

_____

_____

MY BOTTOM LINE Developing a career is not easy. It's hard work even if you truly want the career. Being able to endure the grunt work is a true test of your commitment.

CHAPTER 5

Getting the First Job: Résumés, Interviews, and Other Hurdles

All the preparation you've gone through so far has been for one purpose—to get a job you want. Stay ready during your job search because you never know when or how that great job is going to come.

Achieving your dream begins with projecting a positive image and living your life in accordance with your life-career goals. This is important for any job in any industry. You'll be able to do this best if you've taken time to develop a solid goal based on your capabilities. However, this is only the first step. The next step to turn a goal into the reality of an actual job is to create effective résumés that are targeted to the needs of the prospective employer. Most employers won't have the benefit of meeting you in person until after they've seen your résumé, so it's essential that you develop résumés and cover letters that reflect on paper the same image that you project in person. Think of your résumé as an advertisement—a brief piece of information targeted to the reader's interest and geared to getting you an interview.

Organizing and Managing Your Job Search

If you take time to organize your job search, you will actually save time. You will also be able to conduct a focused search, which will end in not having to compromise in the goal you seek. The following steps will help you get organized.

Create a File for Each Job You Apply for

This information will be useful in networking in the company, targeting and tracking résumés and letters, and responding to questions when you are called for an interview.

Include in the file all pertinent information related to the job or company:

- Company information, contact names, and phone numbers, plus external contacts who can provide information about the company, interviewer, job, and industry. If you followed the suggestion in Chapter 4 to prepare industry checklists, company checklists, and networking contact cards, you can now file this information in the appropriate folder for the job opportunity. If you have not developed this information for companies you're interested in, now is the time to do it.

- The position description as advertised (if you're applying for a posted position).

- The appropriate salary range for the position; if none is listed, do your research and come up with one yourself, in case you're asked to give one during the interview.

- A copy of the résumé and cover letter you developed specifically in response to the ad or, if you sent an unsolicited résumé, based on your knowledge of the company or industry gained from your research.

Get Voicemail or an Answering Machine

Use an answering machine to screen your calls (make sure it has a professional-sounding message on it) so you won't be caught off guard when someone responds to your job search. This will give you time to refer to your information files before returning the call. This is especially important when it comes to salary. A company representative may ask about your salary requirements over the phone if you did not give a specific figure or range in your cover letter.

I want to emphasize the importance of using a professional-sounding recording on your home answering machine. Speak slowly, speak clearly, and don't record over background noise, music, or other "atmospheric" touches. Funny, quirky, or ultra-casual messages are fine for friends and family. But when you're job-hunting, you don't want your answering machine message to get in the way of a potential employer's good opinion of you. Take the time to record a professional message while you're job-hunting; you can put the personality back into your message *after* you get the job.

Be Ready to Take Notes

Be sure to have a pad ready to take notes when you're called. Avoid letting the phone call become a complete interview by emphasizing how much you'd like an opportunity to meet in person. If you go into the company for the interview, document all the pertinent information you remember after the interview, including the names, titles, and phone numbers of the persons you met with (ask for their cards), and add it to your file. (Remember to use the company checklist we provided in Chapter 4.) You can use this information to create an effective follow-up letter and to prepare for a second interview. When you write your follow-up letter, you'll want to mention at least one point that was important to the interviewer and reassure that person that you will be able to address the issue. This shows that you listened and heard the interviewer. She will be very impressed with this type of response.

Your Résumé Is Your Ticket: Where Will Yours Take You?

The résumé is usually the first piece of information the employer sees about you. For this reason, it needs to be concise and compelling. (See the section "What Will You Bring to the Party?" later in this chapter.) Besides piquing the employer's interest so that you get invited for an interview, the résumé can also have an influence on the position you're eventually offered and final salary and benefits negotiations.

I've seen every type of résumé cross my desk—from typo-ridden coffee-stained messes to highly professional, polished masterpieces. Each résumé told a different story about the person behind it and gave a clear indication about whether he or she would be right for the job. I don't want to be negative, but I really believe that it's sometimes easiest to learn from mistakes—especially when we learn from the mistakes of others. Later in this chapter I'll tell you how to craft a winning résumé. But before we talk about the "how to" of creating a good résumé, let's take a look at some sticky traps you'll want to avoid in that process. Here are some examples of disappointing résumés I received while working as staffing manager for a Fortune 100 company. The points that follow each case will help you avoid repeating the mistakes of these examples.

Case 1: Who Wrote This?: Use *Your* Voice in Your Resume and Cover Letter

I received a beautifully printed, eloquently worded, two-page résumé detailing the applicant's numerous accomplishments, which might have convinced almost any reader that this person was a real professional—someone who would add value to the organization. Unfortunately, the cover letter that came with the résumé destroyed that impression; it was written in pencil on college-ruled notebook paper and stapled to the résumé. I guess the sender didn't want to spend the extra bucks to have whoever wrote the résumé also write the cover letter. Or maybe he was just too young and inexperienced to know any better.

Point one: Your résumé is a reflection of your skills and your personality. It should have your voice and style, even if you get someone to help you write it. Most likely, this applicant had his résumé created by a professional résumé writer and then wrote the cover letter himself. The two documents reflected the personality of different people. It's a great idea to have someone critique your résumé—it usually helps you make it more focused and catch any errors in spelling or grammar—but always, always make sure that the language and voice are yours. Make sure to use the same types of words and tone in your résumé as you would use if you were speaking to the letter's recipient. Treat it as a formal business letter, of course, but a business letter written in *your* voice.

Point two: Your cover letter and résumé should always be printed on the same type of paper and have matching styles (fonts, voice, and overall look). The contents and format of cover letters is discussed in the later section of this chapter, "Creating a Great Cover Letter."

Case 2: Are You Applying for a Security Clearance!? Avoid Unnecessary Details

I loved the five-page résumé that could have served as an application for a security clearance. The woman accounted for every moment of her adult life. She even volunteered explanations for the times when she wasn't working, giving specific dates and pointing out that she had stopped working during those periods to raise children. Character-affirming behavior, to be sure, but not information likely to inspire an employer to call her for an interview; in fact, such details might raise a concern in the employer's mind that the woman would have a high absenteeism because she would have to take care of the children.

Point one: You need only include information on the résumé that is relevant to the job opening; don't bare your soul and don't include non-essential information (hobbies, marriage status, kids, and so on). Also, you are not expected to account for all your time between high school graduation and the present. Generally you should not go back in your job history further than 10 years. You are not required to list dates, except on an application form, which a résumé is not. If there are gaps in employment that you do not want to initially bring to the employer's attention, it's best to use a functional or skills-based resume. (We show you an example of a functional resume later in this chapter.) Please understand that you can expect the employer to question you about gaps in your work history, so you will need to be prepared with a good explanation.

Point two: Never, ever supply information that might raise a negative concern in the employer's mind. To make sure you don't, have someone critique your résumé for impact before you submit it.

Case 3: He Actually Sent a Sample? Be Careful When Using Attachments

Another priceless example was the résumé accompanied by a piece of pipe with a bolt on it, pictures of the pipe, and copies of certificates (no doubt from where the person had attended pipe school). He was a draftsman and wanted to provide a sample of what he had worked on. Also, the résumé he submitted went into extensive detail—too much, in fact. Obviously, both the résumé and the sample were the applicant's way of trying to establish without a doubt that he was qualified for a draftsman position.

Point one: Generally, résumés should not have attachments. In some professions such as graphic arts, web design, or other creative and visual fields, it may be acceptable and even expected to send along a sample. In most professions, you can bring samples to the interview to be shown if and when it seems appropriate.

Point two: No matter how well-written or how detailed it is, a résumé will not get you a job. At best, it can only stimulate an interview. Remember, the résumé is only the hors d'oeuvre; the interview is the meal.

Case 4: And What Happened Next?: Less Can Be More on Your Resume

Another example of an overly long and detailed résumé came from an applicant who explained in full detail—on seven pages—all the responsibilities for each one of his jobs. Yawn. He not only outlined his accomplishments (an effective way to market yourself on a résumé), he gave detailed explanations for how he had obtained each positive result. His writing aptly demonstrated the documentary approach to communicating the who, what, when, where, and why of an activity. Yawn. Yawn. Yawn.

Point one: Use the KISS, Tell, Sell method in developing your résumé. KISS—keep it short and simple. Tell—give a summary at the beginning.

Sell—list accomplishments to support the summary and include information on where you've worked and the titles you held, if appropriate. Have someone review your résumé to ensure that the information supports the objective. The best reviewer is someone who has a job similar to the one you're seeking.

Point two: Always try to list examples of your accomplishments, the end results of having carried out a task, rather than simply list the detailed responsibilities of the job. For example, "Trained 300 sales representatives at four locations within 90 days" tells more about your actual skills than "Manager of Sales Training, responsible for developing sales material, coordinating training activities, scheduling, ...and so on."

Case 5: Glad You're Not Sick Anymore: Don't Get Too "Personal"

Another résumé certainly worth mentioning is the one on which the applicant stated, under personal information: "Health excellent, three successful bypass operations." My God! All I could think was my company probably wouldn't want to be responsible for him having a fourth successful bypass operation.

With some things, you can't win. If your health is excellent, why mention it? It's not the type of thing you should try to prove. On the other hand, if you've suffered from some injury or illness, what good will it do to tell a potential employer?

Point one: If you have an illness, injury, or disability that affects your ability to carry out the essential functions of the job, then you are required to admit that to a prospective employer. If not, don't mention health.

Point two: Generally, it's best to leave out personal information. But if you have a hobby or community activity that your research shows would be well received by the interviewer (because it is particularly well-related to the job you're seeking or the company you're interviewing with), you might want to include it. This might be the very information that gets you an interview.

Case 6: The Truth and Nothing But: Don't Tell Too Much, Too Soon

I could go on and on, but I'll end with the example of a programmer who believed in being absolutely truthful on his résumé. Also, he wanted to be recognized for his many years of experience—36 in all. So he emphasized the total years worked as part of his summary statement, which started, "Programmer with over 36 years experience in…." He also used a chronological résumé with actual dates (months and years), listing every job he ever had, as well as his entire salary history. The résumé was four detailed pages long. This approach did not get him an interview. Too much, too soon.

Point one: No company is obligated to pay you for your seniority in life. Employers are only willing to pay the industry standard for the position they've advertised. Communicating your age does show experience, but that can be overshadowed by the fact that it shows your age and could be exposing you to age discrimination. Also, to employers, an emphasis on age and seniority probably implies a high salary expectation.

Point two: Never include your salary history in the cover letter or the résumé—even if it's specifically requested in the job description. Generally, employers don't expect to get it. If a company does ask for this information and you feel compelled to comply, give only a salary range based on what your research has shown would be appropriate for the job you're applying for.

What Will You Bring to the Party?

Leslie offers career advice from two perspectives: as manager for her 15-person department and as recruitment manager for the company. In these two roles, she's seen countless résumés cross her desk. A good résumé, she says, clearly presents the applicant as having a focused direction and a solid understanding of what he or she wants from a job and what he or she can offer a company.

For Leslie, this sense of purpose can be more important than experience. "I've interviewed candidates right out of school who I feel can offer more than someone with experience. For instance, I'm impressed with people who have held internships and summer jobs relevant to their goals because that shows they have real focus. I see a lot of young people who want to get ahead and who have a philosophical drive for excellence, but they don't have a direction yet."

In addition to identifying and clarifying their goals, Leslie encourages job seekers to prepare a résumé that sells them. "It's not often that I see a résumé that is accomplishment-based, yet those are the résumés that I'm most impressed by. Even people who are just out of school or have been working for only a couple of years should be able to find one or two things they are proud of and that they feel have been successful in.

"I look for résumés that sell the applicant—but how do you sell yourself if you are not sure what you bring to the party? During an interview, I'll ask someone why he wants the job and what he has to offer. If he can't sell himself and doesn't know what he wants to do, then all I can do is explain what we have to offer. I tell him that he needs to figure out where his skills might fit in and if what we have is in the direction he wants to go."

Leslie White
Recruitment manager, Walt Disney Feature Animation, Burbank, California
Business: Corporate hiring practices.

Creating an Effective Résumé

Now that you know some of the things you absolutely should not do when developing your résumé, let's look at things that you should do—how to create a résumé that will be a strong self-marketing tool and set the stage for an interview that will be to your advantage. The information in this chapter is aimed primarily at those who are beginning their first "career job" search, rather than people who are preparing to move into a new company or embark on another type of mid-career move. If you are changing careers or have a lot of experience but are now re-entering the work force after a long absence, see Chapter 10 for advice for developing mid-career resumes or see the resumes at the end of this chapter.

Target the Résumé to the Employer's Point of View

Let the situation dictate the information you include on the résumé. If you're responding to an ad, every piece of information and every statement on the résumé should support the job requirements outlined in the ad and be targeted to a prospective employer's needs This will help convince the employer that you have the skills, motivation, and personality for the job. If you have a job description, read the information in the description, sentence by sentence, and target the summary statement and accomplishments to respond to those job requirements. If you're sending an unsolicited résumé (doing a cold mailing) or one as part of a networking follow-up and you are not asking to be considered for a specific position that you know is open, the information should be tailored to the industry or the company. Be guided in developing your résumé by the research you did on the company. (In Chapter 4 you learned some important ways to make the most of your company research.)

An Objective Is Optional

A good résumé is geared toward an objective, which may or may not be stated on the résumé. (In most cases, the best place to state your objective is in your cover letter.) If you do not state an objective on your résumé, you should still have an objective in mind as you write your résumé. This objective will serve as an unseen guide to help you craft a résumé that clearly builds toward your career goal. If you state your objective on the résumé, position it right below your name and address. The objective shouldn't be some grand-sounding statement but, instead, tailored to the job described in the ad or to a position you're interested in.

For example, if the ad is for a sales trainee with retail experience, an appropriate objective might read, "Seeking a position in which I can apply my retail experience as a salesperson to help meet the company's profit goal," or simply, "Objective: Sales Trainee." It should not read: "Seeking a progressive position with a major company where I will be able to advance and achieve my goals in management." The employer wants to know how you are going to bring value (the popular term today) to the company and help meet its goals—not how the company is going to meet yours. What's more, the second one really doesn't say anything; it's vague.

Provide Accomplishment-Oriented Information

The accomplishment statements and job history are the heart of the résumé. Well-written accomplishment statements linked together can tell a compelling story about your capabilities. Accomplishments are not tasks, duties, or responsibilities. Accomplishments are an example of how well you handled all of those tasks, how well you shouldered the responsibility you had, and what success you had with difficult duties. Use numbers, comparisons, and results to demonstrate those accomplishments, as in the following example:

> Job: Telemarketer for professional services company.
>
> Accomplishments:
>> Averaged 93 percent success rate monthly in setting appointments for sales staff.
>>
>> Received the Excellence Award for three consecutive quarters as top performer in a division of 35.
>>
>> Promoted to Sales Associate after 18 months.

All of the accomplishments and job history should be tailored to support the objective. Because each position will have unique requirements, you might have to revise your résumé every time you apply for a job and use slightly modified or different accomplishments as appropriate. For this reason, it is a good idea to keep your résumé on disk and have access to a computer and laser printer so that you can easily and quickly amend it.

Do KISS and Tell

As I mentioned earlier, keep the résumé short and simple. Do not write long paragraphs filled with "high falutin'" words and detailed information about the duties and responsibilities you had in each job. Instead, summarize your background and experience in a few concise sentences (keep it to about six to eight lines); follow this summary with a bulleted list of accomplishments (keep each to one sentence). If appropriate, list the names of the companies where you've worked, your title for each position, and the dates (month and year) you worked. Include equivalent education (ten years experience plus a number of college-level courses and a certificate in a specialty instead of a business degree) as well as transferable experience (experience gained in relevant volunteer activities).

Put a Positive Light on Your Information

To create an overall positive impact with your résumé, consider these tips:

- Include dates only if they enhance your chances (long-term employment with a company) and leave them off if they hurt your chances (a series of short-term positions; large gaps in employment).

- Don't include any demotions. (List department headings or functional titles rather than your actual titles so there is no emphasis on the demotion.

  Example: If you were demoted from Supervisor of Market Research to Researcher, list the position under the heading "ABC Company, Marketing Division" rather than, "ABC Company, Supervisor, Market Research." Then list the accomplishments you had in your job rather than the duties.

- If you have some history of working in the type of job you're looking for and you want to highlight your most recent work experience, use a chronological format—listing the jobs you've held in chronological order, starting with your most recent position first. Otherwise, if your knowledge is primarily based on your education, a skill-based resume is best. With this type of résumé, your educational credentials should be listed first.

If this is a first-career job and your background and experience is primarily education or jobs not specifically related to the new career, use a functional résumé and include specialized relevant courses and school projects. When you discuss non-career jobs you've held, elaborate on your accomplishments or responsibilities and highlight skills and talents you developed and demonstrated that are relevant to the career job you're seeking. For instance, if you worked at a pastry shop as a cashier and you want to pursue a career in pharmaceutical sales, you might communicate relevant skills this way:

> **The Sweet Shop** 10/2000–12/2003
>
> Memorized all the ingredients of 35 different pastries to be able to respond to customer inquires.
>
> Sold $700–800 in pastry daily.
>
> Developed a marketing strategy that increased daily sales by 25 percent within three months.

This example shows the discipline to memorize information, communicate with customers, develop marketing tools, and sell, which are relevant skills for the pharmaceutical sales job.

Don't Mess Up the Mechanics

When you're putting together an effective résumé, you don't want your message to be lost or overlooked because of problems with your "package." No matter how good your education, background, and work experiences might be, if your résumé looks sloppy and contains errors, your image will suffer. Here are some basic tips for putting together a professional looking resume:

- Do the right thing with paper and type. Use only white or off-white paper for both the résumé and cover letter, and use the same stock for both. Print both the résumé and cover letter on a laser printer.

- Do use a cover letter. If you send a résumé in response to an ad, always include a cover letter and reference the advertisement in the letter.

▓ Stapling pages together is a "no no." Do not staple the résumé; instead put your name on both pages in case they're separated.

▓ Résumés with typos and grammatical errors are a big mistake. A misspelling or glaring grammatical error will instantly land your résumé and letter in the reject pile. Be sure to check and double-check your résumé and cover letters and then have others proofread them for you before sending them out.

21st Century People Need a Scannable Résumé

Some companies use computer scanners to read and sort résumés. Creating a scannable résumé is largely a matter of placing the information so that it can be read easily by a computer scanning program. Scannable résumés should be left-aligned, rather than centered, and they should contain "catch words" that apply directly to the type of job you're applying for and the skills used in that job. (The example of the scannable résumé at the end of this chapter will give you a better idea of this format.) It is perfectly alright to send two copies of your résumé: a copy laid out for review by a person and another, scannable copy.

The content of a scannable résumé deserves a much longer description than we can provide here. The chapter called "Resources" at the end of this book points you to many good books written specifically to describe résumé preparation. But there are a few "mechanical" aspects of creating the scannable résumé that you should keep in mind:

▓ Use a laser-printed original on white or light-colored paper; print on one side only.

▓ Do not fold or staple the pages together.

▓ Use 10–14 point standard typefaces and avoid boldface, all capitals, italics, underlines, and shadows.

▓ Put your name, address, and phone number on separate lines.

For More Advice

For more about résumés take a look at Chapter 10, about changing companies. Although it addresses résumés and other job search tools particularly for people who've been working for some time, it has some advice that novices will find very useful, particularly the section, "Check It Out! Selecting and Evaluating Companies." Don't forget to check the "Resources" at the end of this book for great references for writing résumés.

Creating a Great Cover Letter

The purpose of the cover letter is to get your résumé read. In developing the cover letter, you should be guided by the same KISS and Tell principles used in developing a winning résumé. You need only write three paragraphs for an effective cover letter.

- The first paragraph should state what job you are applying for, which would be the job advertised, or a need you hope to address within the company.

- The second paragraph should show how your qualifications match the needs of the company or the job. Here is where you can re-emphasize the points made in the résumé but use different examples to do this; don't repeat the same ones you've included in your résumé.

- The third paragraph should express your interest in setting up an interview and your willingness to supply the employer with references.

The cover letter should always be typed, and it, as well as each page of your résumé (keep it to one page if possible but no more than two), should have your name on it. Your cover letter should have your address and phone number at the top in a letterhead format. (You can make your own letterhead on the computer; you don't need to spend a lot of money buying special letterhead stationary.) If you're responding to an advertised position, list that position as your objective. If you send a résumé and cover letter in response to an anticipated opening, or as part of a cold mailing, then the cover letter should specify your area of interest. When appropriate, include the name of someone at the company whom you have permission to use as a reference. And finally, never *ever* send out a cover letter and résumé without having both of them proofed and proofed again by one or more people who can spot errors in spelling or grammar. Nothing can shut down your chances for a good job more quickly than a typo or spelling error on your professional "introduction" to a prospective employer.

MY BOTTOM LINE Résumés and cover letters represent you. If you send out a badly written, sloppy résumé, the employer will think you'd make a poorly organized, sloppy employee. Why, then, would she want to hire you?

Getting Ready to Succeed in All Types of Interviews

Essentially, an interview is a conversation we have with someone to determine how we might fit with some job purpose he or she has in mind. That conversation could occur anywhere, anytime, and in a variety of circumstances. Overall, the keys to a successful interview conversation are knowledge of self (your goal and skills) and the company (when being interviewed by a company representative), preparation (knowing what to expect), and practice (knowing what to say). Properly armed, you'll be able to handle any one of the following types of interviews.

Over the Back Fence

I don't believe that any conversation is casual when it centers around getting a job, even though the tone might be light. For instance, a conversation about jobs with a neighbor over the back fence (who happens to be employed by a major electronics firm, for instance) could turn into a subtle screening interview or even a decision interview, depending on the person's job level at the company. Whether they take place over the fence, at the supermarket, or at your kid's soccer match, I'd take these conversations seriously. Give responses consistent with your goals and present yourself in a positive light.

Phone Interview

One of the first things I noticed when I started working out of my home was that when I answer the phone, my tone is often dictated by what I'm wearing and, sometimes, the position I'm in when answering. I soon figured out that the best way to answer the phone during business hours is when I am in a business mode. By that I mean fully dressed, made up, and my hair in place (not lounging around barefoot in a T-shirt and sweats) and sitting upright and alert, preferably at my desk.

I've also found a couple of other approaches that help convey a businesslike tone. First, I always keep my answering machine on. That way, if I'm not in a position to answer with the proper tone (that is, at my desk and in a business mode), I have time to get organized before returning the call. Also, while talking to a potential employer, it can sometimes be helpful to stand facing a mirror and smiling while talking because it conveys better energy.

As I mentioned earlier, it's always a good idea to keep your job-search and company research files where you can access them while you're on the phone. In most cases, employers will make advance arrangements with you if they intend to conduct a full interview over the phone. For true phone interviews, you'll want to have re-read your research and prepare as thoroughly as you would for an in-person interview. Have a glass of water near the phone, in case tension makes your throat become dry. Have a pen and paper ready to take notes, and you might want to have a list of potential questions ready because you'll probably be asked whether you have any.

More often, you'll have a brief phone conversation with an employer or a hiring manager that leads to an appointment for a full, in-person interview. In any case, your ability to speak knowledgeably about the company and the position they have available during your phone conversation will help make the right impression. The better prepared you are, the less likely you are to trip up due to nervousness.

If you already have a job, determine whether it will be all right to receive calls from potential employers. This is usually acceptable when your current employer knows that you are leaving. Otherwise, when a potential employer calls you at your place of work, ask to call him or her right back, then go to a quiet place where you can return the call in private.

Informal Interview

A client once told me about an interviewer who had set up a meeting with him, saying that the interview would be informal and conducted on a Saturday. My client arrived at the "informal" interview wearing a very casual suit, only to find the interviewer dressed in a regular business suit.

Surprised at my client's attire, the interviewer commented, "Oh, I see you decided to dress casually."

I've learned that interviews are never really informal, even if the company's culture is. The interview is always serious business, so always put your best foot forward—even if the interviewer says the interview will be informal. Don't ask the interviewer what you should wear; just assume formal business attire. But if the interviewer specifically tells you to dress casually, then do. If you're not sure what "casual" means, ask for clarification: "Slacks and no jacket?" or "No tie?"

Over a Meal

By the same token, an interview is not the time for an "if it's not all over the place, it shouldn't be in your face" burger—and it definitely is not the time for any drink stronger than coffee or a soft drink. The suggestion that you have a chat over lunch or dinner does not take away from the intensity of the interview; rather, it adds to it. Do not be so relaxed that you're unable to stay on point. Also, I suggest always ordering something easy to eat—such as soup. Stay away from pasta dishes, finger foods, or salads, especially the ones with the cherry tomatoes, which tend to slide off the plate when you're trying to cut them.

An interview is usually stressful at best, so it makes sense to keep everything as simple as possible. A complicated and difficult lunch only adds to the stress. Most important, in an over-a-meal interview, mind your manners; the interviewer might be evaluating your social graces. Be kind to the waiters, don't talk with your mouth full, and eat slowly and with moderation.

Stress Interview

A stress interview normally will not occur unless there is a lot of stress in the job and the interviewer needs to determine how you will handle it. The stressors applied will usually be something that a person in that job would be expected to be able to manage. For instance, a candidate for a training manager's position might be asked to make a short presentation to a group of peers or members of the upper-management team. You can prepare for this type of interview by role-playing with friends, pretending you are in a stressful situation similar to something you might encounter on the job. Then, ask your friend for feedback on how well you handled it. Again, being well-prepared—studying your company and industry research, going over potential questions, reviewing your résumé carefully and determining the best way to present your education and experience for the given job—is your best defense in preparing for a stressful interview.

Panel Interview

Some people consider a panel interview similar to a stress interview. Panel interviews have become very popular in this era of self-directed work teams because greater consideration is given to everyone being able to work together effectively. A panel could consist of between three and five members and any combination of people, including a manager, a human resources representative, peers, and an upper manager.

One-on-One Interview with the Boss

Eventually, at some point in the interview process, you'll be interviewing one-on-one with the person who will be supervising you. In some cases, especially at a smaller company, this will be your first and only interview. The one-on-one interview with the boss has definite pros and cons. On one hand, you're closer to the power with this interview; therefore, if you make a good impression here, you'll more likely get the job. On the other hand, it gives you no room to recoup after you've made a mistake or to develop allies who could help prepare you for the big interview, as is possible when interviews are set up progressively.

Prior research is going to be very important before this interview. One of the best sources for information is networking. Usually the more confident (not cocky) and spontaneous you are in these interviews, the better. One client was stumped when the head of an accounting firm snapped, as his first question, "Why should I hire you?" She stammered and couldn't come up with an answer. She told me that if she had been prepared and not thrown off balance, she would have replied, "Because I get along well with all the key people in the department and with people in three of the top companies you represent." Certainly, that answer would have been preferable to the "no answer" she gave, especially because it would have been a natural response.

Progressive Interviews

This is probably still the most common interview process. You interview with a human resources representative first or a search agency representative followed by a human resources representative; then you meet with your prospective manager and then interview with the manager at the next level up. If you "make it" at one level, you will be prepped for the next interviewer. If the interviewer is inexperienced and does not do this, be sure to ask what you can expect and how you should prepare for the next interview.

Light Conversation with the Receptionist

Finally, when you're at a potential employer's place of business, consider every conversation you have to be a potential "interview." Once, my friend Paul arrived early for an interview and started a "light" conversation with a person at the front desk, whom he thought was the receptionist. After about 10 minutes of conversation, she let him know she was the personnel manager and proceeded to escort him back to her office to finish the interview. Luckily, he had not said anything that could have damaged his chances for the job, but he might have, just because he assumed she was the receptionist and that he could relax. Even with the receptionist, it's not a good idea to relax to the point of not putting that best foot forward. Many receptionists have the ear of the boss and, therefore, may have significant influence in the selection of the final candidate for the job.

MY BOTTOM LINE	Being ready for your interview starts with truly believing that you can have the job you want—actually visualizing yourself in the position and carrying out its responsibilities. With such an attitude, you'll project an image to the world that fits your career goal. If your dream is to be a successful manager, then you must project yourself as self-assured and organized. That image will be reinforced by others, who, sensing your confidence and belief in yourself, will feel that you are well-suited for such a career. Projecting this positive self-image and confident attitude is your most powerful tool in any job interview.

Acing the Actual Interview

The interview is the fifth step in a nine-step process to getting the job you want. (See the table called "Nine Steps to a Successful Interview: The Essential Job Search Chain" later in this chapter.) The steps form an interlocking chain, so if a link is weak or left out, it will impact negatively on the effectiveness of the entire chain. Proper planning requires knowing what you want to do, something about the industry and company, the right salary to ask for, and projecting an image that fits the job.

All of this leads to putting your best foot forward in the job interview. The interview is, simply put, a conversation between you and one or more individuals within a company who want to find out whether you have skills and experience and the right "chemistry" to make a good "marriage." If they find that you have best components (better than the other applicants), you will receive an offer. Then ideally you'll be in a position to negotiate for a good salary and benefits, which, combined with the job, will help you move forward on your career track.

Look as If You Fit the Job You Want to Fill

I once heard someone tell a salesperson who had just given a presentation to a group of potential customers that her appearance and presence spoke so loudly about who she was that she hadn't needed to say a word. She looked successful—and the people in the group were sold on her product because they were sold on her. She had achieved this effect through planning, research, and careful execution. By studying her client base, she knew how to appeal to it and, because of this preparation, felt confident in her ability to communicate to the group.

You have within your control the ability to walk into an interview and do the exact same thing this salesperson did. You should always go to an interview looking as though you fit the job you want to fill. You can't expect to command an $85,000 salary with a $35,000 image. On the other hand, you don't want to go to an interview for a $40,000 job dressed in a Chanel suit. Or interview with a law firm dressed in a loose flowery skirt and sandals or a bright jacket and a wild tie. Get the idea?

The best approach, when in doubt, is to dress conservatively—especially when you're not sure about how people dress in that culture. This is definitely not the time to wear an outfit from your "cultural uniform." Only something consistent with your "business uniform" is acceptable here. I know the navy blue suit is a boring idea, but it still works. I've never seen a person yet who didn't look businesslike in a navy blue suit; something about it just says "professional." Even children recognize it: Once, I walked past a group of kids wearing my navy blue suit, and one of them told me I looked "business-y."

This conservative approach should follow through in the rest of your attire: conservative hairdo, moderate makeup, discreet jewelry, no strong perfumes or aftershave. The idea is to keep the interviewer's attention on your sterling qualifications and sparkling personality rather than some distracting element that might cost you the job.

Don't One-Up the Boss

I've known people to lose an opportunity because they appeared not to need the job or they one-upped the interviewer with their image or conversation. According to a high-level executive I know, an applicant should never project an image beyond the job he is applying for—and certainly not beyond the boss's level.

I hate to say it this way, but you'll be dealing with human beings—not perfect beings—which means you'll be dealing with people who have egos. The sad truth is some interviewers don't want to hire someone who seems more prosperous than they. Maybe you don't want to work for anyone like that (and I can surely understand that feeling); however, if you're aware of this potential obstacle up front, you have the option of toning down your image—if you choose to. Who knows, the job might be so appealing that it will be worth making any minor adjustments.

For example, if you're being considered for an entry-level job and you drive a Lexus or a Mercedes to the interview, it may appear as if you don't need the job. If that's all you have in terms of an automobile, be discreet about it by parking in a low-profile place in the parking lot.

You're Always on Stage

Whenever you drive onto the company's parking lot for an interview, there is a chance that you are being observed by someone at the company—possibly even the person who'll be conducting the interview. Be on your best behavior: Make sure that your car is clean, inside and out; don't make unseemly adjustments to your clothes while walking into the building; and carry yourself gracefully and with an air of confidence.

Be nice to everyone—beginning with the parking attendant or the doorman—everywhere, all the time, even in the restroom. You never know who has the boss's ear. An informal procedure at some companies is to ask the receptionist what they thought of the applicants—in terms of how they presented themselves at the reception area, how they acted when they were waiting for their interviewer, and so forth (remember my friend Paul!). In fact, more companies are making this a part of their formal screening process. So keep in mind that the person you may be inclined to ignore might be someone who will have an influence in the final selection.

In Case the Interviewer Doesn't Know How to Interview

It's hard to believe when it actually happens, but there will be times when you will have done everything you're supposed to do in preparation for that very important interview and then end up with a person who doesn't know how to interview. The best way to deal with this is to prepare some questions ahead of time so you can guide the interview and sell yourself. I suggest that you consider beforehand what issues concern you and have questions in mind that you can ask about them. For instance, if you're a creative person and most productive when given free rein to accomplish an assignment, you'd want to know how much freedom you would have in carrying out your responsibilities.

You're more likely to get a true assessment of the situation by asking a series of open-ended questions:

- How are projects assigned?
- How are they monitored?

▓ How do company managers like to work with the staff (with a teamwork approach or specifically assigned duties)?

▓ Which project management style has proven to be most successful in the company?

Equally important is how you ask the questions. Always be open. Don't be judgmental or condescending. Never, ever give the impression that you think the interviewer does not have his act together.

The Top-Ten-Plus Interview Questions

An employer might ask any number of questions to find out whether you have the skills to confront the challenges of the position, the motivation to work through any problems that arise, and the personality to fit into the work culture. If you can handle the following frequently asked questions, you should be able to handle any interview with confidence:

▓ **Tell me about yourself.** Keep your answer short, to the point, and under two minutes. I would give a brief career overview, point to a couple of accomplishments that demonstrate your skills and that align with the job responsibilities, and then mention why you are interested in the job. If you developed your skills doing community work or are just out of school, mention the activities you've been involved with that demonstrate skills related to the job. It's best to avoid discussions about your spouse, children, or personal issues, because it might work against you later, even if the interviewer expresses a positive attitude about it at the time.

▓ **Why are you leaving your current company?** Separate your job search action from any action your former company has taken that has caused you to look for a job. Try an answer like "The company is restructuring, and I've decided to seek a new challenge." Never, ever say you've been fired or laid off because it lends a negative air to the conversation. By the same token, if you've quit a job because of intolerable working conditions, don't speak negatively about the experience or the company. Simply say that you felt it was time to move on and challenge yourself in new areas.

▦ **What are your strengths?** This question could be posed in a variety of ways, such as, "Why should we hire you? How do you see your skills enhancing the department? What would your supervisor (or peers) say about you?" When responding, give examples that align with the job requirements. For instance, as a financial analyst applicant you might say "I've always been complimented by my managers for my analytical ability. I even received a bonus for discovering an error that would have caused the company several million dollars." Or as a public relations applicant, you might answer: "I was asked to head a special community project by a company that contacted me on the recommendation of several community groups, so I believe one of my strengths is that I'm respected within the community." You can prepare for this question by researching the job, company, and interviewer (through networking) to get a clear idea of the specific skills and strengths the employer is looking for.

▦ **What are your weaknesses?** This question might also be posed in a variety of ways, including, "In which areas do you need to develop? Tell me about a failure you've had and what you learned from it." Rather than point to an obvious flaw or make up an answer, focus on the overuse of a strength that you have a handle on. For instance, you can say something like "I know that I tend to be a perfectionist, and sometimes that causes me to put in extra time on a project to satisfy my need for perfection and meet the project deadline." Of course, only say something like this if it's absolutely true.

▦ **What are your goals?** Only discuss goals that are attainable within that company, preferably that particular department. It's always a worthwhile goal to say you want to grow professionally. Don't assert or even hint that your goal is to one day get the interviewer's job; the statement is passé and could be frightening in the current downsizing environment.

▦ **What did you like best about your present or former manager?** Whatever you say, let it be positive because the answer reflects more on you than on the manager. If you felt overburdened with work in your present or former situation, think of it this way; it afforded you an opportunity to grow professionally. Therefore, you could say, "He or she challenged me to develop my skills and take on more responsibility" or something to this effect.

- **What was it like working at your former company?** Your answer here also needs to be positive. Even if the interviewer has something negative to say about the company, don't allow yourself to be trapped into agreeing with a negative comment. If the interviewer mentions something negative, don't argue with him or her; just express, in a nondefensive manner, that you had a more positive experience—and let it go.

- **The psychological questions.** Questions along this line may or may not occur, but if they do, there is no way to anticipate what kind of question might be asked. Although some companies use psychological tests to evaluate candidates, more often interviewers will pose pointed questions to get a sense of a person's outlook and psychological makeup. Some of the psychological questions that I have heard asked include, "If you were a tree, what kind of tree would you be? What would you take with you to the afterlife? What animal would you choose to be?" There are no right or wrong answers to these types of questions. They are usually posed as a way of determining how you would fit into that company's culture. Take the questions seriously and take your time to answer them as honestly as you can.

- **The situational question.** Here, an interviewer might ask you to imagine yourself in a situation likely to come up in the job and describe how you would deal with it. Whatever your answer is, always remember that on the job you'd be expected to get the job done, so make sure your answer ends with that kind of conclusion.

- **The difficult question.** Generally, these are questions unique to your situation or background that you probably would prefer not to answer. Usually, they refer to something on your résumé or in your background that stands out or is inconsistent, and they generally address such issues as, for example, the fact that you have no degree, your erratic work history, job gaps in your work history, and, subtly (or not so subtly), your age. If you ask someone to review your résumé prior to your job search, they will likely spot any issue that might give rise to a difficult question. This way, you'll have time to think about how you might best answer and be better prepared when it comes up in an interview.

■ **What kind of salary are you looking for?** For each job that you go after, have a salary range in mind that is consistent with the industry standard in your geographic location. A little networking with friends, peers in your professional association, or placement agency representatives who specialize in your area of expertise should help you arrive at an average for your locality. Keep in mind, however, that you should only provide this information when you feel you must. When you are first asked in person about salary requirements, your initial response should be that you're open on the question of compensation and that it would depend on the job requirements. If the employer asks again, then state the salary range that you're research shows is appropriate for the job and area. If he or she continues to press and asks specifically what your last salary was, give a range that aligns with the industry standard. Never give an exact salary because it does not allow you room to negotiate later.

MY BOTTOM LINE | The interview is where all the pieces come together. Don't blow it. Practice. Practice. Practice. Go on practice interviews first. Although you think you know the answers, you might be surprised at what comes out of your mouth.

End the Interview the Right Way and Always Follow Up

At the end of the interview, find out what the next step will be. Then, based on the response, ask whether it's okay for you to follow up. For instance, if you're told a decision will be made in a couple of weeks or the next stage of interviews will be in two weeks, you might say, "Why don't I check back with you then?" On the other hand, if the interviewer clearly states that you will be contacted within a week, one way or another, then wait for someone from the company to call you; if you haven't heard from anyone by that time, follow up with a call.

Be sure to write that thank-you letter; it only takes a few minutes. Most people don't follow up, so doing so will help you stand out. The note should be typed, brief, and well-written, with a professional, not casual, tone. If you interviewed with several people, it's all right to send the letter to the primary interviewer and extend a thank-you to the other interviewers in the same letter.

Getting Offers and Negotiating Job and Salary

When the interviewer asks "How much money would it take to get you here and when can you start?" does it mean you've been made a definite offer? No, it doesn't. That question is probably asked of all candidates interviewed. An offer is not a question; it is a statement consisting of a starting date, salary, and title.

Any negotiation should start first with the job responsibilities and accountability because that will be the basis for any salary offer and negotiation. Preferably, issues relating to the job, such as duties and title, should be negotiated before a salary offer is made. When you receive an offer, find out when a response is expected and set a date then and there to get together to discuss your acceptance.

Be sensitive to how much negotiation is possible. (Follow your gut on this one.) You need to be able to recognize when negotiations have gone as far as they will go. You should not negotiate an offer if you have discussed every facet of the job during a series of interviews and there has been some give-and-take on both sides. In this case, you've actually been involved informally in the negotiation process all along. By the time the offer is extended, it is just a formality (or should be). To negotiate at that point is inappropriate, and the employer might think you're playing games and withdraw the offer.

I've known this to happen before. I've seen offers withdrawn when the candidate got greedy or misread the interviewer and overplayed his or her hand. There is no need to negotiate an offer that you know is fair. If you've done your research, then you should know the appropriate salary range for your skills and for the job.

I recommend taking the following approach in handling any offers:

- Know your absolute bottom line—what you must get from the job in terms of salary, title, perks, and so on. I believe in making sure the company meets your most important (non-negotiable) expectations before going forward with any other negotiations. After they've met these considerations, you can think about the factors that would be nice to have (such as a reserved parking space or a membership to a health club). Because every issue cannot have equal importance, you must prioritize your needs. You might have to give up something, so you need to know ahead of time where you're willing to make adjustments.

- Next, consider how the position will help advance your career. If it does not, you might want to ask for additional responsibilities to accomplish that goal. Even if you don't get more money for taking on additional responsibilities right away, the added experience will ultimately pay off.

- Ask for a salary that aligns with your newly negotiated job. If the employer is not willing to meet your salary expectation right away, suggest you be given a performance review in three months, at which time they could agree to meet your original sum or, at least, renegotiate. (Realize, though, that by this time, you may have made an intellectual and emotional commitment to the job and believe that it is a good choice for you, or the employer may recognize the added value you bring and be able to flex a bit on the salary. At any rate, these approaches bring up the issues without backing you or the employer into a corner.)

- Finally, have a list of benefits or other perks that you'd like. Ask for these last. But be prepared to give in on these items, unless one of these is a nonnegotiable item for you, in which case you should have found out whether you could get this item before proceeding to this point.

▦ After you've reached agreement, put everything you've negotiated in an acceptance letter to the employer. It can be simply stated:

> Dear _____ ,
> Per our conversation on (date) I will start working
> on (date) as (title) for $_____ annually. We agreed
> to the following: (list everything you agreed to during
> your negotiation meeting).

▦ If you receive more than one offer and the company you prefer makes the first offer, you should thank the second person and say that you have an offer on the table you're considering. If your second choice makes the first offer, ask for at least two days to respond, then let your first choice know that you have a serious offer on the table and, if they are interested, you will need an offer from them within 24 hours. Sometimes this will make your first choice step up the hiring process; sometimes it won't. I've known people to accept an offer and then get a better one and leave right away to take the second offer. There may be no serious consequences to this kind of action, but it concerns me. It's a small world, and burning bridges like this can possibly damage your reputation.

MY BOTTOM LINE Salary negotiation is a beautiful concept, but don't get carried away because it might not be an option. Most often the company makes an offer, and that's just about it. Once you've made yourself valuable to the company, then you're in a position to negotiate. But keep in mind that can't happen until *after you get the job.*

What If You Think There Was Discrimination?

What I've described is what you can expect if all things are equal. But often they're not. If you are a person of color, an older person, or a person with a disability, you need to know that discrimination might rear its ugly head and affect the hiring decision. It may happen before you even get to the interview. I've heard of situations where the interviewer mysteriously disappeared when it was time for a scheduled interview. In one case, the interviewers were looking out the window when the man drove up. He waited for a couple of hours but was never interviewed.

Discrimination may show through in a comment or question that is made outside the formal interview. An Asian woman told me that an interviewer seemed shocked by who she was—the fact that she was Asian. Her name on the résumé had not revealed this fact. The interview was very awkward; the interviewer seemed uncomfortable, and the conversation was strained. Discrimination may surface when you're greeted in the waiting area, while at lunch with the interviewer, when you say goodbye. ("How did you happen to apply to this company?" or "Do you think a person your age would fit in?")

Questions You Shouldn't Be Asked

Federal law does not expressly prohibit inquiries concerning an applicant's race, color, religion, sex, national origin, or physical or mental disabilities; however, such inquiries must directly relate to a *Bona Fide Occupational Qualification* (BFOQ). A BFOQ is a qualification reasonably related to the essential job requirements in circumstances in which the needs of the group adversely affected by the qualification cannot be accommodated without undue hardship on the part of the employer.

BFOQ has been narrowly construed by the Equal Employment Opportunity Commission and the courts, so the employer must be sure that any qualifications imposed are significantly related to successful job performance. In other words, an employer had better have a very, very good reason for asking any of the following questions. If such inquiries are made by a potential employer, you should ask how the information relates to the job:

- Are there any holidays other than those usually observed that would require you to be absent from work?

- What are the nationalities of your parents?

- Would you like to be called Miss, Ms., or Mrs.?

- Are you single, married, or divorced?

- Do you plan to have a family?

- Do you have any disability?

- How severe is your disability?

- Have you ever been arrested?

- What was your maiden name?

- Where were you born?

- Of what country are you a citizen?

- What is your native language?

- Whom should we notify in case of an emergency?

- To what clubs, societies, or organizations do you belong?

- What kind of discharge did you receive from the military?

- Can you read well enough to take this test?

What Recourse Do You Have ?

Although the employer may consider any such remarks or questions " off the record," the Equal Employment Opportunity Commission may not. If you believe that you have been discriminated against under the law, immediately contact The U.S. Equal Employment Opportunity Commission, 2401 E Street NW, Washington, D.C. 20507, or call 800-USA-EEOC (the TDD number is 202-634-7057) to contact an EEOC field office.

MY BOTTOM LINE If you've mastered all the right steps for getting a job, then there may be cause for concern; no one needs or wants to become a professional job seeker! But to ensure that you maximize each job search you embark on, make sure you cover all the major bases. If you don't, you might spend more time in the search than you need to and—even worse—cheat yourself out of a great opportunity. The following chart summarizes the key steps in the search process and will help you get the maximum return for your effort.

NINE STEPS TO A SUCCESSFUL INTERVIEW: THE ESSENTIAL JOB SEARCH CHAIN

The Link	If It's Weak	If It's Strong
Goal setting	Unfocused search. Poor résumé. Vague answers in the interview, looking for any old job.	Productive search. Winning résumé. Clear responses in the interview. Job on the right career track.
Research	Unfocused search. Generic résumé. No information to prepare for interviewing. No idea of appropriate salary to quote.	Focused search. Productive résumé. Confident two-way interview. Successful salary negotiations.
Multiple strategies	Limited opportunities. Longer search.	Expanded search. Mentors. Shorter, more successful search.
Résumé	Untargeted. Takes longer to get interviews. Interviews for jobs you don't truly want.	Targeted. Significantly increases chances to get interviews for jobs you want. Sets parameters for the interviews. Position in line with career objective.
Interviews	Poor preparation. Poor result.	With a solid foundation of steps (links), this will be a piece of cake. Prior practice will enhance result.
Offers	Probably only one or none.	Most likely one that will fit well with your career goal.
Negotiation	Not likely.	Absolutely. Job first. Then salary. Then benefits.
Acceptance of offer	A job.	A career with a future.
Future outlook	Poor unless the process is improved.	Excellent. Plan your move and repeat the prior steps.

Chronological Résumé Example

Sharon Binyon
6632 Coal Mine Road
San Diego, California 99393

(310) 555-2288

SUMMARY
Track record for demonstrated empathy in dealing with difficult children and adults. Capable of dealing well with public in any arena. Organized and disciplined worker with high standards for excellence. Strong work ethic and good project leader. Teaching strengths are in reading comprehension and math.

EDUCATION
B.S. Elementary Education   June 1999
University of Southern California, San Diego, California

A.A. in Arts & Sciences   June 1996
Pasadena City College, Pasadena, California

HONORS/ACTIVITIES
- Dean's List 1996, 1997, 1998, and 1999
- Awarded Betty Fisher Scholarship 1998, 1999
- Board Member, Association of San Diego Teachers

EXPERIENCE
Teacher (3rd Grade)   August, 1999 - Present
San Diego Elementary, San Diego, California

- Wrote lesson plans and taught 35 students in self-contained classroom.
- Tutored three difficult-to-teach students on weekends and brought them to the appropriate reading and math levels.

Student Teacher (5th Grade)   August, 1998 - June 1999
Bayview Elementary, San Diego, California

- Assisted in preparing and teaching lessons to 87 students.
- Assisted with grading and project assignments
- Arranged three field and study trips for the entire class

PRIOR EXPERIENCE
Service Clerk   June - August, 1999
Toys R Us, San Diego, California

- Received Excellence Award for superior performance in handling difficult customers

Cashier   June - August, 1996 - 1998
Sea World, San Diego, California

- Requested to return to work in summers until I accepted a full-time position.

Assistant Manager, McBurger's   June, 1994 - June 1996
Pasadena, California

- Trained all new hires.

REFERENCES
Work references and letters of recommendation provided upon request.

Functional Résumé Example

CRAIG FELLOWS
1234 Briar Lane
Arlington, New Jersey 33321

(483) 555-4221

SUMMARY OF QUALIFICATIONS

Six years experience in leading and training employees to meet tight deadlines and accomplish sales goals. Excellent communication and people skills. Detail oriented. Enthusiastic, energetic, goal-oriented worker who works well on teams and on individual projects. Enjoys challenging tasks. Quick learner. Experience includes:

Supervision

- Supervised ten employees, and hired and trained four people for two new positions.
- Managed a $125,000 budget with no overages.
- Developed a plan that increased efficiency in the accounting process and helped recover $50,000 in revenue.

Sales

- Generated $1,200 in average daily sales in the cosmetics industry.
- Introduced two new product lines in six stores, resulting in $70,000 in revenue in four months.
- Handled two sales territories for three months while co-worker on sick leave.
- Received High Achiever Award for highest sales revenue in one month.

WORK HISTORY

Salesperson, Home Depot

Assistant Manager, Housekeeping, Green Briar Convalescent Home

Bookkeeper, Little Joe's Shoes

Sales Clerk, Cosmetics, J C Penney's

EDUCATION

B.A. Liberal Arts, University of New Jersey, Cambridge, New Jersey

REFERENCES

Available upon request.

Scannable Résumé Example

The following résumé is the same as the functional résumé. This example shows how to convert that résumé to a scannable format. Please note the slight variation on words in the summary. These changes are more likely to coincide with the scan program.

CRAIG FELLOWS
1234 Briar Lane
Arlington, New Jersey 33321

(483) 555-4221

SUMMARY OF QUALIFICATIONS

Six years as leader and trainer of staff. Meet tight deadlines. Meet sales goals. Excellent communication and interpersonal skills. Detail oriented. Enthusiastic, energetic, goal-oriented worker. Works well as team player as well as on individual projects. Enjoys challenging tasks. Quick learner. Experience includes:

Supervision

Supervised ten employees, and hired and trained four people for two new positions.

Managed a $125,000 budget with no overages.

Developed a plan that increased efficiency in the accounting process and helped recover $50,000 in revenue.

Sales

Generated $1,200 in average daily sales in the cosmetics industry.

Introduced two new product lines in six stores, resulting in $70,000 in revenue in four months.

Handled two sales territories for three months while co-worker on sick leave.

Received High Achiever Award for highest sales revenue in one month.

WORK HISTORY

Salesperson, Home Depot

Assistant Manager, Housekeeping, Green Briar Convalescent Home

Bookkeeper, Little Joe's Shoes

Sales Clerk, Cosmetics, J C Penney's

EDUCATION

B.A. Liberal Arts, University of New Jersey, Cambridge, New Jersey

REFERENCES

Available upon request.

CHAPTER 6

Work Smart and Play the Game

To be effective and successful in a job, you need a thorough understanding of what makes the organization tick and what your real job priorities are. To do this, you've got to learn the work culture, the processes for getting things done, the people and their roles, and the criteria for advancement. When you join a company, you must adjust your general business mindset to one specific to that particular company.

Realize that when you start a new job, you'll be at the beginning of another stage of your career. Expect to experience the discomfort and awkwardness that goes with starting something new. It doesn't matter whether you've just graduated from school, you're starting your first career job, or you're changing jobs, you probably are leaving an environment where you were comfortable and secure, because you knew and operated within the standards of that place. Now your comfort will be challenged as you adapt to fit the objectives and working style of your new employer. To make a successful transition into your new job, you'll have to approach it with an open mind, ready to learn a different way of doing things.

Making a Smooth Transition

What kind of differences might you face as you adjust to your new job? Let's say that in your former environment, everyone dressed casually, the executives interacted very informally with the staff, and it was perfectly acceptable for you or any of your co-workers to join the president at lunch in the cafeteria and bring up any concerns or suggestions. Now, in your new company, you quickly find that everything is much more formal, much larger, and the executives maintain a certain amount of distance from the staff. In this new culture, if you approached the president with an issue without first discussing it with your boss and your boss's boss, you probably would be considered out of line. Two different companies, two different mindsets.

The transition from college to the business arena can be even more dramatic. Here are some tips for making it easier:

- Understand that being new is an uncomfortable feeling and that everyone from the CEO to the receptionist has experienced similar discomfort. If someone you make eye contact with seems reasonably friendly, it might be a good idea to ask them something like, "If I have any questions about how things are done in the office, who should I contact?" Usually a statement such as this will bring some support that will help ease the tension.

- Be the best inexperienced new employee you possibly can. Listen (even if you think you already know the answers), take notes, and express appreciation for any help that you receive.

- Make good first impressions so that your co-workers will be receptive to the contributions you make later.

- Set realistic goals and don't try to do more in your first few months than you should. Give yourself some time to truly know what is going on. Three months is not an unreasonable period of time to spend getting a grip on your responsibilities.

- Remember that you, and only you, are responsible for your success. Ask questions, listen, and learn. And don't be shy about letting others know that you want to learn so you can do your best.

- Transition means adapting, changing, and learning: Be prepared. You will no doubt have to communicate a little differently; watch how others do it in your environment. You will no doubt have to dress differently; watch how the successful people in your environment dress and adopt a style similar to theirs. Watch how the people who are respected behave. Pick up tips from them.

■ Have realistic expectations, which means looking past what you learned from the recruiting process. Sometimes the recruiter's description of your position and opportunity for advancement doesn't quite match the reality of your job. Your job might involve different responsibilities, and advancement might take a bit longer. Be open to finding out a slightly new variation of what is required of you to advance or succeed after you start.

MY BOTTOM LINE | If you take time to proceed the right way, you won't have to backtrack and try to correct mistakes. Take time to learn the ground rules and understand what's expected of you. If you let your co-workers know that is what you are doing, you will have two wonderful results: They will respect your maturity for taking this approach, and they will help you.

How to Achieve Early Success in Any Job Situation

You need to be willing to make the necessary adjustments to achieve early success on the job. If you adjust your mindset and proceed with a positive, open attitude and a willingness to learn and work hard, you are on your way to achieving the success you desire. The following sections discuss some of the most critical tasks you'll need to tackle to get off to a good start in your new job.

Learn the Ground Rules of Your Company and Your Job

Rodney Gee, a black staffing manager, has found through his years at Motorola that learning the boss's expectations is an important part of the first-step process in any new job. "As a new employee you should figure out the company's unwritten ground rules in the first 30 days on the job and make sure that you and the manager have the same expectation level regarding success and failure," he points out. "It may take two or three meetings to get this information, but it's worth it because 12 months later, you'll want the manager to be happy with you. So find out what's in her head, not just what is on paper."

Your race, age, or gender might be an added factor that you'll need to consider—both from a positive and negative prospective. Even with the greater diversity in the workplace today, you might be in a minority in your company. Everything you do may be magnified through the lens of the majority group. This can have its advantages and its disadvantages. (See "Working with the System.") Either way, it will place an extra burden on you to connect with the other team members, but you have to get to know them to become an accepted part of the culture. You might have to be the one to extend yourself first because some of your co-workers might be unsure about how to approach you. This extra burden can be offset by the fact that others will notice your work more easily simply because you are different from the majority.

Get a Mentor

Rodney Gee also stresses the importance of getting a mentor at your new company as quickly as possible. "Once on the job, it's critical to get a mentor, figure out the ground rules, and get a clear sense of your manager's expectations," he says. "The best way to get a mentor is to perform. Let someone see that being connected with you is a positive thing. Be flexible; learn from anyone. Your mentor does not have to be the same race or the same sex. He or she will help you know where the traps and land mines are, and knowing that will enable you to run better," explains Gee.

A knowledgeable mentor is like an excellent attorney, financial adviser, or doctor. He or she can provide key information that might literally save your professional life. The mentor you hook up with should be someone who has been with the company for a while, who knows his or her way around the organization, and who is known and highly respected. Mentors can come from any organizational level; they don't necessarily have to be top managers or executives. Once you find a mentor, stick with him or her and make the effort to learn all you can: Your mentor can serve as your guide and teacher and help you reach your career goal.

Mentors: A Key Factor to Success

With a 25-year career that has culminated in a key position at Chevron, it's safe to say that Gregory knows how to achieve on-the-job success. "People think it's all about working hard and being competent," he says. "Of course, that's essential, but having mentors has been instrumental for me. I was fortunate; when I first came to work, I found a mentor who advised me to get things done within the context of how the company wanted things done and to get a grip on how to deal with the office politics."

Throughout his career, Gregory has relied on mentors to help him handle difficult situations. "The EEOC guy became a haven for me; I could go to him and scream and then go back to work. He was very helpful in discussing strategies and options for getting around a situation so it wouldn't happen again. He made me realize that I faced the same obstacles as everyone; color was not the issue. If there was a 9-foot hurdle, I needed to be able to jump 11 feet or make someone think I could."

Realizing early that he needed a plan to make his success happen, Gregory was willing to follow any positive role model no matter what that person's color. One of his early mentors was a white supervisor who offered to teach him what it took to be successful. Later, Gregory found mentors in two managers who had faith in his ability to get the job done. "I was very lucky. I worked for an organization whose vice president was using visionary principles and optimizing human resources before it was popular to do so. Ultimately, I worked for two guys who did not see it as a risk to put me, a black man, in a management role—because if I didn't cut the mustard I would have been replaced just like anyone else," Gregory explains.

"One of the issues that people of color need to deal with is that the bottom line in corporate America is to make money. I have found that if I can help the company be more profitable, they don't care what color I am. They may have had some issue initially about how I would compare with the white male, but that was overcome when I was able to show my competency in reducing tax costs."

Gregory Redmond
Black manager
Chevron Corporation
Business: Tax planning and coordination

Understand the Significance of the Company's Mission

Know and understand the company's mission: its purpose, the reason it exists. Many companies have a formal mission statement that appears in its employee handbook, its annual report, or its long-range plan. Some promote their mission in slogans and advertisements. A mission statement can be a single phrase or several sentences or paragraphs. Get to understand and accept it so that you can incorporate it into your job. For instance, if a company's mission is to upgrade the physical quality of people's lives through its products and services, it wants to project a healthy image of itself and its employees. For you this might mean not only doing good work but also participating in walkathons and campaigns to ban smoking or to develop healthy eating.

Understand the Culture

The company's culture is its personality. People who are most successful within a culture are those who are compatible with its personality. Observe how the greatest number of people behave in the organization; how things get done; how people talk, dress, and interact with one another. These clues will show you the behavior and values that will be rewarded in the company. Your mentor can guide you in developing an understanding of the company's culture. He or she can help you form a positive relationship with the company by giving you information that will save you from making mistakes or wasting your time in unnecessary or unrewarding actions.

Project a Great Attitude

Learn to cultivate a great attitude no matter what the circumstances. Approach tasks with a "can-do" attitude, changes with a "flexible" attitude, disappointments with a "mature" attitude, projects with a "team" attitude, and disagreeable people with a "pleasant" attitude. The right attitude in all circumstances is a tremendous aid in being successful careerwise.

Get Along with Your Boss

Develop an understanding of your boss, your boss's boss (to the extent you can), and the rest of the corporate hierarchy. Don't judge your boss; that's not your job but someone else's. No boss is perfect, just as no person is perfect. A lot of what your boss asks you to do will be dictated by his boss, who, in turn, is following directives from her boss, and so on and so on. Make the effort to understand your boss and find out what he needs to have done to make his work life easier—and then do it.

Get Along with the Other People on the Job

Get along with the other people on the job—peers, subordinates, and support staff. Remember that everyone has his own cultural mindset, just as you do, so there are bound to be different points of view and approaches to dealing with tasks and issues. Understand that the organization has a collective voice made up of bits and pieces of all its people. If you want to be included in that voice and respected for the part you contribute, learn early to respect and get along with others.

Learn How to Get Credit for What You Do

Keep in mind that you and your peers are all in competition for promotions, top jobs, the boss's approval, whatever. So balance friendliness, helpfulness, and team play with a sense of responsibility for taking care of your own career. If you have been clearly designated as the primary person on a project that turns out well, don't worry about tooting your horn, because everyone will already be aware of your role in the project's success. But if you support one of your colleagues on an important project and she takes the credit, make sure that the right people know of your contribution. The best way to do this is to subtly communicate your achievement to the people who matter. For instance, if you have not received credit for a project, ask your mentor what you should do to avoid that situation in the future. His advice will help you later; at the same time, you'll be alerting someone else in the company of your contribution to the project. Another approach might be to mention your involvement during lunchtime conversations with your peers or to include your final contributions in your regular status report to your manager.

Make the Most of Meetings

I used to think meetings were a waste of time (when I was younger and in more of a hurry), but I've grown to appreciate the benefits of a good meeting: The synergy produces some good ideas and allows you to reality-test your own concepts. Meetings provide an arena where you can express ideas, observe other styles of management and problem solving, and learn who in the organization has clout and who doesn't. A lot can be said about meetings and how to make the most of them. For instance, when it's a show-and-tell meeting, make sure you have something to show; at a brainstorming meeting, let loose and contribute your ideas if the meeting is truthfully set up for that purpose. (Your idea might be the winning one and score big points.) Be aware, however, that people sometimes set up brainstorming meetings simply as a forum to get their message out. As you become more familiar with the people in your business and the tone of the meetings they hold, you should be able to spot such "fake" meetings and determine whether your contributions will be welcome.

Maintain a Business Mindset

Evaluate the things that happen on the job against your business mindset and not your cultural programming. For example, if your cultural programming values status and titles and a department reorganization causes you to change positions from, say, manager to project leader, you might have an immediate negative reaction from your cultural viewpoint. You might feel embarrassed to tell your friends because you expect them to think you've failed or lost face. But in evaluating the change from your business mindset and with your goals in mind, you need to ask yourself if that's really the case. Will this position actually advance your career in the long run? Are the responsibilities ones you would enjoy handling? How critical is the project to the company? If your answers are positive, then accept the position for the good opportunity it is and forget about losing your old title.

The most successful people in any business are those who make decisions and guide their actions based on sound business thinking, rather than operate strictly to protect or enhance their own egos. The more you can keep your ego in check, the better employee, co-worker, and leader you'll be— and the more successful you'll be in any career.

Follow the Social Rules for Business

Whether at work or in a social setting, when you interact with colleagues you're still, in a sense, "at work." You are being watched and evaluated. Because of this, the one absolute no-no is to hang out with your boss or peers and to drink or participate in any kind of unacceptable behavior. I've seen several careers derailed because of this. Drinking with your boss is as bad as drinking during an interview. It should never be done. On occasion, of course, you will attend social functions (such as the office party) with your boss and your peers where alcohol is served. Remember that a party with your co-workers is still an extension of work. I avoid alcohol, and that is never a problem because a lot of people, like myself, don't drink for health reasons. An occasional drink or glass of wine is probably fine, but it is never a good idea under any circumstances to get tipsy.

Know That Every Level Has Its Price

Accept that the business arena is a tough, competitive environment where you will have to start at the bottom doing grunt work and carrying out "gofer" duties until you work your way up the ladder. Everybody has to go through this; it's called paying your dues. The reality is that every time you join a new organization or move to another division or job in a company, you'll have to go through a process of paying your dues, to some degree. Also, understand that as you move up the ladder, the price will be progressively stiffer at each level. As you consider your moves forward, carefully evaluate each one against your whole life-career plan to make sure that the price is worth the sacrifices you might have to make.

 I believe that opportunities are not accidents; they come when we are ready for them and when we have developed the skills to handle them.

Facing the Realities of Your Job

It's very possible (maybe even probable) that the responsibilities of the job you interviewed for will change when you come on board. No matter what you anticipated the job and the company would be like, both are likely to be different; they may be better or they may be worse, but they will definitely be different from what you expected. Look around, take an inventory, and compare what you expected to what you actually got; then you can begin to get an idea of what you'll be dealing with on a day-to-day basis.

Any number of circumstances can lead to a modification of your job from its original description: For instance, the person who was to have trained you has since left the company (and took the training materials); the company has undergone a major redirection; your department has agreed to take on a new, unexpected project; or a new manager has taken over in your department.

Whatever the case, you start the job only to find that you won't be doing what you thought you would be—at least not right away. If this occurs, you might want to give the situation a couple of weeks and then discuss it with a mentor and sit down with your manager to clarify the modified responsibilities, accountabilities, reporting relationships, projects, and priorities. If you find, after talking with her, that there exists a serious discrepancy between your original understanding of the job and the new parameters, you have options. You might want to ask your manager whether you can have a couple of days to consider the impact of the change. Then, after thinking it over, get back to her to discuss and resolve your concerns and present any modifications you feel are appropriate.

If it looks as though your modifications will not be accepted, you might want to consider changing jobs (perhaps within the company). First, evaluate the job at hand and its potential against your goal. Even though it is not what you bargained for, would succeeding at it help advance your career? If so, then it might be wise to stick with it. If you don't want to do this or the job doesn't support your career, it may still be best to stick with it for at least a year, because leaving so soon might not look good on your résumé. You might find it worthwhile to bide your time until another change comes about. The boss may change, the job may change, or you might find a temporary or volunteer way to do more of what you want to do outside of the job, which would then increase your value to the company or at least to your résumé.

Case in Point: Two Tales from the Front

Once, while working on consulting assignments for several companies, I had an opportunity to meet two newly hired marketing representatives— Pam and Kurt—who were both going through the process of adjusting their expectations for their new jobs to the realities of what they found. Pam had been recruited by one of my client companies to fill a junior marketing role; Kurt had been hired by another company for a senior marketing position. They were both in the same profession but at completely different places in their careers: Although Kurt brought 30 years of business experience to his new job, Pam had only been out of college a few years.

Interestingly, Kurt's prior business experience didn't seem to give him any edge in adjusting to his new work environment. With his experience and seniority, he expected the same special consideration he had received at his former company. Instead, the managers and executives treated him as they did any other new employee. They did not immediately recognize capabilities that Kurt considered obvious, and he felt insulted by the oversight.

Pam faced similar difficulty in adjusting to her new job. In her junior marketing role, she had expected to be meeting with clients from day one. Instead, for the first few months on the job, she functioned primarily in a clerical role. She complained angrily to me that she had not been hired to be a clerk.

After I counseled with them, both Kurt and Pam decided to stick it out and make a go of their jobs. Eventually, they both made friends within the company who were very supportive of them. These colleagues helped them over the initial hurdles and encouraged them to keep plugging away until they had established their reputations and niches within the companies.

Making the Most of the Real World Versus the Ideal

Both Pam and Kurt did adjust to their situations. They let go of their original expectations, accepted the reality of their jobs, and figured out how to make the most of them. You can do the same by understanding that adjustments take time and by accepting these basic realities:

- No matter who we are, where we come from, or how much experience we have, we all have to prove ourselves in a new setting. Whether you are a novice or an experienced professional, you are still an unknown entity to a new employer and the people in the company. You have to prove yourself within the framework of values that exist in the department and conform to the culture. Not to worry, though—cream always rises to the top. If you're good at what you do and sincerely want to do a good job, your value and commitment to the company will be recognized by the people who matter.

- You have to accept your place in the pecking order of whatever group you're in. One of the best examples of this that I've seen was a new vice president bringing coffee and otherwise catering to the company president. Because they were both white males, neither race nor gender was not an issue. Rather, the vice president simply recognized that as the new person in the group, he would need to go through a type of initiation to be accepted in the new culture.

- Even if everyone in the group has the same job title, the person who's been there longest, is the highest producer, or in some other way shines above the rest will always be higher up on the ladder. It might be subtle, but an invisible pecking order exists in every company. It's always a challenge being the person at the bottom of the pecking order, but remember, it won't last forever. It will get easier—I assure you—once you've demonstrated your unique capability and you start to advance in the pecking order.

- It's essential, when joining a new company, to become part of the team. You won't automatically be accepted as a team member because of the authority implied by your job title. No matter what your position, you will have to earn that acceptance by sincerely pitching in, doing your part, and then helping others in the group who need it. You need to emphasize "we" and not "I" in your attitude and actions—being quick to compliment others for their contributions rather than seek compliments for your own.

New Job Reality Checklist

The following checklist will help you to objectively evaluate your new job and identify areas that are different from what you expected and that could affect advancement of your career plan. Once you've pinpointed these areas, you can then discuss ways to gain the skills and experience you need with your manager, determine whether you want to alter your plan and follow a new career direction, or decide whether you want to look for another job in a year:

Whom did I expect to report to?

Whom will I actually be reporting to?

What kind of people did I expect to be working with?

What kind of people am I actually working with?

What hours did I anticipate working, and what responsibilities did I expect to be accountable for?

What hours am I working and what responsibilities am I actually accountable for?

What kind of working culture did I expect?

What is the culture like?

In what ways did I expect the job to impact my career path?

In what ways do I now see it affecting my overall career path?

Overall, is the job different but better?

If so, has that caused me to want to change my career path to fit this new discovery?

MY BOTTOM LINE

To stay competitive, dynamic organizations are constantly in a state of change, and this change invariably impacts everyone in the company. Thus, the job you interview for could easily be different by the time you actually start. Be prepared to adapt if this is the case. If you have done your research and know your ideals align with the basic ideals and mission of the company, a slight variation of the job you get from the one discussed in the interview shouldn't negatively impact your career plan.

Starting Over

At 26, Adnane received a Ph.D. in physics from the University of Paris, making him one of the youngest non-French people to receive a degree at that level from that university. Although his degree guaranteed him a job with status and a smooth career path in Paris, outside of France he had to struggle to make his mark.

"I had a career in France planned, but a family illness forced a move to the United States," he remembers. "With no job and no connections, I faced a lot of problems here. People were not familiar with what I had done, and I did not have a degree from the United States."

Adnane solved both the job and the education dilemma when he made a cold call to the head of the physics department at University of California, Santa Barbara (UCSB). He explained that he had his Ph.D. and had been doing some of the same work they had been doing. In his first interview, Adnane impressed the department head by clearly stating what he wanted from a job with UCSB and by showing his confidence in his abilities to achieve it. He got the job and, while working at the university, obtained a master's degree in nuclear engineering.

Interrupting his career in the United States, Adnane returned to his home country, Algeria, to complete a military commitment; when he returned to the United States, he found himself, once again, starting from scratch. "My wife suggested that I give training classes at Delco since they were planning to send people to the Middle East. I had a knowledge of the culture, which could help with business transactions, so I approached management with the idea and started at the company on a contract basis. The training contract led to a full-time position as a senior process engineer."

In addition to training, Adnane also worked with the marketing group, serving as liaison between customers and management. Eventually, moving another step away from physics teacher, he became a business development manager.

How does Adnane align his original career goal in physics with what he does now? "Physics is almost metaphysical for me," he says. "It's my continuing goal, to study how the universe was created. But at heart, I'm an entrepreneur; all the jobs along the way have presented a challenge to me. And I love what I am doing. That's 50 percent of what it takes to succeed.

"The rest is hard work."

Adnane Boumediene
Algerian manager
Hughes-Delco Systems Operation
Business: Business development for the Middle East

Setting the Stage for Progress

You have a perfect opportunity to start setting the stage for progress in your first weeks on the new job, as you start to have informal conversations or lunch with peers and management. People will be curious about you; they'll wonder what you're about and what you have to offer. In a way, those first several weeks will be like a mass interview. Some of your new colleagues might ask questions about your background or comment about it in relation to the department's needs. Often this dialogue is just an effort to be polite and welcoming, but it does provide an opportunity to let people know about your capabilities and your goals.

In Informal Conversations

Let's say you're a financial analyst with a volunteer background in social services. During lunch one day, a new colleague might say, "The department manager mentioned that you've done some work with underprivileged children." Keeping a friendly and conversational tone, you might respond by describing the volunteer work you did for a social services organization, where, as part of the finance committee, you helped develop a budget and set up an accounting system. Then, if it seems appropriate, you might mention, still in a casual tone, how much you enjoyed doing that kind of work and that you'd like to do more if time permits.

Now you've left your colleague with a clue about something that interests you for the future. He might later be the one to suggest your name for a human services role, simply because you planted that seed early. Of course, having a specific goal in mind will help you maximize these opportunities.

In Career Planning with Your Manager

A key opportunity to lay a foundation for career development comes when you sit down to talk with your supervisor about goals. During your initial conversation after joining the company, you probably talked about goals in general. After the first three or six months in the job, many managers review new employees' job performances, and they usually do it regularly about once a year after that. If a review doesn't happen within the first year, I'd ask for a meeting to synchronize your expectations with the manager's goals for the job. At the meeting, keep the conversation low-key as you ask questions. Focus on getting a clear understanding of what the manager expects of you first before making comments about your future goals. Part of establishing a reputation as a team player means performing well at the job for which you've been hired and not just using it as a stepping stone to the next opportunity.

In Anticipating Problems

Beyond this, informal exchanges with your peers will help you lay a foundation for working with them by giving you a sense of what they expect from you and how they see you fitting with their team. For instance, you might find out that your presence in the department is stepping on someone's toes. Armed with this information, you'll be prepared to deal with a potentially problematic individual and handle any conflicts that arise. Also, in talking with your colleagues, you'll likely find out how your predecessor performed on the job. If he or she handled some aspects poorly, then you can avoid making the same mistakes.

Dealing with Office Politics and Avoiding Land Mines

Based on the situations I've experienced and observed, I believe that the tasks associated with performing the job are usually easy compared to the challenge of dealing with the people. Unfortunately, office politics and dealing with various personalities and styles are unavoidable in any work environment. Often, I hear people say they want no involvement with politics on the job; all they want is to do their work. I think it's impossible to function in a job without being involved with others, especially in the team-oriented environment that is so common in business today, and if we're involved with others at all, then we're involved with office politics.

In dealing with people in the workplace, I have found that three key factors will help you master office politics:

1. Work at a job that aligns with the goal in your soul. If you do work that you respect and enjoy, you'll be in an environment that's a comfortable fit, with people in tune with you. Your shared interests will make it easier for you and your co-workers to bond and work harmoniously—reducing the potential for uncomfortable conflicts or stressful office politics.

2. Treat others the way they want to be treated, which is not necessarily the way you would want to be treated. Really, this is just a matter of showing consideration and having good manners. Acts of consideration are like planting positive seeds; they will surely bear the fruit of returned consideration from the people to whom you show kindness, as well as from others who observe your behavior. But be sensitive about this because not everyone wants the same treatment. What might be respectful behavior in one culture might not be respectful in another.

3. Avoid situations that are potential land mines. Avoiding land mines requires sensitivity to the impact of subtle nuances and changes in your environment (for instance, being sensitive to the fact that two people who are key players in the organization have stopped communicating with one another). At the same time, it's important to understand that people have personal issues they may be dealing with and that sometimes negative behavior toward you is a result of those issues.

Although the first two points of my list are self-explanatory, the last point begs discussion. The ability to sense and avoid land mines might ultimately determine whether you succeed in a given position—and whether you are happy in it. One of the most challenging consulting contracts I've ever had was with a company whose complex, volatile politics made interacting with the decision makers seem like dancing with an octopus. As soon as I got a handle on the arm of one problem area, I would be encircled by another. The situation challenged me on many levels, but I came out of it with an enhanced ability to recognize and deal with the political nuances of an office.

Although you can't possibly anticipate or avoid every land mine that might be planted in your career path, the following sections describe some common ones that could cause a big ripple in your plans. Know how to handle them.

Power Shifts

Power shifts occur when the person you report to maintains the title, the responsibility, and the office but has been replaced in power by someone else from behind the scenes, whom you may or may not know. In this situation, your boss is a lame duck; he doesn't have any clout. When someone else at your boss's level or higher starts showing authority toward you or your department, you can assume that a power shift has occurred.

Sometimes a power shift is not so obvious. Instead, it might be evident in the lack of action or decision making shown by your boss in instances where you would normally expect her to take action. Even though you realize this is occurring, continue to treat your boss with the same respect and deference you always have. Respect the authority that goes with the position, even if the person in the position has lost her power.

Me, Not Thee

You might discover, after starting your new job, that someone else in the department wanted the job you were hired to perform. Now, unfortunately, you find yourself working side by side with a resentful, possibly bitter, co-worker. This can be a real challenge because even if he behaves badly and refuses to cooperate fully, he might have the sympathy of the other people in the department. After all, people more often identify with the underdog.

To handle these potentially volatile situations, do your best to work with such individuals. If they refuse to cooperate, however, don't try to do them in. Instead, just step back and let them do it to themselves, or let someone else in the department call them on their behavior. You can only survive and win in this character-building situation by taking the high road in every instance. The person will either have to meet you at that place or leave when you refuse to stoop to her level.

The Shadow Boss

Sometimes a supervisor will form an emotional attachment with someone in the department or the company and let that person manipulate her decisions and actions. Everyone in the department might know about this "shadow boss," but no one will risk being beheaded by talking about it. This person has the boss's ear and uses that power to pull strings in the shadows. Unlike a power shift, where upper management knows who is really in charge, upper-level personnel in this situation usually have no inkling that a shadow boss is manipulating the power.

Some of these shadow bosses can get cocky with power. I remember one such woman who approached me in the ladies' room and asked me what job I wanted in the department; she informed me that all she had to do was speak to the head of the department and the job would be mine. I couldn't decide whether she was overcome with her own power or so disliked in the department that she was looking for an ally. Probably it was a bit of both. I avoided her offer by saying that I didn't know what job I wanted and I'd have to think about it.

It's not up to you to blow the cover off the boss or advantageous to get into a confrontation with the shadow boss. Treat them both with respect, and wait for the situation to blow over. It will. If it appears, however, that this situation will significantly block your progress in the company, then start looking for another job. You will lose if you try to fight, and you might damage your reputation during the process.

Who Did You Say You Were?

Another potential land mine might occur when you walk into work one morning soon after starting your new job only to find that your boss has been replaced—with no warning—by someone else. You're in trouble if this new boss is someone who would not have chosen you for the job and for whom you would not have chosen to work. What should you do? Be cool, cooperate, and give yourself some time to truly assess how well the new arrangement will work for you. If you find this person impossible to work for, immediately start looking for another job. In the meantime, congratulate her on the job and say that you look forward to working with her. (Practice before doing this, and try to do it with sincerity!)

The Come On

It is possible for true love to occur at the office—and it's such a rare find that I would not tell anyone to refuse it, no matter when or where they found it. Just realize that every person who pursues you romantically is not necessarily motivated by love (especially if he or she is married). If you're being pursued by someone at the office, mention casually to some of your co-workers that a particular person has been very nice and friendly. Keep your tone light and casual, and do not make any judgments about the person's behavior. Your co-workers' responses will help you determine the intentions—and the reputation—of the person pursuing you.

If he or she is the wolf of the department (in plenty of instances, women do the pursuing), you'll want to steer clear of any involvement. A casual fling is not worth losing your reputation or credibility. Of course, if the person is your boss or has become relentless, vulgar, or otherwise inappropriate in his or her behavior, then you're dealing with sexual harassment. Address the situation immediately with the appropriate people in your human resources department.

Birds of a Feather

Be courteous to everyone, but stay focused on the job that has to be done. Unfortunately, in this superficial world of ours we are often judged by the people with whom we spend time. I learned this lesson years ago, when I submitted an application to lease an apartment and mentioned that my friend, a former tenant, could serve as a personal reference. The manager looked at me oddly for a moment and then said she would rent it to me in spite of this connection. Apparently, my reference never paid her rent on time, although she appeared to me to be a very credible person.

MY BOTTOM LINE | The ability to stay effective when working among land mines takes time to develop, so as you're gaining it, it's best to walk softly, maintain a pleasant attitude, and keep your eyes open and your mouth shut.

Working with the System

Judy followed an ideal model to get her job with Hughes Delco. First, she worked for the company during the summer while attending school. Then, after she obtained her Bachelor of Science degree in electrical engineering from California State University, Chico, Hughes Delco management asked Judy to join the company as a full-time employee.

"I started as an associate engineer and worked my way up to a project manager within a three-year period," she says. "I have to admit, though, that it's twice as difficult for a woman engineer to succeed, because it takes longer to be taken seriously. Many times, people thought I was the secretary coming into meetings. But I did my homework and studied everything, often working until 10 or 11 at night. I proved I was just as good as the men, and after that I was able to ease up."

Part of Judy's success has come from learning how to deal effectively with people, especially her bosses. "I like to learn about people and what makes them tick. I learn the preferences of people and then I adjust accordingly," she explains. "For example, I had a supervisor who liked one-on-one interaction; a written report meant nothing to him, but if I explained the issue to him in person he was very impressed. Another supervisor was just the opposite, so for him I would write a report."

Judy has experienced some of the downsides of being a woman in a male-dominated profession. "I've had to deal with men coming on to me, especially powerful men who are customers. I've also had to deal with the jealousy of peers, especially other women. I've even been verbally attacked and ridiculed in meetings. At first,

I would ignore incidents like this, hoping they would stop. When they didn't, I knew I had to confront them. Before doing so, I always did my research, making sure I knew my area of work and that of the person who was attacking me so that I could respond knowledgeably to the person's comments."

Although Judy believes that the disadvantage of being a woman might initially mean not being taken seriously, it's outweighed by the advantage of standing out and being noticed. This, she says, can help in your career progress—as long as you're willing to prove you're competent. "My advice to a person coming out of college is to give it your all. The first year is extremely important. Work 16 hours a day if you need to in order to establish a good reputation. After that, you can relax a bit."

Judith Schulte
Hispanic-American engineer
Hughes Delco Electronics
Santa Barbara, California

More Education, Training, and Skill Development

It's a given that no matter how much you already know and how much training and experience you brought to your present job, there will be something new you'll need to know and some new skills to acquire as you move ahead in your career. New people join the company, bringing different perspectives, ideas, and approaches. The company restructures and takes a new direction. A key person moves on and you have to adjust and learn how to deal with new leadership—and on and on.

I find it easier to make adjustments if I feel I have some control over the when, where, and what. If you agree, take the initiative to assess the people, processes, and systems that support your new job. Determine the additional skills, education, and training you need, and then make a plan to acquire that knowledge. You can gain a sense of control by considering the following areas that you can continually improve in any job.

Systems Skills

Almost every department in medium and large corporations has computerized systems. Even though you may be familiar with computers, you might need to learn the software systems being used within your company. Most companies use standard packages, but some have software programs designed specifically for their operations.

Don't assume that just because you're familiar with personal computers you will automatically understand the company's computer programs. Instead, plan to find out about those systems and learn them right away. If you are not computer literate, take some night classes; you cannot afford to be out of the mainstream of communication and efficiency. The sooner you get up and running on a company's processes, the better you'll be able to perform your new job and advance to the next step.

One of my clients, Janet, found this out the hard way in her new job as a college recruiter. Unable to format her own documents or go online, she had to wait for administrative support from the department secretary and others to format her work and perform research on the Internet. After showing up at several meetings with poorly prepared or late assignments, she lost her boss's sympathy. The boss expected her to take the initiative to learn the system. (Because most bosses do their own typing and computer work these days, they expect the same of their staffs.)

Process Skills

No matter how you learned to do something in school or at your former job, you're at a new company now. Learn how to do things right—their way. Do it their way for a while, and then, if you see a more efficient way that something can be done, begin to make suggestions for improving the process. These suggestions are likely to be better received if you've been a team player and tried the systems first in the way they've been established.

Communication Skills

If you don't speak well in front of groups, join Toastmasters International or some other organization that will provide you with an opportunity to develop your speaking skills. You will definitely need this skill for presentations (formal or informal). Writing skills are equally important. Because you'll probably be writing for yourself and possibly for your boss as well, you need to be able to compose clear and concise letters and memos, as well as organized, well-written reports. Get prepared. If you know you have weak writing skills, take a business writing or English composition class to bring them up to speed.

Interpersonal Skills

Getting along with others is a must, especially in the new team environment. Most jobs are now interdependent, and the new style of project work demands that we have the flexibility to change roles. In the new culture, it's possible to be a project member on one project and project leader on another at the same time. Joining a professional group, preferably one where you'll be able to work on committees, will allow you to develop professional interpersonal skills in a safe environment. The people in these groups represent the norm in business, and the way they interact as part of the committee mirrors how people interact in the profession. I've gained a tremendous amount of knowledge just by observing others in these committees and then adopting successful approaches I've seen them using.

State-of-the-Art Knowledge

It's important to know about the latest whistles, terms, concepts, trends, gadgets, gurus, and books relevant to your business and your field. You should read at least two or three trade or business magazines regularly so that you're conversant and up-to-date on current ideas and innovations. For general business information, I like *Fortune* magazine, but I also recommend subscribing to a technical publication that specifically addresses your professional area.

MY BOTTOM LINE | I remember asking a wise minister how long it takes to learn everything we need to learn so that it all comes together. "Forever, " he told me. "We keep learning as long as we keep living." This is especially true on the job.

Keep an Open Mind to All Possibilities for Advancement

Accept the fact that it might take you a while to figure out the realities of the job. Throughout the process, be sure to stay flexible and don't rush into making any rash decisions. Keeping a flexible and open mind helped Harry, a former client of mine, switch directions and get into a career that was much more satisfying for him. At first, Harry joined a large company as an accountant, with the intent of gaining experience so that he could start his own accounting business within five to seven years. He believed that owning a business would ultimately provide more variety and personal satisfaction than working for a company. Within three months on the new job, however, he changed his mind.

Drawn to the auditing function at his company, Harry decided that the travel and cross-divisional interaction within that position would provide him with as much variety as he wanted. Plus, he realized that he liked the security and benefits the company offered. After refocusing and settling on a new career path as an auditor, he set about getting mentors to help him achieve his new goal.

Harry found his mentors not by asking for their help but by asking for information about auditing and the types of assignments he should request to prepare himself for an opportunity when it arose. He made every person he talked with aware of the fact that he wanted to move into auditing; in this way, he made them potential mentors. He clicked with a couple of those people in a special way, and they offered to help him.

Re-Evaluate Your Original Career Plan

Once the realities of the job and your role become clear, you can start thinking about what adjustments (if any) you need to make so that you can continue to advance. For example, you might realize that you need more training to develop new skills to succeed in your new position or get to the next level. It may be as simple as learning a new computer program or as challenging as learning to function under an entirely different management approach.

At the same time, you might want to re-evaluate your overall career plan to get a sense of where this job will ultimately take you, now that you know its realities. You may decide that it's exactly the right move to propel you on the career path you initially planned. On the other hand, you might determine that it could lead you in a different, though equally or even more rewarding, direction than your original goal, in which case you'll have to change your plan. Within three months, however, if you find that the reality is so far off from your expectations that the job will be a negative career move, you need to cut your losses and start looking for a new job immediately. If you can find one soon enough, you won't even have to show your current job on your résumé. But if you stay where you are longer than six months, you're running into time that will have to be accounted for; in this case, it's probably best to stay with the present job for at least a year so your résumé reflects that you're a stable person and not a job-hopper.

Jobs That Lead to Other Jobs

Even with a well-thought-out career plan, it's possible to end up in a job that seems to be a total deviation from your original plan. (See "Starting Over.") This can happen, for example, when company managers recognize that a very pronounced technical or administrative ability of yours would fit well in a specific job that differs significantly from anything you've ever done. This happened to Steve, who was asked by the high-tech pharmaceutical company he worked for to take on the role of technical recruiter; his firm was having trouble identifying and recruiting the talent it needed. Steve's background as a chemist, combined with his outgoing personality, enabled him to identify and bring in several strong candidates to fill the company's needs.

For Rick, a career switch arose completely out of the blue from an entirely unexpected opportunity. An aspiring engineer, his career plan was moving along technical lines. One evening he went with some friends to a network meeting for the marketing of a health supplement, and although the meeting and the product had nothing to do with Rick's job, he found himself intrigued with the product and the sales process. He could not stop thinking about the presentation or talking about it with his friends. You can guess the rest. He got involved with marketing the product on the side, and within nine months, he quit his engineering job and went to work for the health supplement distributor. Within a few years Rick advanced to a high level within the organization and started earning a very good salary.

Rick's story shows how important it is to always be open to new directions and interests because doing so can lead to unexpected rewards. Regardless of how an opportunity surfaces, when it does, be willing to examine it for the potential it offers.

MY BOTTOM LINE

People who know how to deal effectively with people of all cultures and every socio-economic level will succeed even if they have mediocre skills. Advancing and mastering the job is hardly ever about technical skills. After all, how long does it really take to learn those? It's usually about how well one can work with and through people—sometimes difficult people—to get things done. Here's where your knowledge of the company's internal process and application of the business mindset will be most important.

Lest you become arrogant enough to think that the problem of being difficult rests entirely with someone else, let me clarify this point for you. Sometimes you can be the problem—for someone. Remember that what goes up can also come down. Learn to be a team player with everyone both up and down the ladder.

PART THREE

Make Your Career a Work in Progress

Have you attained the success you want at your job and in your profession? Are you satisfied that you have challenged your skills and talents to their fullest capacity? Or is there more that you can and want to do?

Part Three carries information geared toward those who have been in the workforce for some time and who are now moving into the critical "middle years" of their career development. It's never a good idea to sit back and coast on the initial "steam" you attained at the beginning of your career. A good, strong career path requires ongoing attention and effort. If you've been on your career path about five years, maybe you're now wondering what it takes to move up to the next rung of success. You're probably ready to refocus your goal and reassess your plan so that you can continue moving forward. You need to take the time to evaluate any new internal and external factors relevant to your career and incorporate them into your plan.

Part Three addresses the issues that are likely to impact continued career growth. It provides tips and methods for re-evaluating skills and clarifying or setting new goals. It highlights the significant factors that can contribute to your successful advancement to the next level of achievement, and it looks at how you can grow professionally either within your company or by changing companies. The chapters in this section explore the full cycle of career growth.

CHAPTER 7

Do You Still Want to Do What You Thought You Wanted to Do?

Just where are you along your life-career track now? Is your career progressing the way you want it to? Is it as challenging and interesting as you hoped, or have you begun to feel that your job is boring or that your career has somehow been derailed? Maybe you're exactly where you want to be. If so, great! But even if you're happy with your career and the direction you're headed, if you've been in your career for at least five years, it's time to take a look at your original goals and re-evaluate the way they fit with your current career trajectory. Think about the changes in your life over the past few years; is your career path still leading you toward the right career goals?

If you're moving as you expected you would, where do you want to be in six months? In a year? Will your original plan still get you there? Perhaps you've reached a career plateau. Are you truly at the right place—or have you more or less settled for what you have?

Perhaps you're not really where you'd hoped you'd be by now. If so, you're in good company. Many people reach a point when they feel disappointed and frustrated with their career, for all sorts of reasons. What's yours? Are you stuck in a dead-end or stagnant position? Are the skills you've learned quickly becoming obsolete? Maybe you've maxed out with your present skills and can't move ahead without more training. Or maybe you began working without ever really committing to a career, and now you're longing for the satisfaction and meaning that comes from making that true commitment.

If you're pretty content for now, then the first section of this chapter, "Staying Alert and Staying on Track," will help you explore your short- and long-term goals. This exploration will help you to enjoy a career plateau for now or continue to advance at your present pace, without cutting off future opportunities for advancement. If you are not completely happy with your progress, the second section, "Jump-Starting a Stalled Career," will help you get refocused and move onward and upward.

Staying Alert and Staying on Track

Time waits for no man—or woman. As time passes, subtle changes and seemingly minor circumstances can have a long-reaching impact on your life-career plan. If you don't have a regular, organized practice of self- and career-examination, you might be in jeopardy of being caught off guard by unexpected changes. Many people have been dramatically deterred in their career goals as a result of poor planning. As you'll see in the following case studies, Craig and Anita let this happen to them.

Case 1: The Dangers of Tying Your Career to a Specific Company

For Craig, a company restructuring turned his life upside down. Although he'd heard rumors for three years that the company was going to downsize, Craig did not worry or explore alternative options because he felt secure in his job. He had a good track record in facilities planning, and his career plan, which he had geared to the company, was right on track. So when a cost-cutting effort to support the downsizing eliminated both his depart-ment and his job, Craig was shocked and caught without any options. He hadn't prepared a strong backup plan that would help him through an unexpected circumstance. He hadn't explored options and alternatives for his career that were independent of his current company. Just as important, he failed to continually update and expand his skills so that he always had transferable skills to offer. By doing so, he may have been able to survive the restructuring by moving into another position within the company that would still utilize skills that tied into his career goals. Perhaps Craig's biggest mistake was not keeping an eye on industry trends and develop-ments. Had he done so, he would have been more likely to predict the downsizing that took his job, and he would have had a better sense of what transferable skills he should have developed, where the jobs in his area were moving, and how compatible his career goals were with the changing industry.

Case 2: The World Doesn't Stop When You Do

For Anita, complacency was her undoing. Anita worked hard to get through college and followed all the ground rules for getting into a career in a professional services firm. Five years after joining the firm, she had progressed to a manager's level. At the same time, she married. Her spouse had worked and sacrificed as much as she had and was equally successful in his position. When they married, they both decided to relax a bit and enjoy the fruits of their labor. Anita felt comfortable in pulling back somewhat from all the activity she had exerted in achieving her success. After all, her team was doing well and she had established a good reputation with her company. On a subconscious level, Anita felt that she had arrived and thus did not have to work quite as hard as she had when she first started out.

When a couple of new hotshots joined the company, she noticed they were real go-getters, as she had been when she joined. They had definite aspira-tions for moving forward. "Good," she thought. "Let them pay their dues, as I have." She continued enjoying the fruits of her labor and working in "maintenance mode" on her job for another 18 months, at which time, to her surprise, the division was reorganized. One of the hotshots was made her new director. She felt that the directorship was in line with her career goal and that it should have gone to her. When she discussed this with the vice president, she was told she had been considered, but the powers-that-be felt that the new person would bring fresh thinking and innovative ideas to the team. Although she was able to keep her title, Anita was in effect demoted. She could have avoided this demotion if she had prioritized her time, remained involved with her team and its activities, and kept her skills updated and her knowledge current.

Revisiting—and Revising—Your Action Plan

Like Craig, Anita probably would have fared better at this critical juncture of her life with more planning and regularly scheduled analysis of her action plan. Periodic reviews of your action plan (the one you created in Chapter 3) are essential for maintaining your job focus and career track. They give you an opportunity to make sure that the career path you're on still leads toward the right goals.

Alfredo Arguello, a marketing manager for GE Medical Systems, offers some great advice for staying on track: "The first step is to understand your goals. Review and update them every 6 to 12 months, and ask for participation from others so that you can uncover areas in your career where you can develop new skills and grow personally. The second step is to manage job performance daily. Look in the mirror every morning and ask, 'How am I doing?' Also, develop your communication skills and develop outside of the job through extracurricular activities. Use the skills you develop away from the job to add to the knowledge base you use to meet your career objectives."

Some of Alfredo's other suggestions include doing everything with the purpose of achieving results related to work. For instance, he sees lunching with colleagues as a powerful tool to gain knowledge or skills that will help him succeed on the job (See my earlier comments on the importance of this type of contact in Chapter 1.) He also believes in stretching beyond his comfort level to promote professional growth. "One way to do this is to take assignments outside of your job requirements. For example, learn how to use the Internet and make it a useful tool within your company, or look at special problems and participate in their solutions."

Alfredo's advice is well worth remembering and following. Here are some sound steps I recommend for keeping your career alive and on track:

- Be sensitive to ways you may have changed in the last few years. You might have new psychological needs that you need to address and incorporate into your plan. (See the section "Recognizing New Psychological Needs," later in this chapter).

- Stay current on the company research you gathered before starting your current job so you will know where other opportunities exist. Develop contacts with at least two other companies where you can market your skills. If you did no research before you got your job, reread Chapter 4.

- Stay current on your industry so that you have a good sense of where you can transfer your skills and still keep your career on track.

- Be sensitive to changes within your company. Most rumors have merit. Mergers, sales, and other changes in management and ownership are likely to have an impact throughout your company. Be prepared to respond to change by revising and updating your plan often.

- Stay active in a formal professional group or be part of informal social activities with people from a variety of companies. This will help you to remain current with industry news and trends.

- Toward that same goal, subscribe to (and read) at least two professional magazines a month.

- Meet regularly with your mentors, either formally or informally, to stay connected, gain knowledge about company and industry activities, and seek feedback on the progress you're making toward your goals.

- Research the additional education or training that you need. (Reread Chapter 3 and review the chapter "Resources" at the end of the book for sources, if necessary.)

- Review your career goal annually against your life-career plan to be sure that your career plans harmonize with and support your life goals.

- Revise your action plan every six months, and use it to chart the progress you've made and stay on course.

MY BOTTOM LINE	There is no room for complacency if you want to maintain a successful career. You have to work to reach the goal. You have to work to maintain the goal. You can never stop honing and developing skills to support your profession; if you do, you might as well leave the job willingly before someone replaces you.

Jump-Starting a Stalled Career

Are you satisfied with your job, or do you feel you ought to be more successful? I remember as a teenager thinking that if I could ever make a certain amount of money a month, I'd be in heaven; I'd know for sure that I was successful. It wasn't that I planned to measure my success by the money I made, but the money was my way of keeping score. But years later—when I was making that amount of money every *week*—the feeling of success was only fleeting. By that time I had grown and changed; other needs had surfaced and become priorities, replacing old goals and expectations. I needed a bigger goal to shoot for.

Perhaps you've felt this way too. Maybe you're where you wanted to go, but now you're not sure it's where you want to be or it doesn't satisfy you the way you thought it would. Now you find yourself wanting more—something different, something to bring back the excitement of meeting new challenges. Or you could feel that your values have changed and are not in line with the work you are doing. Maybe you've discovered new strengths (and weaknesses) that weren't apparent when you first developed your original career plan. Do you feel a need for new professional challenge and growth that are not part of your job now?

No doubt, if you've been working for 5 or 10 years at the same company, in the same job, or on the same career path, and you're feeling dissatisfied as though there's something missing, it might be time to reassess your original dream and bring it into sharper focus. You need to look at whether it's time to change your career path or maybe just revitalize the one you now have, either at your present company or somewhere else. Whatever the answer is, you can find it by taking a long hard look at where you are in your career, how well that "place" suits you now, and whether it leads you in the direction you want your future to take. The worst thing you can do is refuse to analyze your situation for fear of finding that you need to assume new challenges. Don't confuse stagnation with stability. Ongoing professional assessment and growth are the only means to a truly stable—and satisfying—career.

Clarifying Your Goal

After working for 5 or 10 years, maybe you have come to a realization that you've never actually committed to a career. Maybe now, for the first time, you're ready to establish a goal—based on your dreams, skills, and strengths—and commit to it. During the process, you might discover that you're happy on your current path, but that you need to define your expectations, make specific plans for advancement, and search for new challenges and opportunities. On the other hand, establishing a goal at this point might mean switching directions and committing to an entirely new career.

Those of you who have been working for some time might want to read Chapters 2 and 3 of this book, and apply the processes outlined there on goal-setting and job research to help you identify your goal. In going through this self-assessment process after you've been working for a while, you have an advantage over a person just starting out: You can analyze the activities and accomplishments you've enjoyed on the job thus far to help find your success pattern.

It's a safe bet that you're working toward the right career goal if you would still do what you're doing—or at least some parts of it—without getting paid. But you might still need to refocus your goal if you're dissatisfied with some aspects of what you do or the circumstances surrounding your work. For instance: You enjoy training but also want to design training programs; you like sales but would prefer not to travel extensively; you enjoy leading a group but dislike being accountable for hiring, firing, and performance reviews. The following exercise can help you sort through the good, the bad, and the "ugly" of your current work and use that information in re-directing your career path.

Career Goal Checklist

If you're not sure where you are in terms of your career—whether it's time to redefine your goal or switch directions—take a look at the following checklist. An analysis of your responses to the statements should help you in clarifying your career goal.

Ten years ago my career goal was (or I had no specific goal, but my objective for work was): _____

_____

I am involved in the following social, professional, academic, or other activities to support that goal (or just because I enjoy them): _____

_____

These activities appeal to me because they satisfy my need for (leadership? creativity? skill development? autonomy? service? challenge? fun? friendship?): _____

_____

_____

During the past 5 or 10 years, I've developed the following skills that I enjoy using but didn't consider when I was planning my career: _____

_____

_____

My interests, plus the new skills I've developed and past skills I enjoy using, are an indication to me that my original career goal is (good/not good and needs changing to a different goal) because: _____

_____

_____

Based on these considerations, my career plan (is on target/has changed). I will now be pursuing a career as/or move my present career forward by:

_____

_____

A Road Map to Success

Sometimes it's difficult to identify a career goal simply by naming a specific profession. Combining the activities that interest you with the skills and knowledge you enjoy using will help you to identify a profession where those skills will fit. When you use the same skills that you enjoy over and over, consider them strengths and use them as a basis on which to establish a career goal. The following steps will help you discover the group of skills on which you can set a career goal to which you can commit:

1. List at least 15 accomplishments you've had on the job or in extracurricular activities. These accomplishments should be examples of how you've carried out responsibilities. They should start with an action verb and show a result when possible. Here's an example:

   "Led a team in setting up an accounting system; coached a girls' softball team to first place; elected president of condominium association; developed a training manual and conducted classes on new accounting process."

2. Alongside each accomplishment, list the skills and functional knowledge it reveals. Focus on people and administrative and technical skills. Do this for each accomplishment, even if the same skills are repeated several times. Follow this example:

ACCOMPLISHMENT:	SKILLS:
Led a team in setting up an accounting system.	Leadership, problem solving, selling, motivating.

3. After analyzing each accomplishment, circle the skills you see repeated several times. These skills are the first component of your success pattern.

4. Determine whether there are common themes running through all the accomplishments. You might need help doing this, so get someone to review your list of accomplishments and indicate what he or she sees as common themes. Here's an example:

   "Most of the accomplishments focus on creating, initiating something new, solving problems, implementing processes, and so on."

   This is the second component of your success pattern.

175

5. Develop a list of interests—those things you enjoy, extracurricular activities, things you read about, hobbies, or an avocation.

6. Combine your success pattern (predominant skills with common themes) with your interests and knowledge to develop a career goal you can commit to and enjoy.

Example: Discovering Your Success Pattern

Here's an example of one "success pattern," just to show you how the list might look. When considering and mapping your own skills and accomplishments, be honest; neither false modesty or gross exaggeration are helpful in this exercise.

ACCOMPLISHMENT	SKILLS/KNOWLEDGE
Worked with the systems group to develop a new process for conducting market research; program implemented companywide.	Analytical Conceptualizer Team player Marketing savvy
Initiated a cross-functional market-support team that helped develop a new marketing strategy with sales projections exceeding $10 million for the first year.	Leadership Conceptualizer Marketing savvy
Convinced upper management to establish a new product line in a unique location, which increased national sales by 17% in three months.	Communication Marketing savvy Implementer
Appointed to head a special task force for the city to uncover problems in major planning projects.	Leadership Analytical

Common Themes

- Creativity (develop, initiate, establish, uncover)

- Leadership (worked with group, developed team, convinced management, headed task force)

- Marketing savvy (market research, marketing support, product line)

Outside Interests

- Politics (supported various initiatives)

- Social causes (served on the boards of organizations to help children and people with disabilities)

- Fitness buff (ride a motorcycle, work out three times a week, scuba dive, play tennis)

Possible Jobs

- Marketing position in the fitness industry

- Fund-raiser for a social organization

- Fund-raiser for a political party

Will Just a Modification Do?

If you discover that you like the skills you use in your job but dislike the culture in which those skills are applied, it might be time for you to modify your career goal. For example, you might feel strongly about developing social programs for those in need but do not enjoy working directly with the recipients of the programs. In this case, you would probably be more effective in a government or corporate program-development role, or working in a fund-raising capacity, rather than be involved in the hands-on "frontline" implementation of the program. If you enjoy the work you do in a large corporation but hate the surrounding politics, you may find that changing to a smaller company or starting your own company is the answer, as it was for Barbara.

Case 3: Same Place, New Career

It was her divorce that started Barbara thinking about where she was going with her life. At 33, after eight years of mediocre performance as a personnel assistant with a major electronics company, she decided it was time to start looking for more from a job than just getting by, time for her to commit to developing a career. Money was not an issue, because the company paid her well. Rather, she was motivated by boredom and the sharp realization that even if a prince came into her life to take her away from it all, she would no doubt have to help him buy the horse as well as polish his armor! And she realized she wanted to do more than just work; she wanted to be truly productive. To this end, Barbara decided to seek guidance outside of her company on how to redirect her professional path.

An officer in one of her professional groups helped Barbara target a career goal based on the skills she enjoyed using. She realized that her current job did not draw on her strong points; as a personnel assistant, she spent a great deal of time alone, interpreting and processing detailed benefit information to prepare long, intricate reports. Working in isolation and handling so many details left her feeling uninspired and unmotivated. Actually, she did her best work among a lot of people in a fast-paced environment.

Over the years, Barbara had met those needs by working on committees with professional groups to which she belonged. Although she had been relatively nonproductive at work, she played an active and dynamic role as a volunteer for professional and community-based organizations. These extracurricular activities gave her the sense of challenge and satisfaction that was missing in her job, and they'd helped her refine her organizational, communication, and leadership skills. Barbara decided to focus on a career in the area of community and public relations.

Realizing that she could achieve her goal at the electronics company where she already had eight years of contacts and experience, Barbara decided to focus her efforts on seeking a promotion to the company's community affairs or public relations department. Her mentor recommended that she get a list of available openings within these departments and start networking with the appropriate people to let them know of her interest and the extracurricular activities that had helped her build relevant skills.

As she networked within the company and made her ambitions known, Barbara quickly found out that she had two major obstacles to overcome. Her poor attitude about her job had preceded her so she had to establish a new positive image. She started that process by asking supervisors and managers in the public relations and community affairs departments for help in changing her image. The fact that Barbara had taken the initiative to seek advice demonstrated her desire for self-improvement, which impressed company managers; as a result, her image began to change for the better.

She had a second obstacle to overcome: education. Although she had an undergraduate degree in psychology, her company expected managers to have M.B.A.s. She enrolled in a night school to start working toward an advanced degree. This combined effort at improving her image and going back to school for an advanced degree resulted, within seven months, in Barbara's promotion to an entry-level management position in the community affairs department.

Build a Solid Foundation

Being uncertain about your career goal or spending time on non-job-related activities while at work can have far-reaching effects beyond your immediate position. For example, poor performance can give you a bad reputation—one that might precede you when you are looking for another job. In a company such as GE Medical Systems, which emphasizes employee development, poor performance on the part of an employee or a potential applicant would be hard to hide and difficult to overlook.

"At GE, when we have an opening, we work with the manager to develop the qualifications needed for the job. For candidates, we first look at employees within the company up to a certain job rank, and then we look at candidates from outside the company," says Marc Saperstein, global resources manager. "We do midmanagement-level recruiting at agencies, and the agencies do a lot of networking within companies to fill positions." If a person has a reputation for mediocre performance, the word could easily spread within the company or through the network of corporations and agencies with which GE networks.

If you're unhappy with a job, it's better to cut your losses early and move on, rather than risk developing a negative profile, Marc advises. "You may be concerned about projecting a lack of stability by changing companies, but this shouldn't be a problem as long as you have the necessary experience and don't change companies continually. Here at GE, we look for what's in a person's background. In reviewing résumés, we look for clear, concise accomplishments that are easy to read. It doesn't matter if a résumé reveals someone's age; we expect someone with a lot of experience to be older. Job gaps might be a problem, but if they've got the experience, we'd address the employment gaps in the interview."

Even so, Marc thinks too much fluctuation in a career—in other words, a number of different jobs or repeated layoffs—might signal a problem. If you do decide to change jobs, make sure that you've identified your goal very clearly and have chosen a path that you'll be able to stay on for a while. "If a person has been laid off from five or six companies, that may tell you something. They should have either switched careers or changed their approach. After all, results don't lie."

> **Marc Saperstein**
> White manager
> GE Medical Systems, Fairfield, Connecticut
> Business: Global human resources

Recognizing New Psychological Needs

You may have reached a point in your career where you're bored with duties and responsibilities that once motivated you, and you're anxious to take on new challenges and explore new interests. If you're feeling this way, there's probably a simple explanation: You've changed. You're no longer the person you were when you first started in your career.

For instance, early in your career you may have been satisfied sitting back and following someone else's lead, even if you didn't completely agree with his or her approach. Lately, however, you've been speaking up. You've observed the inefficiency of certain processes and want to revise them so they'll be more efficient. You've become curious about certain roles and wonder what it would be like to function within them.

These needs you're expressing might not even be new; they may have been lingering for years but were more or less ignored. If you don't address them, though, they could sabotage your job performance, as they did for Edith.

Case 4: Let the Real You Out of the Box

Edith worked as a financial analyst at an insurance company. Ignoring her needs for creativity and leadership caused her to develop a serious performance problem at work (See the section "Build a Solid Foundation.") Like Barbara, she participated in many outside community activities and, because she felt bored and unchallenged in her work, spent most of her time on the job handling extracurricular projects. At the same time, she actively promoted her volunteer causes and sought support from others in the company.

Before long, word spread throughout the organization about Edith's activities. A performance evaluation, calling her on the carpet for her inappropriate use of company time, forced Edith to admit that she had no real interest in her job and that she was only hanging on because she was afraid to change. Finally acknowledging her frustration, she set about developing a new career goal that would motivate her. Eventually, she left her corporate job to take a position where she felt she could make a worthwhile contribution—working for one of her state senators, whose views she sympathized with. By finding a career into which she wanted to channel her at-work time and energy, Edith improved both her working life and her job performance.

Case 5: Make a Secure Change

Unlike Edith, Bruce managed to satisfy his psychological needs while still performing well in his primary job as a systems engineer. He did this by working two jobs for 12 years. In addition to working full-time as a systems engineer, Bruce also owned and operated various businesses. His primary job provided benefits and financial security for him and his wife and their five children, whereas the three businesses that he owned over the years satisfied his strong entrepreneurial urges. For a while, the arrangement worked out fine, but at a certain point, Bruce became frustrated—and tired—of walking two paths. Just about this time, his employer restructured and offered employees a severance package to reduce staff.

After calculating the financial risk, Bruce decided that his need to be creative and control his own destiny was now a higher priority than financial security. He had long lost interest in his "day" job and, like Edith, found himself spending more and more time on that job handling work for his own business. The severance package proved to be the catalyst that forced him to address his frustration and finally go into business for himself full-time.

Have Your Needs Changed?

Sometimes it's difficult to recognize your own psychological needs, especially in the early stages when they might simply present themselves as vague yearnings. If you ignore them, you may very well find that they grow and fester, affecting your attitude, your performance, and your sense of self-worth and well-being. To explore your own feelings and see whether you've developed new psychological needs in the past few years, take a couple of minutes to answer these questions:

Ten years ago, if I were part of an informal team gathered to complete a project, I would tend to take on the role of (leader, follower, mediator, scribe): _____

Today, I would take on the role of: _____

Ten years ago, I felt challenged by the process of moving up the corporate ladder because: _____

_____

Today I would feel challenged by: _____

_____

Because: _____

_____

The greatest need (desire) I had ten years ago was: _____

_____

· The greatest need (desire) I have today is: _____

_____

My current career goal of _____
(satisfies, does not satisfy) my greatest need.

The career I (intend/will continue) to pursue is:_____

_____

It will satisfy my needs for: _____

_____

That Was Then, This Is Now: Time to Revisit Your Priorities

As you progress through your career, time, circumstances, and experience will cause you to develop new values and priorities. The priority you give your career will be relative to its importance in carrying out the other priorities of your overall life goals. For example, if you value a secure, comfortable, and stress-free existence above anything and are not concerned about earning a great deal of money, then you probably won't give your career a very high priority. You may be satisfied with a nice job as long as it offers reasonable security and is relatively stress-free.

On the other hand, if you place a high value on personal freedom and living well, you need to earn a good amount of money to support these ideals. Because a successful career will be the means toward that end, you will have to give your career a high priority. Ultimately, then, the more you see your career as a means to achieve high goals, the greater priority it will have in your life and the more committed to it you will be.

This is why it's important to identify and understand your current non-negotiable values and how they are supported by or in conflict with your career goal.

Case 6: The Risks of a High Priority Career

Paul's priority had always been to develop a solid financial base that would support his and his intended wife's lifestyle and give them the time and freedom to travel. To achieve this, he decided to use financial and business skills as an independent businessperson. After graduating from college, he took over the family's car repair business and spent five years overseeing the operation. The business, however, proved to be more demanding than Paul had expected. Spending almost all his waking hours either involved in car repairs or in managing the administrative details of the business, he had no time for a social life, which caused strain on his relationship. When his fiancée gave him an ultimatum, he decided he had better make a career change or risk losing her.

Paul decided to rearrange his priorities. He sold the family business and, using his alumni contacts from college, got an accounting position with a major company. The discipline he had developed in managing his own business served him well in his new position, and within three years he had advanced several levels and accumulated enough capital to collaborate with other entrepreneurs to start financing small real estate projects. These investments helped secure a future for Paul and his wife. After several years, he was earning enough income from the real estate holdings that he was able to cut back to a part-time position and finally begin to enjoy the freedom and travel that had always been his first priority.

Your Career Priority Assessment

What priority do you give your career? Your answer to the following questions might help you decide whether you need to modify or change your career goal, based on shifting priorities:

- I am only working to pay my bills or to upgrade my lifestyle a little bit. I would not have a problem giving up my career when my finances improve.

- My job is not part of a career plan; I just "fell into it" as a result of convenience. I wouldn't work if I didn't have to.

- If I did not have my career, my life would be different because I would have to find another way to get the same psychological needs met.

- Because of my career, I have improved as a person, and it helps provide a boost to my self-esteem.

Be very honest with yourself about your answers and what they reveal about your true desires at this point in your life. When you consider your life-career goals, always keep in mind that work is only a part of one's life. Some people are not cut out for a career (this includes men and women). For some, there is another road that they are destined to travel. At this juncture of the road, after having some actual work experience, and knowing the demands that are required to either advance or maintain your career, you should know deep in your heart whether a career is part of your destiny. If it is, accept the demands that go along with it, give your career a high priority, and then give it all you've got. If it is not, and simply having a nice job is what you desire because you have another higher priority, then accept this as well. Make the adjustment and follow where your true path leads. Either way, don't be half-hearted with your choice. Choose and then follow your choice with commitment.

MY BOTTOM LINE It's never to late to get on the right track or to change tracks if necessary. The good news is that skills are never wasted. They can be an excellent basis for a wonderful new change.

CHAPTER 8

Moving Up or Moving On: Are You Ready for the Next Level?

Moving forward with your career means more than just reviewing your plan and refocusing your dream. It means adding to your skills and knowledge, expanding positive character traits while minimizing negative ones, and being more self-directed and willing to take calculated risks to move past obstacles. It may mean developing new character strengths and skills and maybe even making more sacrifices to move your career forward. At this point in your career, you've no doubt had some successes and from them have gained the confidence that even more success is possible. I hope by this juncture you've passed the point of *can't* (if you were ever there) and all your energy can be focused on *how*.

Do You Have What It Takes to Reach Your Goal?

If you've chosen your career goal well, it will be something that you're good at, you're interested in, you enjoy doing, and you think is worthwhile. It will be something for which you are willing to work and make sacrifices. Now you're ready to look at what else you may need to reach your goal.

Following are fundamental personal qualities that can go a long way toward ensuring success in your career journey. I believe that, to some degree, everyone needs all of these qualities to reach their goals.

Faith

You have to believe that the dream you dream has been given to you to accomplish. You have to believe that you have the skills and talents (which may need developing) to achieve your dream. If you believe this, it will be evident in your behavior—and if you don't, it will also be evident. A positive belief will surround your actions with an air of confidence that will draw people to you who can help you accomplish your goals. Also, your positive mental attitude will help you to recognize and grasp opportunities in every situation, which can bring you closer to achieving your objectives. When you discuss your goal with others, you will refer to it with the anticipation of succeeding, speaking in terms of *when* you accomplish your goal, not *if* you accomplish it.

A Plan

Turning a dream into a reality can seem as insurmountable as eating an elephant—if you look at it as something that you must accomplish all at once. But the task is not as daunting if you take it one step at a time. Break down your dream into sequential steps, make those steps your objectives, and then develop a plan for each objective while keeping your overall goal in mind.

Remember Barbara in Chapter 7? She set a goal to develop a career in public affairs and community relations but had two obstacles that she had to address before she could accomplish it. She had to overcome a poor professional image that came from years of mediocre performance as a personnel assistant, and she needed to go back to school to get an M.B.A. She began by adjusting her attitude so that instead of seeing these things as obstacles, she approached them as objectives. Then she set about tackling both objectives simultaneously.

The same steps she took may help you advance your plan:

■ Let your management and other people who could mentor you know of new plans you have for advancing your career— such as school, volunteer efforts, the desire to participate on internal task forces, and what you hope to accomplish with this new effort.

■ Ask for advice on what you can do to advance.

■ Make sure that you are performing at a very high level in your current job, and if there is a deficiency, set about correcting it right away.

■ Prepare to get additional schooling or training if necessary.

■ Maintain a very positive attitude in all actions and interactions with everyone.

Time

Implementing a plan and developing a career takes time. Often those "overnight successes" you hear about or see on television accepting awards as bright new talents spent years preparing to get to that point. I recently met a 30-year-old man who was frustrated at his lack of ability to get a decent job. Then he came to terms with his dilemma and accepted the fact that it would take time and work to get his career on track. "It looks like I am going to have to change my career direction," he told me. "I think I'd like to be an engineer, so I'll need to go back to school. I realize I'll be 35 when I finish, but if I don't start now and put in the time, I'll just be 35 without a career instead of 35 with a career." A wise man, he realized that time passes no matter what we do with it. If we use time constructively and patiently pursue a goal, we will find ourselves a few months or years from now that much closer to achieving that goal. You might need to reprioritize your current activities or eliminate some altogether to find the time needed to handle new activities associated with your advancement.

Self-Discipline

No one is going to hold your hand and remind you to do the things you need to do to make a satisfying career for yourself. This is your career, and you're on your own. You have to make up your mind to do something and then not let anything get in the way of doing it. Still, that's easier said than done.

I realize how challenging it can be to cultivate self-discipline because I had to work hard on it myself. I've always had a strong pleasure principle that is easily activated; it doesn't take much to make me want to drop everything to have fun. In establishing my career, I had to learn to discipline myself to stay on track with my plan. At first, I found it a real challenge, but it became easier as I gained new pleasure from setting and achieving my goals. By exercising self-discipline, I developed more self-confidence in my ability to get important things done.

Perseverance and Patience

As you work toward your goal, you will undoubtedly experience setbacks and you will have to overcome unforeseen obstacles. All these things are part of life—part of the character-building process we all have to go through. You will find that you have more perseverance in a career that you truly enjoy than you would in a job you just tolerate.

Do you have the ability to endure, wait, and persevere without whining? Then you have the patience necessary to succeed. Attaining your goal is going to be difficult. If you accept that this is true for everyone, then you won't be expecting sympathy along the way—empathy maybe, from others like yourself who are also on the path, but never sympathy.

I find that it is easier to be patient when I can achieve little successes along the way toward a bigger goal rather than wait for the one end goal. If you set your career plan up so that each objective represents a milestone, however small, then accomplishing each one will give you cause for celebration. This will help you remain patient and continue until you meet the next objective; pretty soon you will have reached the winner's circle.

Flexibility

Absolutely nothing is going to go exactly as planned. That's a guarantee. At best, your career plan will be an excellent guide. The training and skill development that comes from handling a series of related positions and the mentoring you receive (more about this in Chapter 9) will lead you on a steady path to your goal in spite of some obstacles. At the very least, your plan will be a point of departure. You may follow all the rules to make it work, only to discover partway through that it's not what you want at all. A disappointment, to be sure, but now you know what you *don't* want. You will then have to exercise a lot of flexibility to make a change to a new direction.

Remember Judy in Chapter 3, who dreamed of owning her own realty company? Flexibility enabled her to keep herself on track when she discovered that being an independent real estate agent was not what she wanted to do. She redirected her interests and, using some of the same skills and knowledge, got a job managing the office for a large real estate firm.

Commitment and Self-Motivation

To me, being committed means that not accomplishing the goal is not an option. It's just that simple.

Your goal needs to be compelling enough that it instills in you a deep and abiding desire to go after it. If you're self-motivated, you'll take the initiative to reach out and do or learn the things you need to move through your objectives. This includes taking any necessary steps to correct personal deficiencies that stand in your way.

Objectivity

Objectivity enables you to make the most of suggestions and even of criticism from others regarding your professional strengths and weaknesses. If you can listen with an objective and open mind, then you can consider others' ideas rationally and decide whether to follow their advice. Even if you think you know it all—as many of us so often do—you can usually benefit from picking up even one significant piece of information that can help you move a step closer to your goal.

Resourcefulness

A measure of resourcefulness can go a long way toward making the process of achieving your goal easier. Resourcefulness is closely tied to creativity, which is a natural talent for some people. It means being able to take any problem and draw on your abilities and available resources to find a creative workable solution. If you find that this is not one of your strengths, then spend more time with people who are good at being resourceful. By bouncing your ideas off people who can instinctively come up with workable solutions to problems, you'll probably discover new ways to overcome obstacles. Most likely, the more you work with such people, the more you'll learn to tap into your own creativity, trust your instincts, and draw on your resources for solving problems.

Take a few moments now to reflect on whether you have the characteristics and personality traits you need to move ahead. Think about activities or situations that have required you to give an extra measure of yourself and which traits surfaced prominently to enable you to do that. Think about the positive comments that people make about you and what traits they point out. If you receive written performance reviews at your job, they will probably emphasize certain characteristics you've demonstrated that coincide with these.

MY BOTTOM LINE Natural talent can sometimes be a burden because it can cause you to believe that the talent is all that is required. This is simply not true. Success in most endeavors is based on 90 percent perspiration and 10 percent inspiration. Do not allow your talent to be a stumbling block to developing the characteristics necessary for accomplishing the goal.

Refining Your Personality Traits

The older we get, the more we become who we are. As one of my accounting teachers once said, "People don't change; they intensify." The problem is that this sometimes means that the very traits that are our strengths can also be our downfall—if they are carried too far or become too intense. For example, detail-oriented perfectionists might focus so much on the little parts of a project that they lose sight of the big picture—and drive others crazy in the process. People who like to talk and interact with people might let socializing get in the way of their job performance.

To avoid allowing a personality trait to become a liability, you need to be sure to keep it in check. Here's where you can use objectivity to help you stay on track. If you make it a regular habit to seek feedback about your personality style, especially as you take on positions of responsibility over others, you'll be able to curb extreme traits or flaws and develop strategies to ensure that they do not cause your downfall.

Take a look at the following extremes that we'd all be better off avoiding.

The Wall

Many times over the course of my career, I've met professionals who are absolutely inflexible. I call this type "The Wall." They follow the policy book to the letter. This behavior might be expected and even desirable in a security guard, but not in a person managing or working with people as part of a team. Wall types usually come across as very rational and logical in their communications. They present themselves as balanced, fair, and open to hearing what others have to say. They may even encourage employees to express their ideas and to offer suggestions for resolving problems. Then they reject everything. After this happens a few times, co-workers and staff members feel discouraged and, ultimately, unmotivated. Wall types completely stifle creativity because they're driven by their emotions. They're afraid. And in most cases, they're afraid of making a mistake.

You cannot advance without some risk because there is no safe and secure path for anyone. It's human nature to be apprehensive when trying something new, but when apprehension develops into irrational fear that immobilizes you, it can be detrimental to your career growth. If you recognize behavior in yourself that might define you as a Wall type, then you need to develop relationships with people at your level or higher whom you trust, respect, and can seek advice from. Bouncing ideas off these people and getting input on your decisions may help minimize the risk of failure. Because you will probably be more comfortable connecting with someone outside your company, seek such relationships in professional associations and social groups.

The Nitpicker

I know, I know. The only reason you're so careful about everything is that you want it to be perfect. Nitpickers are fascinated with and involved in every detail of a project. Not only that, they're also involved with perfecting everyone else's role in the project. They think they have their finger on the pulse of what is happening, when actually they're so caught up in details that they may be missing the big picture.

These people come off as condescending (after all, no one can do it quite as well as they can), and they immobilize and demoralize people who report to them. After they correct and change everything that is done, they leave their co-workers feeling as if there is no point in creating anything, because the Nitpicker will only change it. This personality trait is often combined with a blazing wit sprinkled with liberal portions of sarcasm, both of which impede the development of confidence in others and are not conducive to effective team-building. Overall, the actions of Nitpickers discourage initiative and growth.

If you recognize this trait as part of your personality, you can keep it in check by seeking feedback (from peers and subordinates—or both if you dare) and allowing room in your planning to encourage initiative in others. In planning a project, you should include as part of your outline those elements that you have determined must be included and a description of the format in which they should be developed. After that, allow others some creativity and freedom in developing the aspects for which they are responsible, as long as their ideas are consistent with the overall goal and timelines. Then, accept their approaches and suggestions if they meet the bill, even if it's not exactly the way you would have done it.

The Philosopher

Philosopher types see all and know all, so much so that they have a hard time getting anything done because they are more interested in talking about a project than doing it. Seemingly very astute about everything (and everyone) in the department, they often cannot be pinned down to carry out in a timely manner very specific tasks for which they are directly responsible.

Philosopher types tend to create a great deal of frustration among their co-workers because they often deviate from the issues at hand and take up a lot of unnecessary time dealing with peripheral issues surrounding a project. For instance, if a Philosopher were planning a series of meetings to discuss a certain issue, he or she, during the planning stages, might go off on tangents about how people behave in meetings, the difficulties of organizing such meetings, and other points totally irrelevant to the main issue.

If this behavior sounds familiar, you can work toward correcting it by writing out very specific interim objectives with a time schedule—which you must follow on a daily basis—to enable you to meet overall goals by keeping focused on *doing* rather than *thinking*.

The Super-Expediter

The extreme opposite of Philosophers, Super-Expediters are action-oriented and do everything quickly. They may even ride roughshod over the feelings of others without meaning to. They just don't make the time to take those feelings into consideration because they are so focused on accomplishing their objective. Their extreme independence can leave people feeling breathless and uncared for, as if their input on a project were not important.

If you've demonstrated behavior similar to this, you need to factor in extra time to accomplish each objective; you should focus not just on getting the job done but on taking the time to ask for and listen to input from others who are involved in your projects. They may share some information that will make the outcome even better than you anticipated.

Take an Objective Look at Your Personality; Then Act on What You See

Now that you have some idea of personality traits that can block your success, take an objective look at your personality and working style. Also, because most of us have a blind side that prevents us from knowing completely the personality traits that we show to the world, input from others will help us gain that objective view. Get input from people you know—friends, peers, mentors, your boss—about the personality strengths and weaknesses they see. The more objective and detailed these people are, the more helpful their comments will be to you.

A friend once asked me for such a critique and then laughingly added, "I've buried all the sharp instruments, so I won't hurt myself after you give me your opinion. So go ahead, I'm ready to hear the truth." You need someone whom you trust to be honest with you for it to be meaningful. Once you have the information (your self-critique plus feedback from others), then you can develop a plan for modifying some of your more extreme personality traits.

Wisdom Is Knowing Yourself—and Your Impact

"My ancestry defined my identity," says Sam Chan, whose mother is a Midwestern American of mixed white-European heritage and whose father is Chinese and Mongolian. "I was raised in a traditional Chinese culture, but, because of my mother, with her Midwestern roots, I felt at home in mainstream American culture. From her, I inherited a gift for gab and an ease in being entertaining and publicly visible. From my father, I got the traits of humility, hard work, and sacrifice. My paternal grandmother, who must have anticipated the challenges I would face with my mixed heritage, gave me two Chinese middle names that mean 'patience' and 'anything possible.'"

As a biracial child of the fifties, Sam learned early how to harmoniously blend his diverse personality traits. That kind of blending carried forth into both his studies and his work, and it allowed him to advance rapidly in his profession. He currently manages two major and complex programs: a youth and family services consortium and a diversity consultation and training program. Both programs focus on ethnically diverse populations in underserved communities. "As an administrator, I continue to look for the new and different, while working to bring people together without conflict," he explains.

The lessons learned early in managing the conflict of his double heritage serve Sam well today in his relations with others. "I do not try to exacerbate conflict and I don't run away from it either. I view conflict as a gift of energy, and I direct it somewhere for the good. After all, some energy is better than no energy, and having it is an opportunity to create something positive—for example, bringing about harmony between Asians and blacks, who are often pitted against each other."

Part of Sam's self-refinement comes from expanding beyond his field and placing himself in new environments where he encounters new challenges, people, and ideas. For him, this continual stretching beyond the familiar and comfortable brings personal growth. He says this has increased his appreciation of shared efforts. "In encounters with others, I appreciate the blending of personality traits to achieve a group voice. This group voice is something different that each individual brings to the table and is owned by everyone there. I believe this is the value of sharing versus an individual competitive interest, because shared work leads to a group investment."

In sharing, he believes the most important thing he can give is himself. "My knowledge is your knowledge," Sam asserts. "The most important source of power is information, and wisdom is knowing clearly about yourself and who you are and your impact upon other people. As one of the Zen masters says, 'The greatest gift one can give is the essence of one's self.'"

Sam Chan, Ph.D.
White and Asian-American executive
Director, Professional Services Center, California School of
Professional Psychology, Los Angeles, California
Business: Youth and family services and training

MY BOTTOM LINE Others will let you know what your personality quirks are—sometimes in a serious statement, sometimes in jest. You simply must *hear* what is being said and have the courage to take corrective action.

Upgrading and Expanding Your Skills

As you move ahead toward your goal, some of the new challenges you might face are dealing with unfamiliar technical or business information, mastering new technology, or learning to effectively supervise people. The wise professional will take the initiative to gain an understanding of what new challenges he or she is facing and then find the best ways for gaining the skills and knowledge necessary to conquer those challenges.

Bob Kemp in Chapter 4 provides an excellent example of someone who recognized a deficiency in his skill base and then set about correcting it. When he achieved a leadership position at a financial institution, he knew that his engineering background was not sufficient for the task so he enrolled in school to secure a degree in business. Charsetta in Chapter 3 is another good example; she obtained her M.B.A. to advance in the human resources field.

Gaining Additional Training

Your next job might not require returning to school for a full course of study, but it probably will require additional education or training on some level. As a matter of fact, you should expect that at each higher job level you'll need some new skills—ones you may be able to acquire right on the job or through outside training courses. To determine what new skills you may need for a job you might like to advance into, do a bit of research. Get a job description if you can and talk with two or three people who hold a position similar to the one you're interested in. Find out what additional training they acquired and also what skills or training they already had that proved helpful in the position.

Then sign up for courses or classes to upgrade your skills in those areas as necessary. (Refer back to the information in Chapter 3 on education and training for resources and ideas.) Additionally, if you work in a larger organization, you can ask someone from the human resources department to provide information on recommended training programs.

Improving Your Non-Technical Business Skills

Even if you find that you do not need to upgrade your specific technical or business knowledge, you'll no doubt have to upgrade your peripheral skills For instance, you might have to take a class on business and report writing or upgrade your computer knowledge to develop and produce effective business reports. Also, in most business environments, you will be expected to make oral presentations. The higher you go, the more likely it is that you will be speaking in public—at conventions and seminars, for example—so you can certainly benefit from training in this area at any point in your career. (Consider joining Toastmasters International, a professional organization established to help people develop and build confidence in their public speaking skills. It has hundreds of member groups all over the world.)

Without a doubt, you'll also want to develop your people skills; many business models are now constructed around the concept of teamwork. To prosper in a team-oriented work environment, you'll need to be effective at guiding and motivating others and building productive, self-directed work teams. Fannie's story in Chapter 4 offers good examples of some ways to develop these leadership skills. Now might be the time to step forward and volunteer to head up one of those committees in your professional organization or any other social or professional group that you belong to. Another excellent way to get personalized and customized support in moving to the next career level is through an executive coach.

Developing a Management Mindset

Are you ready for management—in all its forms? Ultimately, the most important thing you need to manage is you—your responsibilities and your time. As you take on increased responsibility, you'll need to free yourself to function at that new level by letting go of some of the responsibilities of your previous position—or at least by managing them differently.

For instance, if you are promoted from laboratory assistant to laboratory supervisor, you'll probably have to leave the day-to-day preparation of the laboratory experiments to the new assistant. As your role shifts from doer to planner, your responsibilities will involve using new skills in interviewing, selection, and employee development, as well as in communication, training, and delegating. If you spend your time performing laboratory tasks instead of directing activities, then both your job and the assistant's job will suffer. As you move from a supervisor's role to a manager's role, you will have to deal with more accountability and less direct control. You will need to develop very effective leadership and executive skills and be able to operate with a vision from a broader perspective. If you're moving into a consultant role, expect to be challenged to influence change and implement a vision without having direct power and authority.

When you have a handle on your strengths and weaknesses, and you are capable of functioning effectively within a progressive and diverse work environment, you are ready to move forward to that next opportunity.

An Interview with an Executive Coach— Your Invisible Mentor

Executive coaching is designed to assist technically proficient professionals and executives in maximizing their strengths and overcoming personal barriers to success. Using a coach is an excellent option when other, more traditional forms of employee development are either unavailable or do not address your individual development needs. You can hire a personal coach on your own (and pay for it) or get your company to hire a business coach to work with you.

The following interview with Diane Sanders, senior partner in Corporate Coaching International, LLC, Los Angeles, provides more highlights on coaching.

What is business coaching?

"Just as a sports coach gives his or her players ongoing feedback about how to maximize their strengths and overcome obstacles to success, business coaches work with technically proficient men and women who encounter difficulty along their career paths. The job of a coach is to help employees understand how their behaviors may be going out of bounds and to illuminate appropriate alternative behaviors that will ensure long-term success.

"No matter how talented a person may be, unspoken success factors such as the ability to build positive workplace relationships and work effectively as a member of a team and the willingness to go the extra mile can and do affect career mobility. Good coaches have the courage to speak the unspoken, whereas a staff member's own manager may be hesitant or lack the skills to help the person develop."

Who should use a coach?

"Traditionally, coaching has been confined to senior managers and high-potential fast-track managers who are being groomed to move up in the hierarchy. With the rapid changes occurring in the new corporate environment, development tools, including coaching, are being used now by some mid-level managers as well because of their added responsibility and authority to affect decisions. Coaching provides an opportunity for the company as a whole and for each individual to better understand the perceived environmental factors that may affect their future success."

How do business coaches know what's needed within a particular culture?

"Good coaches have often worked in more than one corporate or business environment and understand what it takes to succeed. Capable coaches work in partnership with the organization, the employee, and the employee's management."

Can you give me an example of a coaching situation?

"I coached Jack, a highly competent industrial engineer who worked for a large oil company. Jack's technical competence was great and the company did not want to lose him, but his interpersonal behavior was so out of bounds that no one could work with him, and the company had nowhere else to move him. Jack's manager explained that Jack appeared to have mood swings; he'd lash out at his peers and his customers at inappropriate times. Jack was described as a technically proficient 'loose cannon.' When Jack and I discussed the feedback he got from his assessment and his management's concerns, he admitted that he always tried to do perfect work, but his peers and often his customers were just too unsophisticated to understand what he was trying to explain; he'd respond by exploding in frustration and anger.

"As part of the coaching process, Jack began to see that it wasn't his peers or his customers who were at fault; he was. When he understood and accepted his responsibility for the problem, he realized that what he was really experiencing was burnout because he always had to do perfect work. He also acknowledged that the company's structure had changed to a more team-oriented environment and that he no longer fit in; he worked better as an individual contributor.

"When he reached these conclusions on his own, he could then specifically ask for help to move out of the company in order to start his own consulting practice where his technical competence and ability to work on his own would be of value. He worked with the company to develop a plan to provide consulting services rather than stay in a traditional employer/employee relationship. Both Jack and his company benefited in the end."

What information does the coach share with the company?
"The coaching relationship is a confidential one. Coaches share only information directly related to helping employees achieve specific behavioral goals. Coaches do not reveal any information obtained from interviews, meetings with employees, or feedback instruments."

How much time does coaching take?
"Once the assessment phase of the coaching process has been completed and goals and objectives have been outlined, the coaching process, with follow-up, may take anywhere from three to six months to, in some cases, a year."

How does a person know if having a coach is right for her?
"If a person wishes to further develop her leadership, interpersonal, or communication skills and is flexible about making changes, open to feedback, and willing to see herself as others see her, then she will find coaching useful."

Where does a person find qualified business coaches?
"The best way to find qualified business coaches is by referral. Check with your organization, business journals, business and professional training and organizational development networks, training institutes, organizations that provide coaching skills training to individuals, and even the Internet."

MY BOTTOM LINE | A desire to advance in your career means you've no doubt mastered the initial steps for success. To move ahead you will need to learn more processes and possibly some new technology. But the primary factor will be learning how to work effectively with even more people. A critical step in this process is learning about yourself and how to impact others in a positive way. Do what is necessary to master the art of effective interpersonal skills because higher levels require working through people to get things done.

Having a Career in America

Tony Okonkwo has met the challenge of overcoming obstacles to relocate to America from Africa and start a new career. He is the publisher of *African Torch Magazine*, which provides support to black immigrants living in the United States. "I am glad to be able to contribute my quota in a democratic society. First to my people, the poor, deprived, squalid African-Americans, and then to others in the society who will benefit."

Tony learned early in life about some of the factors necessary for success in the American business structure. "If you want to move up the ladder in corporate America, the best thing is education. Education is an absolute must for moving up. You see, people are often born with a specific talent. I've seen many instances of this even back home. When you have the talent for something, you just seem to know how to do it. But talent is not enough. The white man is born into the system in America, and because of this it is easy for them to get the introductions necessary to move ahead. People of color do not have this advantage naturally. White people can go to banks and get loans; they can move ahead because they have contacts. They control the system. Going to school helps give this advantage to others. It helps one to build character and makes one a sound person so one can interact with everyone. School also expands a person's horizons socially. It allows for networking contacts and this sort of thing. All of this is helpful later in building and expanding a career."

Tony has grown his business so that the distribution channel for *African Torch Magazine* has expanded to Houston, Dallas, New York, New Jersey, Atlanta, Rhode Island, and North Carolina. He has done this through learning how to interact effectively with others. "To progress you need to see everybody in the work environment as a friend. Everyone counts. White people have been taught to smile and act in a way so that everyone says 'That is a friendly person.' People of color must learn the same thing. Also, we must learn to compete, get a good education, and read more often. We have a shortage of information that we can make up for simply by reading."

Tony Okonkwo
African immigrant
Publisher/Editor-in-Chief, *African Torch Magazine*,
Atlanta, Georgia
Business: Publishing

CHAPTER 9

Grab That Big Opportunity

If it's time to move on in your career, moving up doesn't have to mean moving out to another employer. There may be many benefits to staying where you are, as long as you can find and take advantage of new opportunities there.

Many people might advise against this and tell you to start sending out résumés and networking to find work somewhere else. After all, it's a common belief that people get ahead more quickly by changing employers. But I disagree with this "common wisdom." Of course, you may face some obstacles in moving from one level to another (for example, if you've been pigeonholed in a certain job or at a certain level), but the advantages of staying with the same company are many. If you've already established a reputation for excellent performance, as Jacquelyn tells us in "Strive to Deliver Excellence," you'll be in a perfect position to go after a promotion, and it will probably be easy for you to find support for doing so. After working at the same company for some time, you'll likely know about potential land mines and how to avoid them (see Chapter 6). Once you've won your promotion, you'll also probably know how to access resources and the right people to help you meet your objectives in a job that carries added responsibility.

Are You Ready?

Before initiating a plan to move up at your company, consider the following factors that contribute to upward mobility. If there are any obstacles you may have to deal with, incorporate into your plan a strategy for addressing them:

- **How is your personal image?** Does your attire reflect the level to which you want to move? If not, buy two or three suits, a new briefcase, shoes, and such. The expense will be worth it because your new image will give you a psychological boost as well as make you look like someone on the way up.

- **Do you have a good track record?** Any glitches there? If so, check with your mentor or an understanding supervisor (if you're fortunate enough to have one you can confide in) for the best way to address this at your company.

- **Are you likely to encounter roadblocks because of your age?** If so, a haircut, makeup, and some alterations to your wardrobe can help you project youthfulness and openness or seriousness and maturity. If you work with a fashion consultant at one of the better department stores and let him know of your concerns and the image you want to project, he can help you get outfitted. A cosmetologist in the same store can help with the appropriate makeup to accomplish your goal.

- **Do you anticipate a gender issue?** Do your homework; unfortunately, women often must work harder and be smarter than men just to overcome ingrained biases. Be sure you know what is required to move into a higher position, and make sure you have the bases covered.

- **Do you anticipate a racial issue?** Strive for commonalities and chemistry; they usually win out. (Refer to Chapter 6 for guidance in ensuring that your personality is a good match with the company culture.)

- **Are you qualified?** Stay focused on how your qualifications fit the needs of any job you plan to interview for. The barriers you may face in trying to get "hired" into another department or into a higher-level job in your current department could be similar to those faced by people seeking employment with

another company. If you suspect this is true, take a look at
my book *101 Great Answers to the Toughest Job Search Problems*
for more suggestions on how you can address a variety of
difficult issues.

After you've anticipated and planned for any negatives, you're ready to
evaluate the potential for moving forward at your company.

Establishing the Plan for a Promotion

If you're with a large organization, arrange to meet with people who can
give you an idea of your potential for advancement: managers, department
heads, and human resources people. This will help you determine not only
where and how far you can go within the company, but also whether you'll
be able to accomplish your long-range career goal there at all. The people
you meet with will be favorably impressed with your show of initiative,
willingness to do your homework, and your ambition. These factors indicate
to decision-makers that you have potential to move up.

Prepare to Speak with Your Manager

If you're with a small or medium-sized organization, talk directly with your
manager (or the owner) about the potential for advancement. Because
smaller companies generally have fewer job slots (and, therefore, fewer
places to which you can advance), you might need to focus more on working to rearrange responsibilities than on getting promoted. This will enable
you to take on more challenging tasks so that you can develop further skills
and, in turn, enhance your marketability in the future.

Whether you work for a large or small organization, timing and tact are
important here. It's best to have been in your current job for at least a year
before broaching the subject of career advancement, even if you've been
with the company longer in other positions. The best time to discuss
advancement is during the goal-setting phase of your performance review.
If you're with a small company or if performance reviews are not a part of
the company's culture, ask your manager for a time when the two of you
can get together to discuss your performance—without using the formal
term *performance review*.

Before approaching her, you'll need to develop your strategy. How receptive is she likely to be to the discussion? Are there any factors that would prevent her from supporting the idea: a heavy workload? Reluctance to lose a key team member? Not naturally inclined to help subordinates advance? Then determine the best way to approach her based on her personal style and yours. Discuss your approach with your mentor or a colleague, and role-play the conversation if possible.

Ask for Your Manager's Buy-In

Once you sit down with your manager, the primary purpose of this conversation will be to get input on your capabilities and potential. Moreover, it's politically correct to let your manager be the first to know that you're interested in advancing; you don't want her to think that you're going behind her back to make a move or trying to separate yourself from her supervision. Also, if she plans to put up any roadblocks to your advancement, you'll want to know this right away so that you can address these issues before proceeding; it's called covering your bases. Ideally, once your manager knows of your goal, she'll help you.

Plan to discuss the skills you want to use and explore the functional areas and specific jobs within the company that would fit those skills and interests. Your side of the conversation might go something like this:

> "I'm interested in advancing my career and focusing more on my artistic skill and mechanical ability. I have some ideas about how I could contribute those skills in the company, and I would like to discuss my ideas with you and get your feedback."

At this point, you're setting a course toward a goal within the company, so you want to get a sense not only of a specific job several levels above where you are, but also of the interim jobs needed to get to that level.

Handling Worst-Case Scenarios

What if your manager seems unreceptive to your advancement? Then make the effort to find out why (if she will tell you). If she makes a good case that you still need to develop skills in your current job, find out specifically what you need to do. Then, it might be best to back away from the advancement idea right now and instead talk about setting goals within your current job to build a stronger foundation for advancement down the road.

If your manager is not receptive to your advancing because she needs you for a critical project, try to get a commitment for a time when you will be able to go after other jobs. If it's not too far in the future, then it will probably be best to just wait it out. If, on the other hand, she gives you no definite timeframe, then you might want to let her know that you'd like to look for new opportunities within the company anyway and that if something does open up, you will do your best to make the transition as smooth as possible for all involved.

If she doesn't have a valid job-related reason for not supporting you or a timetable as to when you can proceed, you'll have to take a different approach. If you work in a large organization, meet with your human resources representative to talk about how you can advance. If you work in a small company, forget the advancement avenue at that company and shift your focus to your other options (start sending out your résumé!) because the other managers (or principals) will probably support your manager's assessment.

Contacting Others in Your Company

The preceding examples are worst-case scenarios. The truth is, it's unlikely that your manager will refuse to support you without giving you a legitimate reason; she won't want to be stuck with a disgruntled, unmotivated employee.

If your manager is supportive, she may volunteer information about her own career progression. If not, ask her how she advanced to her current level, and ask her for advice on your own approach. I've always found people to be more than willing to share this kind of information. Also, find out whom else in the company you should talk with and then ask your manager whether it's all right to tell them that she referred you.

Your next step is to make an appointment with each of these people. When you set up the meetings, mention that your manager suggested you talk with them and that you'd appreciate about 30 minutes of their time, and then give them a clear idea of the reason for the meeting and what you expect from them. Stick to your word; stay focused on your objective and specific about your goals. You don't want to ramble in these meetings and waste their time. If you prepare questions before going to the meeting, you'll be able to keep these informational interviews on track.

Finally, you'll want to meet with your human resources representative, who should be able to recommend a career path for you within the company, discuss the likelihood of relevant job openings in the future, and give you a sense of how you can prepare so that you will be considered for these openings. Additionally, the human resources representative should schedule an interview between you and the manager or a representative from the department you're interested in working in. This will give you not only a clearer understanding of the department and its needs but also the added advantage of alerting the right people about your skills and goals.

MY BOTTOM LINE | Be ready when opportunity knocks...because it will. If you're not ready, it will pass you by and you might have to wait a very long time before something as good comes by again.

Finding Mentors (or Allowing Them to Find You)

As I've noted in previous chapters of this book, the best way to get a mentor is to demonstrate good performance so that you'll be selected by someone who takes an interest in your career and decides that mentoring you would be worth the time and effort.

If you have reached a point in your career where you are ready to seek a promotion within your company, you most likely have been working with one or two mentors within your company for some time. Of course, you can give others an opportunity to mentor you by approaching them and asking for their advice on how to advance in your field or for feedback on your performance.

As you advance in your career, however, it becomes somewhat more difficult to find just one person to mentor you. In her book *Women Breaking Through*, Deborah Swiss offers good advice for finding a number of mentors rather than concentrating on just one individual. Pointing out that it is not necessary to even like your mentors, Swiss includes a quote from Mary Rowe, ombudsperson at MIT, who suggests considering the broadest possible pool of mentors and forgetting about finding a saint or a perfect role model: "Seek advice from anyone who is competent and responsible. Seek out several mentors and learn different things from different people...even your peers."

Any conversations (networking or informational interviews) in which you seek or are given advice are opportunities to connect with someone as an adviser or guide. Most likely, if some chemistry or connection exists between you that supports a mentoring relationship, the other person will be forthcoming with help.

As you expand your network, you increase your pool of potential mentors. Here again, people in your professional groups, associations, social groups that include people who work at your socio-economic level, associates in other companies—all have the potential to mentor you.

At this juncture of your career you have made quite a few advancements, so you'll need to be aware that the mentoring relationships that you developed in the first part of your career may change, and the opportunity for mentors may not be as frequent going forward. The following tips will help you understand how and why your mentoring relationships will change, as well as provide some advice for new mentors:

- People can't mentor you beyond their capability. When someone you've trusted for advice seems reluctant to be forthcoming to your inquiries, hesitant in their responses, or in some instances even negative in their responses, it may simply be because they no longer know how to help you. You have moved past them. The next level of advancement is one they could not or did not want to make; therefore it is the unknown for them. The unknown can be a frightening place and this can result in them giving advice that may seen negative because it is filled with fearful caution. A person like this may have been your peer or even your manager. They still may be your friend, but they can no longer be your mentor. Often, even the friendship will be strained and become somewhat distant.

■ People who won't mentor you any longer may feel you're in competition with them. These may be people who have been your mentor and may even be at a higher level than you but now see you as a threat. You are now competition for them, and they are not likely to help you advance into a position they may also want. These people may even be in another company but can tell that your advancement will soon put you at their level or beyond. It's very difficult for someone to support your advancement past theirs, even if it would not be for the same company. These people can no longer be your mentor—and sometimes they can no longer be your friend.

■ People who may benefit from your advancement will mentor you. The people who are most likely to mentor you as you start moving past the middle ranks of the corporation are those who would benefit by your continued success. Their advice will generally be geared to making you more useful to them and their personal advancement. The suggestions they give will usually be very subtle, as opposed to the more specific kind of coaching you received early in your career. At the higher levels of an organization, you are much more on your own because risk-taking is a large part of what it takes to get there, so listen to the advice offered, consider the source, and understand that you are responsible for the results of any action taken—not your mentor. Nevertheless, you don't need to discard their advice if it, in fact, helps support your goal. Because of the risk of career injury involved in the next levels, be sure that you have anticipated and planned as much as possible for all the consequences of your decisions and that you have contingency plans for your future.

■ Silent mentors help you by example rather than words. These are people whom you may or may not be closely associated with. They have advanced or failed because of circumstances or behavior patterns that were inconsistent with advancement or with the company culture. Or maybe because they made some big mistakes. Find out as much as you can about why they've advanced, or why they've failed, and incorporate that knowledge into your strategies for advancing to the next level.

I hope as you seek advice in how to move forward, you will gain mentors along the way. If you keep your eyes open and finely tune your listening skills, you might be able to pick up clues for identifying potential mentors.

Speak Up

"Networking is something that, from a cultural and personal point of view, we don't do. It's difficult for Hispanics to blow their own horn—and it takes a while for us to understand that it takes more than doing a good job to succeed.

"I am forever grateful to a person who unofficially mentored me early in my career. When I was first starting out, I used to bury myself in my work; I didn't look up or say anything to anyone. I felt that if I did a good job, it would show for itself. But then, the person who started mentoring me began to come over each morning and say, 'Put your head up and say hello,' until I finally started doing it on my own."

This lesson, early in his career, helped teach Juan the value of speaking up, being visible, and reaching out to others. It is a lesson he has never forgotten.

Juan can't emphasize enough the necessity of networking, especially for people of color, who might not be used to this concept. "You should establish a network that will allow you to call on others if you need help.

Employee-initiated, company-supported groups are great for that. At NYNEX, we have groups like our Hispanic support organization and a multicultural association where one can find good role models."

Juan advocates networking because it has been instrumental for him in achieving his own career growth. "I was on the technical side for a number of years and was sponsored by the company in a master's [degree] program. After I finished, I wanted a position as a technical trainer. I finally got the job as the result of knowing the district and regional managers. I had decision-makers on the lookout for me, and it helped."

Juan knows that you cannot succeed by yourself and believes that his ability to develop relationships and get consensus has been invaluable to him. "If I could say just one thing to people who are trying to communicate with others and advance, it would be words that Jesse Jackson spoke: 'Look for the common ground to seek the higher ground.'"

People have more in common than we think. Juan knows from his own experience that success depends on reaching out and communicating our ideas, our goals, and who we are in order to make valuable connections.

Juan N. Rodriguez
Hispanic executive
Director of Human Resources, Manhattan Market Area,
NYNEX, New York
Business: Corporate human resources

Going After a Job

Planning, persistence, and patience will help you get the job you want. Beyond this, there are no set rules for advancing at this stage of your career. Now you're more on your own than you were at the beginning. At this level, you are expected to be willing to take some risks for advancement. Quite often, people secure more advanced positions by using unique strategies and approaches to go after them. Usually these approaches involve some risks and a measure of creativity; in fact, the more unique, creative, or daring the strategy, the more it will distinguish the accomplished veteran from the less confident novice. Of course, your approach should not be foolhardy. But by developing a strategy based on knowledge of the culture and the manager's personality, you won't make any big mistakes.

One experienced executive once told me of a particularly creative approach he used when he was working toward advancement in his company. He timed his visits to the water cooler to coincide with those of the general manager; once there, he would casually mention projects he wanted to promote or inquire about. Cassie, who you'll read about next, took an even more inventive approach.

Case 1: A Strategy for Success

Cassie, a career consultant with a major organizational development firm, did an excellent job of going after the position she wanted—and getting it. It took 18 months, an interim job with another organization, and a 6-month volunteer stint with a social services group before she accomplished her goal. Six months prior to completing her master's degree in psychology, which she was working on while holding a full-time position as an office manager, Cassie decided she wanted to move into a consultant position at the firm. She started the process of establishing her career track by introducing herself to one of her company executives, whom she first met at a professional association meeting, and arranging to meet with him for an informational interview to discuss her career.

In the interview, Cassie learned that her degree would not be sufficient to qualify her to handle the organization's clientele. As part of its marketing approach, the company used only consultants who were highly experienced. In other words, they had no room for an entry-level consultant.

Now Cassie realized that she was either stuck in her administrative position or would have to leave the company. After obtaining her degree, she elected to leave the company and join a smaller organization where she could gain the experience she lacked. At the same time, to supplement the skills she was developing at her new interim job, she worked two evenings a week and on the weekends volunteering for a community-based social services agency. All the while she maintained regular contact with her former employer. Her dedication and commitment paid off. She got the experience and then rejoined her original company, moving into the consultant position she aspired to from the beginning.

Case 2: Working Around a Log Jam

As Cassie found out early, there are two key considerations in going after a specific job at a company: whether the opportunity is worth the effort and what your chances are of getting it. John also learned this after he set his sights on the spot of vice president of finance at his company. He knew that before he could compete for the job, he would need to work at two interim jobs to gain the necessary experience. The problem was that employees with more than 15 years of service were already well-established in those two interim positions. As the situation stood, John would have been wasting his time going after the top financial job in his company. Instead, he opted to transfer to another division in the company where he could get the experience he needed so that he would be prepared to eventually compete for the top position when it became available.

Know Your Challenges

Both of these examples point to the importance of thoroughly assessing your potential for advancing in your company before you establish a career track there. If you discover through your interviews and research that it will be all but impossible to reach your goal at your current company, then it's best to cut your losses and move on. On the other hand, you may learn that the job you want is attainable but that you will need to gain more experience at another company or within another division before you can compete for it.

Expanding Your Current Job

Expanding your current job may be one of the most viable avenues for advancement because it allows you to develop your position specifically around your strengths. To do this, you need to take the lead role in restructuring your job and convincing your supervisors to work with you.

Case 3: A Proven Performer

George, a senior marketing executive for a Fortune 100 company, managed to restructure and expand his position to become lead marketing executive. Noted for his ability to land very difficult clients as well as being able to work well with the staff, George had established himself as an excellent employee. Not only did he willingly put in the extra effort to close the loop on every deal, but he also made himself available to train other marketing executives and to pitch in when one of them needed help.

Before long, others in the department came to rely on George's help, and, as a result, he eventually became overloaded with the additional responsibilities of training and coaching his peers. At this point, he approached his division head about rewriting his job description to incorporate his expanded responsibilities. He also asked for an administrative assistant to help him with some of the follow-up activities and administrative work connected with servicing his clients. Because he presented his needs clearly and realistically (and because his firm recognized George as a real asset), he got all that he requested. The company officially rewrote his position to cover his new responsibility as lead marketing executive; he also got an assistant—and a raise.

Going Above and Beyond

The key to expanding your position is to meet a need your employer has by using additional skills that are outside the scope of your current responsibilities. Some possible ways to accomplish this include:

- Take on the responsibility to initiate activities that will upgrade your skills as well as those of others in the group. For example, provide training or suggest a program of cross-functional activities that will train and expand the capabilities of key individuals.

- Take responsibility for some task that needs to be done but that no one wants to do—for instance, serving as liaison to sources external to your department or company in order to carry out necessary tasks.

- Demonstrate problem-solving skills by working to find a solution to an onerous situation that has bothered a lot of people.

- Volunteer to assume some of the responsibilities that are cumbersome to your immediate manager.

Creating a New Job

Another means of advancing your career within your current company is to create an entirely new position. The key to doing this is to identify a significant need that is not being met, which could either increase revenue, cut costs, or improve efficiency—and then volunteer to step in and fill that need. Because this approach requires the greatest amount of initiative and creativity, many people are not up to the challenge.

It's more common for people to stay in their current job, hoping that someone will recognize their hidden capabilities and then offer to create a new job for them. They want to advance but they're waiting for either someone else or circumstances to create opportunities that will move their career along. Instead of taking the steps to determine where they could add value to the organization, they get stuck by giving in to prevalent career-stopping attitudes.

Don, for example, relied heavily on his good relationship with his boss as an avenue to advance, but he did not use the relationship to its fullest potential. He hinted to Mike, his boss, that he wanted a more responsible position, and he waited with the hope that something would eventually materialize. Nothing did. Don was right to use the relationship as a tool, but he would have been better off talking with Mike not about a problem but about a solution. Rather than ask how he could have more responsibility, Don should have offered to take on more responsibility by presenting a list of needs he could address. If he had looked around the organization to determine where he could add value, he probably could have enlisted Mike's help.

Be Part of a Solution

Most any department or company has areas where productivity is low and work gets bottlenecked or where a number of complaints originate.

By discussing problem areas with the people involved, you'll have a good chance of hitting on workable solutions. Often the people with the problem also have a solution for how it should be handled; it's just that someone in the group needs to be willing to take the initiative for addressing the problem or the responsibility for implementing the solution.

As an example, suppose, as the manager of a marketing department, you were constantly requesting a variety of statistical information that your team needed for developing proposals. You could either develop a retrieval system for accessing the information quickly or research and provide information on programs that could accomplish the goal. You could put this in the form of a proposal with recommendations for your boss's signature. Your boss would then have something he could react to or forward to the next level of authority for approval.

Another career advancement avenue is through the ability to think outside of predictable patterns. When needs arise that must be addressed, tunnel vision may translate to "It's not my job," followed by "It's so-and-so's job. Let him do it. He's getting paid for it." The interesting thing about such an attitude is that people who have it will never be paid for "it," because people who continually pass off responsibility to others are also passing up the opportunity to increase their own earning power.

I encountered this kind of thinking recently when talking with a peer about an assignment that had been offered to me and that I knew would be difficult. The client wanted to implement a huge project on a very tight deadline. My colleague advised me to stay clear of the project because it seemed destined for failure; why risk having the failure fall on me? Fortunately, I ignored that advice and worked hard to help make the project a success. When we did meet the goal, my credibility increased tenfold, ensuring future business with that client. Of course, people can always think of reasons to avoid taking on a challenging job or, in some cases, doing any work at all. Harry is a classic example of someone who held to one of the popular career-blocking attitudes: "That's too much work; I don't want to do it." Seeing himself as someone who possessed true leadership ability, Harry felt he should not have to get stuck in the trenches doing dirty work. After all, he had already paid his dues. He made a point of avoiding projects where he had to "get his hands dirty," or he tried to enlist the help of someone else to handle the difficult tasks. He did all right with this method of managing, but it caused him to lose out when a prestigious position that he really wanted became available. The person responsible for filling the position wanted someone with enthusiasm, high energy, and flexibility. Not surprisingly, Harry's reputation kept him out of the running.

Case 4: Three People Who Advanced Through Initiative

Smart people who take responsibility for their own careers will take a different approach—an approach that will lead to advancement. Consider the examples of Susan, Julie, and Diane, three professionals at the same consulting company who took the initiative to create new jobs for themselves. Susan conducted management training sessions, and after working with several organizations from a variety of industries, she noticed a recurring theme in the complaints from the participants. She saw a need for programs that would bring together managers and employees for discussion and problem-solving and encourage them to form closer working relationships. She developed and sold a team-building program for addressing these issues to the executive management of her company and convinced them to implement the new program nationally. Her concept resulted almost immediately in a significant increase in revenues—and a new job for her.

Julie, a branch manager, used her management and leadership talent to cut costs significantly. After three staff members left through promotion or attrition, Julie realigned the responsibilities without refilling the positions. The district director soon noticed the tremendous savings in overhead, combined with the more efficient operation of the office. He met with Julie to determine what it was that she was doing that made her so much more efficient than the other unit managers. Based on his findings, he promoted her to senior manager, directing the efforts of five other managers and offices.

Diane's new job came out of her ability to conceptualize and implement on a broad scale. In its start-up phase, the consulting company had operated very efficiently and consistently delivered a quality product and service. After about seven years, however, Diane noticed that staff members were experiencing frustration in trying to meet the needs of the clients. She also recognized inconsistent service and duplication of effort. Meeting with management, she suggested consolidating the administrative and system functions in the five offices in the district so that they could be managed at one office, with the aim of improving efficiency. She did so well that the responsibilities eventually grew into a new senior operations position for her within two years.

Finding Your Own Opportunities

Opportunities for creating your own job may exist right under your nose if you are willing to be part of the solution instead of the problem. The following suggestions might spark ideas about needs in your organization that you could explore.

- Check out areas that a number of employees have been complaining about. Make a point of listening for the consistent theme of the complaints, and then explore ways they could be addressed.

- Discuss job issues and problems with members of your professional groups. One of the advantages of participating in professional groups is that they provide a forum for discussing issues that might bring forth a solution. Some of these "solutions" could be significant enough to create a new position or expand an existing one.

- Stay current on industry news. Often reading about other organizations and their leadership approaches can give you ideas for solving problems in your own company.

MY BOTTOM LINE | Opportunity may come down an unexpected avenue, through an unusual source, or disguised as hard work. Watch out that you don't let it pass you by.

Strive to Deliver Excellence

Jacquelyn attributes her rapid career growth at NYNEX to her ability to facilitate change; her transferable skills, reputation, and presence; and, above all, her ongoing commitment to excellence. "I joined the company with 12 years' corporate staff experience but no direct operating experience. NYNEX gave me my first hands-on operating opportunity: handling customer service and managing a staff of 120 people."

Jacquelyn focused on the tasks of the position and directed her energy toward upgrading the customer service effort and delivering excellence. As she did, she successfully elevated the level of service and quality of her role, which ultimately led to her promotion to a position created specifically around her capabilities. She attributes her advancement to Vice President, Quality and Ethics, at one of the company's subsidiaries to her commitment to getting the job done well. "You must have standards for yourself and not be level-conscious—to do a good job no matter what level you're at. I believe that motivating my customer service team to deliver quality service signaled to management that I could lead a quality effort throughout the company, and that led to the vice president position."

Maintaining a practice of meeting high standards never goes unnoticed. Two years after her promotion, a reorganization took place within the company and Jacquelyn moved into a more corporate position as director of corporate culture initiatives and then into her current position of Vice President, Quality and Ethics.

For Jacquelyn, visibility is a final critical element for success. "Visibility means you need to join organizations and volunteer for projects and task forces," she explains. "My participation in these organizations gave me visibility in my company that I never would have gotten otherwise. As a matter of fact, that was how I met my current boss. He was at the back of the room in a group where I was speaking, and a year later he called me about a job. Being visible is important."

Jacquelyn Burch Gates
Black executive
Vice president, Office of Ethics and Business Conduct,
NYNEX, New York
Business: Corporate ethics and quality management

Make Restructuring Work for You

Restructuring has become a constant in most businesses today. If you have the ability to function in the midst of chaos, you can make a restructuring work for you. This can be a real challenge because, naturally, a reorganization creates a tremendous amount of stress for everyone involved, especially if it is also associated with downsizing.

Everyone is wondering what will happen to his job and hoping he has sufficiently proved himself to ensure that his job is secure. This anxiety can cause people to react in several ways. They may close off communication with others and try to protect their turf, potentially shutting down some important processes because they are not feeding the necessary information into the pipeline. Others, assigned to complete certain projects, may delay completion by dawdling or intentionally making mistakes, assuming the company won't lay them off because it needs them to finish the work. Still others may deliberately sabotage the efforts of co-workers to eliminate competition.

Case 5: A Cool Head Draws Attention

Obviously a person who can maintain some objectivity and perspective on work that needs to be done in the face of this kind of psychological upheaval will clearly stand out in a positive way. Janice, a trainer for a major chemical processing company, learned this when her company restructured and decentralized the corporate staff groups. Her whole department was eliminated overnight. Janice and 12 other co-workers were given four months to find a position in the company or they would be declared surplus, given a severance package, and terminated.

As angry and devastated as she was, Janice managed to maintain enough clarity to realize that she needed to focus on getting another job either at the company or somewhere else. Prepared to relocate if necessary, she started sending out résumés and networking all over the country. In the meantime, her responsibilities had been removed and she didn't have anything to do at work. Being idle increased her frustration and she felt very isolated not being part of the mainstream of activity.

She seized her opportunity to change the situation when she encountered the division vice president in the hallway. When he asked how she was doing, she engaged him in a conversation and let him know that she was bored and wanted some work to do while going through the restructuring process. She mentioned that she thought the human resources group could use some help. (Ironically, companies that are downsizing are often hiring simultaneously.) Janice knew of this opportunity through some friends in that department who had told her how extreme their workload had become since the restructure. The executive looked into the situation and the next day had Janice working on a short-term staffing project for the personnel department.

Janice completed the project quickly and went on to provide additional support in the department. This came to the attention of the executive, and he stopped by her office to compliment her on how impressively she had handled the work. Ultimately, Janice was offered three jobs within the company, primarily as a result of how well she had carried out the temporary project. She accepted a newly created position that handled centralized professional staffing.

Look for the Door That's Opening

If your organization is being restructured and you see or feel in others frustration similar to Janice's, keep your ears and eyes open for new opportunities. If you notice any one of the following situations and you have the necessary skills to step in, don't waste any time; seize the opportunity and go for it:

- You notice a need for new leadership skills and knowledge. (In the midst of a major restructuring, human resources might need someone with labor relations skills.)

- A project comes to a standstill because of discord and tension among the group members assigned to work on it.

- Someone suddenly leaves, is transferred, or is promoted, removing key skills from the organization.

- Two or three departments are merged into one, causing some important responsibilities to fall through the cracks in certain areas and duplication of effort in others.

A department or a co-worker has an excessively heavy work-load, and you have very few responsibilities.

Any restructuring, whether it's a reorganization, merger, or downsizing, will result in a wealth of new opportunities. In spite of the potential offered by such changes, the majority of people within the organization may focus on resistance and occupy themselves with pointless speculation, gossip, fear, and work-avoidance. This is your opportunity to step forward and prove your value as an employee. Find the new "doors" that present themselves as a result of company changes, and open the one that's right for you.

MY BOTTOM LINE When you are ready for advancement, the opportunity will be there. That's the way the universe works. You have some control of when the opportunity will be presented by making yourself ready for advancement. After that, you need to be open, listen, and look for the perfect opportunity for advancement.

CHAPTER 10

The Grass May Be Greener on the Other Side of the Fence

After 10 years or so with the same company, you can easily fall into a predictable and comfortable routine, even if you're working at a job you dislike. Most of us, either consciously or subconsciously, resist the idea of making a change from a position that feels secure. So it's no surprise that some of us remain stuck too long in jobs going nowhere.

In Chapter 9 you explored the possibilities of moving up within your company. But for some of us, that type of move isn't the best career decision. In this chapter, we talk about ways you can really assess whether the best move for you is out—out of your current company and into an environment better suited to your career growth. If you've been in your current position for five or more years, you may need a bit of a "refresher" course on résumé preparation and interviewing techniques. We'll talk about those things here, too. Don't be afraid to get back into the market because if you do, you may be pleasantly surprised at your marketability. Statistics show that most people can advance more rapidly by changing companies. You can maximize your experience and career savvy to make this important transition and keep your career on track and moving forward.

You Know It's Time to Go When...

Either internal or external factors will give you signals when it is time to move on. As an ambitious person, when you look at your company structure and needs and do not see an opportunity for you to advance or expand in your current role...you know it's time to go. If you have created an untenable situation at your company...you know it's time to go. If you are no longer motivated by the company's mission or the idea of advancement at your company...you know it's time to go. If none of these situations exist and there are factors in the company that can impede the company's growth, and thus your growth...you know it's time to go. Even if you feel comfortable in your present job and company, if any of the following situations sound familiar, it might be a good time to consider making a change.

Decreased Revenues

When a company starts losing money, it's just a matter of time before managers begin cutting overhead expenses. This means downsizing, which means eliminating projects and people. A company in a downsizing mode is not the most pleasant place to be and certainly not conducive to career growth for most people there.

One of the more negative aspects of downsizing is the politics. People in power tend to make decisions and act on their own behalf and on the behalf of those in whom they have an interest. This often means that if you're not affiliated with the right person or people, you could end up in an undesirable position or out the door, even if you're the most qualified person for a particular job.

The positive aspect of downsizing is that it sometimes brings with it the opportunity to pick up new skills and experience. As managers cut full-time permanent positions, stand-alone short-term projects and temporary positions often become available. Handling one of these projects may be beneficial in adding skills while looking for another position. If you opt to do this, try to take on a project that will allow you to develop skills that could be transferred to another company.

Bad Press

If you've blown it pretty badly, the resulting bad press may make it impossible for you to advance for a long time. In fact, you may not be able to move up at all until an almost entirely new regime comes in—and possibly not even then because bad news is always passed along. The type of bad press you've received will dictate how much it will inhibit your career. For example, advancing in your career after an extensive history of nonperformance, bungled projects, missed deadlines, poor attitude, or not being a team player will require tremendous effort. It would probably be easier in the long run to start over again at a new company, in a new career, or possibly, in a new location.

Less serious transgressions that have resulted in undisciplined behavior or a limited contribution—such as a short period of laziness, an instance or two of poor judgment, or letting outside problems distract you from doing your job for a certain amount of time—are less likely to leave a permanent mark, as long as you demonstrate a true willingness to change and leave the negative behavior behind you.

Incompatibility

One of the best reasons for changing companies is that the culture is no longer compatible with your personality, goals, interests, or values. Networking has long been considered the number-one way to connect with people and move ahead in a career. Naturally, networking, which is simply "word of mouth," is most effective when it occurs between two people who have something in common. It stands to reason, then, that if you are not in sync with the company's culture, you're probably not going to be compatible with a majority of the decision makers there. Most likely, this will limit your ability to effectively network in order to create opportunities for your own progress.

Dead-End Job

A popular belief holds that there are no dead-end jobs, just dead-end people. I have to agree with that to a certain extent, because a "live wire" is not going to allow herself to remain stuck in a position that offers no opportunity for growth. Upward advancement is not necessary for growth. Depending on your career goal, a job that may appear to outsiders to be dead-end might actually be a great growth opportunity for you. Before changing companies, evaluate the potential of the position to get all that you can out of it to help your career goals.

Frank's goal was to start his own consulting practice, and when he landed in a dead-end job, it turned out to be an excellent bridge to achieving his career objective. The position was not geared to any of the company's career tracks; rather it dealt with a lot of external companies. It provided Frank with the perfect opportunity to start building credibility with outside organizations, which he was able to later use as networking contacts when he started his own consulting practice.

A Merger

The rumor mill is probably one of the most accurate avenues of communication in the company. If you hear of a pending or possible merger, it is probably true. A merger can effectively end your career at a "gobbled-up" company, especially if you are in management. Generally, the acquiring company will bring in its own people for all key positions. This usually happens over a period of time, but often it happens immediately. If you are in this category and it does not happen to you right away, it may be because you have a skill or knowledge that the new company needs. But once they have acquired your knowledge, your continued employment is in jeopardy. True advancement in this situation is not likely. Does this mean that the company can be acquired and you cannot advance? No, it does not. Sometimes, it's to the acquiring company's advantage to promote you. In this case, your continued employment may still be in jeopardy once they have gained the knowledge from you that is needed to sustain the company. Accept the new situation if you must, but start the process right away of exploring your external options in case you need them.

An Executive Change

When the CEO, president, or several other top executives leave (or are removed) from their positions of power, it's time to consider a change. The head of the organization establishes the philosophy and tone of an organization. A change at this level produces a ripple effect that may create an atmosphere with which you're no longer comfortable. When a major change occurs within your organization, take the time to research the background of the incoming executive for insight on what the new corporate philosophy might be. Information on how the new executive managed a former company would be helpful.

I remember working at a company whose top executive strongly supported philanthropic causes, which was reflected in the activities to which he committed the company's efforts and resources. When he was replaced, the tone of the company changed considerably. The new head executive significantly minimized the philanthropic effort, as well as the company's presence in the community, and focused on relocating the company to another region.

To get a sense of what you might expect when a major change occurs, ask your public relations department and the executive's former public relations department for literature (such as a press kit) on the company where the new executive previously worked. Also, search your public library for articles on either the executive or the company. Members of professional groups may also provide a networking link through which you can gain information. An additional source for information is the web site of the new executive's previous company, where you would be able to read the press releases about the company. You could also do a search, using any major search engine, on the executive's name or the name of his or her former company to find articles (newspaper, professional journals, and so on) about the executive and the company.

A number of services are available that provide information on databases about companies. These services can be pretty expensive, though, and may not be readily available at your local library. In addition to the databases, such services generally publish a variety of reference materials, so you can get the information that way as well. *Dun & Bradstreet's Million Dollar Directory* is one such source, as is *Standard and Poor's Register of Corporations, Directors, and Executives*; both these publications provide information on companies and officers within publicly held companies. Some Dun & Bradstreet publications can be accessed online by using one of the major search engines. Financial institutions (such as stock brokerage firms) and large corporations are likely to have these database services at their company. A good networking contact at one of these organizations could probably get you the information you need.

A Significant Restructuring

A significant restructuring may come after a change in top executives or as a result of market influences. A major organizational shake-up can initiate a process in which departments within the company continue to be reorganized for a while and no one actually settles into a position for any length of time. This can severely impair your ability to establish a meaningful networking system or develop a career track. It can also remove or consolidate some responsibilities you had hoped to take on as avenues to reach your goal, possibly leaving your career at a standstill.

Should You Stay with Your Company or Go? Making the Decision

Although the examples you just read are not the only factors pointing toward change, they are some of the most common ones. If you've arrived at a juncture where it would be best to change, you should take the time to plan your move carefully. This will give you a better chance of hooking up with the right company, one that will offer you the greatest potential for progress.

To ensure that the energy around your career objectives is truly focused, take into account all the factors that may influence your decision whether to stay or go. For example, perhaps you've been looking forward to relocating to one of your company's offices in another state or region, or you may be reluctant to let go of certain benefits, such as health insurance or a retirement fund.

Taking Stock: Do I *Need* to Go?

The following questions will help you sort out any doubts you may have about changing companies and confirm that your final reasons for deciding to stay or go are based on factors that will promote career growth. An analysis of your responses should help you decide whether such a change is necessary for you to progress in your career at this time. Respond yes or no to the following statements:

- I have been in the same department and job for the past five years.

- I have accomplished the goal that I came to this company for.

- The philosophy of the company has changed, and it negatively impacts my ability to progress.

- The culture of the company has changed, and I don't fit in as well as I did in the past.

- I have identified new objectives and determined that it will be difficult to accomplish them in the current culture.

- There are a limited number of positions for the kinds of job I'd like to advance into and all are filled by people who will not likely move for a long time.

- I have had some performance or attitude problems in the past that I might not be able to overcome.

- I have heard serious rumblings that the company will be downsized or sold.

- My boss and I do not get along well and I need his or her support in order to advance.

- I believe that the management at my current company is poor and will inhibit the growth potential of the company.

- Since joining the company, new skills, interests, and values have surfaced that I could best develop in a different environment.

If you answered yes to any of these questions, it may be time to change companies.

It's equally important that you make an honest evaluation of why you want to change companies. If you feel you must change in order to grow, that's a positive reason. If, on the other hand, you're trying to escape from something (such as poor performance or bad press), changing employers will not help if you take your behavior with you to the new job. To succeed, you will have to improve your attitude at your current job or devise a solid personal plan for establishing a higher standard of performance at your new job.

Taking Stock: Am I *Ready* to Go?

Finally, even when you've decided that a move to a new company is essential, you should take a few moments to assess your current "readiness" for such a move. This will help you confirm that you're making the right move—before you make a change that you can't undo:

- I've evaluated where I am with my career and determined what the next growth step should be.

- My performance and capabilities reflect that I'm ready in every respect for the next step.

- I have explored all possibilities at my current company and know for certain that I cannot accomplish my next goal there.

- I'm certain that the obstacles preventing my advancement are not within my power to remove.

- I'm willing to let go of certain benefits (such as a good retirement fund or a generous vacation and holiday schedule) to go after my goal.

- I've determined that my next career step can only be achieved at another company.

MY BOTTOM LINE Fear of change and complacency can be the death knell of a career. Don't be afraid to accept what is going on around you and to make a decision about the advancement of your career as a result of what you see. Not acting when you should is still a decision, so choose to act and make a decision for progress when you see that you should.

Setting Goals

When all signals indicate that it's time to change companies, you first need to determine the next career objective you want to fulfill through your move. The analysis you did earlier should have provided that. Stay focused on why you wanted to move to another company in the first place, and use those reasons to keep on track with your goal. I hope you've already brought your career goal into focus and arrived at a stage where you can identify objectives and implement a plan to get there. Some key steps in setting a goal and implementing a plan follow:

■ Decide on the next career objective needed to move you closer to your ultimate goal. Examples of next objectives could be a need to develop a particular skill for later; a need to move closer to a school where you will be taking additional courses; a desire to get into a different industry that is more conducive to advancement for people in your profession; a desire to take on more of a leadership role; and so on.

■ When the objective has been set, you should rework your résumé to align with the new objective as well as demonstrate to potential employers that you have the skills they are looking for. For instance, if you want to move more into a leadership role in your next job, use a functional resume and highlight the type of leadership activities you have been involved with. These activities may include projects in professional associations as well as on your current job where you have taken the lead and successfully brought the project to conclusion.

■ You need to set up an action plan to research companies, network, respond to ads, and register with an agency to help with your search. Use the techniques outlined in Chapter 5 and later in this chapter to help with this process.

Taking the steps to plan and implement will not only save you time, but it will also help re-energize you and renew your commitment.

When your commitment is renewed, it will be expressed outwardly so that you send off positive and self-directed energy to the universe. You will walk with more confidence, be purposeful in your activities, and convey very clearly that you know what you want. The universe will respond and your opportunities will arise in direct proportion to the energy you've projected.

Choose Carefully Before You Make a Move

As you shop around for new employers, base your choices on your psychological needs as well as your career needs. If you don't carefully consider these factors before you make a move, you could end up in an organization that doesn't support your goals. For instance, if you enjoy using your leadership ability or you're a creative, independent contributor, and you discover that the new company is very rigid in its culture, policies, and organizational structure, you probably won't be happy or successful there.

Remember, too, that you should look at the big picture when changing companies. Base your decision on more than just a single promotional step. You need to ask yourself whether you'll be able to continue advancing forward within the new environment. Will there be opportunities to advance upward or laterally, and will you be rewarded for doing so? Will there be peer support for projects? Is the company advancing along lines that will provide continued challenge and growth opportunities for you? Will you have any influence in developing new directions?

Art learned too late how important it is to carefully consider the corporate culture and opportunities for personal growth before making a move. A systems engineer, he decided to switch companies several years into his career because he felt uncomfortable in his present company's highly political environment, where upward mobility depended almost completely on whom you knew. An old college friend helped him land a job at his company, and for a time, Art enjoyed his new position. However, after five years with no advancement whatsoever, he became frustrated and discontented.

In his new company, advancement depended solely on seniority. Because the department heads were entrenched in their positions, and Art had less seniority than others in the division, he had virtually no opportunity for advancement. Eventually, be decided to change companies again, but this time, he took the time to evaluate the move against a set of criteria that he developed—a series of questions about the new organization—that helped him determine whether he would have opportunity to advance there.

Making the decision to move to a new company is truly a classic example of the need to "look before you leap." Your change can—and should—be a positive move. You don't need to rush through the first open door. The next section "Checklist for Your New Job Search," will help you to evaluate the move carefully so you get all the benefits possible from this important career decision.

Checklist for Your New Job Search

The following checklist will help direct you in researching, evaluating, and selecting the companies you target in a new job search. The information you gather will make you more knowledgeable about the companies at which you eventually interview, which can only help make you more comfortable during the interviews and show employers that you've done your homework.

- ☐ I've compiled a list of companies based on my interests and skills. I developed the list from information I obtained through networking and from sources such as the Internet, the Chamber of Commerce, professional journals, and business references at the public library.

- ☐ I've read literature on companies that I'm interested in working for and, through networking contacts, have spoken with their employees whenever possible. In the process, I have narrowed my search to those companies whose major policies and culture are compatible with my own values, style, and work ethics.

- ☐ Through my contacts, I've learned the names of the department heads for my profession at the companies that interest me so that I can write to these individuals directly about developing job opportunities.

- ☐ I've selected only companies where I would want to work for a long period of time.

- ☐ The companies I'm interested in all have good compensation policies and opportunity for advancement.

- ☐ The companies I'm interested in all have stable management teams.

- ☐ All the companies are in expanding or growth industries.

- ☐ I believe I could make a contribution and add value at any of the companies I've chosen.

MY BOTTOM LINE | Sometimes situations at your company will dictate that you should make a job or career change, and sometimes your personal situation will dictate a change. At any rate, the important point is to recognize the need and act appropriately when the time to change is obvious to you.

Revising Your Marketing Tools (Résumés and Letters)

If you haven't looked for a job in some years, not only is your résumé undoubtedly out of date, but also it's out of style and does not reflect your current capabilities. Ten years ago, almost all résumés were written in a chronological format; as a result, they often included superfluous company information and emphasized previous job duties. Résumés today either use a modified chronological format (leaving out the superfluous information) or a functional format (for people with a lot of experience). They are viewed as marketing tools that display accomplishments rather than responsibilities. And they are more concise (one or two pages)—not the long documents of years ago. (To read about the different types of résumés, see Chapter 5.)

Because most of us do not think about the skills we draw on to accomplish our jobs on a day-to-day basis, we're often at a loss when we try to describe our capabilities in a résumé or interview. The further we move forward in our career, the broader our skill base becomes, making it difficult for us to break down our skills into specific categories. These issues become even more common for people as they move into a second phase of their career or as they prepare to move to a new company. The following sections help you explore the best methods for updating a professional resume to accentuate the achievements of your career to date.

Emphasizing Accomplishments

In your current position, you may have successfully brought projects to completion, proposed an idea that helped the company move in a productive direction, or identified and capitalized on an unknown talent in an up-and-coming employee—all very valuable accomplishments that demonstrate your capabilities. But how do you categorize these achievements into a superior skill set that you can list on your resume?

Here are some sample accomplishments that illustrate the strong people skills, leadership ability, and technical competence that one can develop over time. They are concise examples of the action and positive results associated with handling a specific task that involves some degree of difficulty, such as working well with a limited staff, tight deadlines, and budget constraints. Any of them is an asset to a résumé:

- Assumed responsibility for and implemented within 90 days a high-priority, past-due project that generated $5 million in revenue.

- Replaced a member on a three-person project team and helped bring the $2 million project to completion on time and under budget.

- Combined three manual financial processes into one computerized system, which was adopted throughout the company, resulting in annual cost savings of $500,000.

- Smoothed out a political bottleneck and recaptured a key account worth $3 million in annual revenues.

As you will note, I've included quantifiable results for somewhat non-quantifiable skills. Where possible, this kind of detail should be added to the accomplishment to demonstrate the real benefit and value to the company. You might need to talk with a manager or someone else in your office to get an approximate idea of the impact of your accomplishment. One good way to determine its impact is to ask yourself what was going on before your action, how did your action cause an improvement, and to what degree things improved.

If you can find examples along these lines from your own experience, include three or four in the body of your résumé to emphasize your skills. If you're using a chronological format, present your accomplishments after the company name, job title, and statement of responsibility. In a functional résumé format, highlight your accomplishments all in one place—such as in a bulleted list—following the summary statement. You can also include one or two of these accomplishments in your cover letter to demonstrate a specific qualification that the prospective employer is looking for.

Let the position, company culture, advertised requirements, and other "knowns" of the company and position you're applying to dictate how many accomplishments to use and which ones best demonstrate your skills. If you're answering an ad, make sure that you highlight accomplishments that demonstrate qualifications appropriate for the need advertised. If you're sending an unsolicited letter and résumé to a company, use accomplishments that align with the information about the company that you gathered in your research.

Updating Your Résumé

A review of the information in Chapter 5 will provide you with the basic foundation for developing your résumé. Completing the following steps should help you bring your information up-to-date:

1. Compile a list of 10 or 12 of your job-related accomplishments. If you, like most people, tend to forget what you've done after the work is complete, you might find it helpful to ask colleagues, friends, and family members who are familiar with your work to help you to remember some of your accomplishments; you can also draw examples from copies of your performance reviews, memos, letters, and other documents in your career files.

2. Refine and focus the accomplishments so they emphasize the skills necessary to support your goal. For instance, a writer might say: "Wrote and edited a monthly 10-page training and development newsletter that was distributed companywide." A training manager responsible for a similar newsletter would have a different focus: "Developed a corporatewide training and development newsletter that provided state-of-the-art information to update the technical staff."

3. Choose a résumé style that fits the type of jobs and industries you will pursue. I suggest creating your résumé in both a chronological and a functional format and see which works best for you. The chronological format is probably most appropriate when you're seeking a job exactly like the one you have or that advances your career to the next logical step. Even so, use a chronological format only if your career has proceeded in a steady upward fashion with no glitches. The functional résumé works best when you have a broad range of experiences and you want to highlight just the information necessary to support your goal.

4. Review the résumé to ensure that there are no negative pieces of information and that all the information is pertinent to the goal. Be sure that your résumé does not include any negative attention-getters, as outlined in "Oops! I Didn't Think," later in this chapter.

At the end of this chapter, you'll find examples of chronological, functional, and scannable resumes that represent good uses of those styles for presenting a well-developed career. And don't forget to refer to Chapter 5 for basic advice on resume preparation.

Oops! I Didn't Think (Avoiding Mid-Career Résumé Bloopers)

In Chapter 5 you read about résumé bloopers that are common on first-career-job résumés, and you learned how to avoid them. Here, we take a look at those mistakes to be avoided when you're preparing a mid-career résumé. If you can avoid the common mistakes listed here, you will be well on your way to creating winning résumés and cover letters that have a high probability of passing the screening process and being forwarded to a decision maker rather than to the reject pile:

- **Showing more experience than the job requires.** The ad asked for 5-plus years' experience, and you show 20. The result? The company may think you're overqualified. Better to say "experienced" in the summary and leave off dates in the body. Or better yet, apply for jobs that fit your experience level.

- **Making it too long and too detailed.** More than two pages is too much. Get to the point; keep paragraphs to two concise sentences.

- **Highlighting demotions.** Demotions are easy to spot when titles are used. When there has been a demotion, don't list any title for any of your jobs; just list the department name and show your responsibilities or accomplishments in that job. Be prepared to explain why you were demoted in an interview.

- **Highlighting job gaps.** If you show dates, it will be glaringly obvious where gaps have occurred. Consider leaving off dates on all jobs when there have been job gaps. This will give you a chance to explain any significant job gaps in person in the interview.

▓ **Presenting information inconsistently.** If you leave off dates, titles, and so on for one job or in one area of the résumé, then leave off the same information in all areas of the résumé.

▓ **Making it too general.** Target the language in both the résumé and the cover letter to the company (if unsolicited) and to the specific job (when responding to an ad). Every résumé sent in response to an ad should be targeted to the needs of that ad—and the language in the résumé and cover letter should be targeted to the industry.

▓ **Stating a weak job objective.** Be sure to be specific. For example, say, "Seeking a responsible human resources position in which I can apply my skills in benefits development, staffing, and compensation at (name of company) to enhance the department's efforts." Don't say, "Seeking a responsible human resources position."

▓ **Including irrelevant information.** Do not include salary history, personal information, marital status, or references to race or gender. If membership in a culturally based association supports your objective, it is all right to list it.

Job Hunting While Employed

You certainly want to keep the job you have while you're looking for a better one. Proceed with care and be discreet. The following sections explore some of the most frequently asked questions and some of the most common issues confronted by people who want to keep things on an even, positive basis at their current jobs while they pursue employment elsewhere.

Should You Tell Your Boss That You're Looking for a New Job?

If you tell her, how should you word it? You need to consider the circumstances and the personality of the manager. If she is open-minded and supportive of your advancement, no problem; tell her. You can take your cues from how she's reacted in the past to other employees who've left the company for greener pastures.

If you've already explored opportunities in the company, and the two of you have discussed what's needed for your career advancement (maybe as part of a performance review process), then she may support your action. On the other hand, if she is the type of person who believes that leaving means you're being disloyal to her, you've got a problem. In this case, be very discreet about your search because if she hears of it, you are likely to injure your relationship with her or you may even be fired. She might not be happy about your leaving, even though it is for your advancement, simply because it will create a vacancy, which means that she has to take the time and effort to find your replacement or do without someone in your position.

If your manager finds out anyway, explain that you are investigating opportunities at this point. (If you've had a discussion about your advancement, tie it in to that.) Also assure her that if you do find another position, you will discuss a departure date with her before you accept so that projects can be turned over to someone else as part of a smooth transition. Then reinforce how positive your relationship has been for you, how you expect to maintain that relationship, and that you hope she understands you're seeking a change purely for your own career growth.

Whom Do You Use as References?

Most companies (if not all of the larger ones) do not allow their managers to give references in their official capacity as a representative of the company, so prospective employers are not surprised when you do not give your former manager as a reference. Some managers will give a reference anyway and just ask that you call them at home. They will let you know when they are willing to do that.

Other good references are peers or people in your professional groups who have worked on projects with you; clients or customers; and public officials and high-ranking service professionals (such as doctors and lawyers).

A word of advice: Choose your references wisely. You want people who you trust will give you a strong reference and who can be discreet about your job search. (You don't want word getting back to your manager.) As a professional courtesy, you should speak with all potential references before you give their names—both to confirm their support and to remind them to be discreet.

What Reason Should You Give for Looking for a New Job?

Be prepared for prospective employers to ask why are you leaving your current job. They may be concerned that you're being fired or are a deadbeat. You're in great shape if your current manager knows you're looking because you can simply state that she knows, that you have a great working relationship, but that the opportunity you seek for growth does not exist at your current company. Then move right into the reason you're talking with this employer—because you believe that opportunity might be with him.

Never, ever say to anyone that you are making a change because you are unhappy (even if you are). It smacks of negativity and can give rise to the suspicion that you are a disgruntled employee who has a negative outlook on work. So scream in private if you must, but put on a happy face in your search.

Should You Take Job Search Calls at Work?

Making a job change is a personal matter. Get an answering service with voice mail (on your home phone or through a personal service) and receive your calls there. Even if your manager knows you're looking, you don't want your job search to take time away from the work at hand. After all, you want to maintain this job; you might end up keeping it.

How Do You Schedule Interviews?

Explain to the prospective employer that because you are currently employed, you prefer to interview in the evening or on a Saturday. But expect that most will want you to accommodate their schedules, and you will, too, if you're serious about your job search. When you explain your situation to prospective employers, they may be willing to do some initial screening by phone. If not, arrange to take personal or vacation days for interviews.

Doing Your Best in Interviews

Having a clear sense of your prospective employer's and the company's culture can save you time and eliminate some of the anxiety about interviewing. Obviously, the best way to find out some of the inside scoop on employers is through networking, but you can also gain some insight by checking resources at a public library or by contacting the company's media relations office (if it's large enough to have one); it will usually be happy to mail you an information packet. If your research uncovers information that makes you aware it would be impossible to work in a particular culture, then you won't have to waste time pursuing opportunities with that company.

Preparing for the Interview

An interview is simply an exchange of information carried out in a conversational vein. You'll do your best in an interview when you know what to expect and have prepared yourself accordingly. I suggest you reread Chapter 5 for a refresher on the basics of effective interviewing. Here are a few tips that will make the process easier and help you prepare to talk with people in both formal and informal settings:

- **Prepare for sensitive and tough questions.** Decide beforehand how you will handle sensitive questions. Often it's the executives who ask the very direct questions (no matter what their human resources people advise); therefore, the higher the job level you seek, the higher the probability you will encounter questions that challenge your overall technical knowledge and vision about the work, as well as your maturity. In addition to demonstrating your functional or technical knowledge, you'll want to give answers that reveal your motivational level, political savvy, and management style, as well as your technical and administrative strengths and weaknesses.

- **Prepare to defend your answers.** As a person of color moving into a key position in a predominantly white environment, you may be asked questions about how you would handle situations on the job. You might have a challenging situation described to you, be asked to respond, and then have your answer probed or challenged to get your reaction.

- **Prepare to quickly assess the reason for the question.** You might want to divert personal questions or look for and respond to the underlying reason that the interviewer is asking the question. For example, when an interviewer asks, "Are you married?" you might respond by saying, "Is there a family-oriented culture here?" Although it's usually appropriate to deflect such personal questions, my own experience tells me to just answer them frankly. Experienced people generally rely on the value they are perceived as bringing to the company, rather than on issues that may be detractors for people just starting out.

▪ **Be prepared to explain why you want to change companies.** It's not unreasonable to change because your philosophy is inconsistent with the former (or new) management or because the growth potential is limited at the company. However, avoid any explanation that would come across as petty. For all questions, honesty in your responses is the best course.

▪ **Be prepared to state your goal and how this position fits that goal.** Keep in mind that in an interview, you can enhance the very positive impression you make initially by demonstrating that you have a goal to which you're committed. I remember being impressed with a client who, at first glance, seemed to have all the tickets—brains, education, style, and wit, as well as options. And that was the problem; she had difficulty committing to any of her options. After probing for a while and receiving only evasive answers, I concluded that she really needed to think more about her priorities so that she could decide which of her options to pursue. I could understand her dilemma, but my opinion of her capabilities diminished simply because I felt that if she really had it together, she would have had a goal before initiating her search, and as a result, she would have been more focused.

▪ **Be prepared to present yourself in your best communication "style."** After years of working and interacting with others, you've probably received some consistent feedback about your communication style. Now is the time to take note of that feedback so that you can develop a strategy for using the behaviors for which you've been complimented and minimizing any less desirable traits (such as taking too long to answer a question).

▪ **Be prepared with some "success stories."** These are also accomplishments—activities carried out with a positive result—that you can (briefly) share in interviews to answer questions like, "What was one of the biggest challenges you faced in your last job?" or "What contributions did you offer to help your department run more smoothly and effectively?" The following section takes a closer look at how you can prepare to fully promote your strengths during the interview.

Developing Your Success Stories for the Interview

A well-phrased (and well-timed) story of how you successfully handled the responsibilities on a former job can do a lot to help you ace an interview. It allows you to display your talents, skills, and accomplishments without having to be obvious about "tootin' your own horn." And it's a much more comfortable and natural way to communicate information about yourself than just responding to questions. Here are some guidelines for effective success storytelling:

- **Choose your story ahead of time.** Your story should be based on the research you've done on the company and about the job. You want to choose a story that will display skills that are in line with the position you're going for.

- **Write the story ahead of time.** Even though you will be communicating a story about something you know, you can still approach the telling from several angles. Writing it out before the interview will help you decide which would be the best slant and what you want to emphasize. Leadership? Communication skills? Team work?

- **Make sure to include your accomplishments.** Don't forget the point of the storytelling: to establish your capability for the job. Get the right accomplishments in the story.

- **Practice relating the story back to the job you're interviewing for.** Don't forget why you're telling the story. Get back to how it relates to your qualifications for the job. For example: "Do you ever have that kind of thing happen here?"

- **Rehearse.** The story may sound great when you're by yourself reading it back. No pressure there. Go through a mock interview with someone, and tell the story in this setting. You'll find it takes a little practice. Plus, the role-playing will allow you to time it. Don't go on and on with your story; keep it under 2 minutes. If you don't have a ready audience, then audiotape or videotape yourself.

Handling the Interview

As you know, if you've been through several interviews yourself, there is no set format as to how the process unfolds. You may start by interviewing with a human resources person, or you may be interviewed right away by the hiring manager. Generally, you will have at least two interviews before a decision is made, and many times three. Some interviews might take place by phone—or even by email—if you are a good distance away.

Most often, interviewers will ask questions specifically based on the information provided on your résumé. For this reason, you should include information that you know you want to be questioned about so that you'll have a better chance to sell yourself. Here are some key points for effective interviewing:

- **Build rapport.** Have a conversation—as opposed to behaving as if you're being interrogated. As a person with work experience, you are more on a colleague level with the interviewer than on the novice level of a person just starting out. Listen to questions, repeat for clarification if necessary, and then respond succinctly. Ask questions yourself. Have an exchange while seeking areas of common interest and benefit (such as "We seem to have a similar vision about the function.").

- **Avoid canned answers.** Be prepared to share concepts about the industry, the direction the company should be going, effective management styles, and the like. Think beforehand about questions you may be asked so you'll know what information you want to communicate. Consider what issues would be important to you if you were in the decision maker's shoes, and, during the interview, allow that information to flow naturally into the conversation.

- **Model the behavior that fits the job.** Your attire, smile, attitude, conversation, and energy should all project intellectual

curiosity, confidence, self-motivation, and personality traits
that indicate you will fit into the company's culture.

▓ **Close on a positive note.** If you're interested in the job, say
so and ask what the next step will be. Then follow up with a
thank-you note. Most people don't, so you'll be ahead of the
game when you do. If you found out about the opening through
a networking contact, follow up with that person so that you
can obtain his or her support in getting the job.

For more basics about résumés and interviewing, take a look at Chapter 5
in this book. Although it addresses résumés and other job search tools particularly for job search novices, it has some advice that people who've been
working for some time will find useful, especially the sections "Questions
You Shouldn't Be Asked" and "Nine Steps to a Successful Interview."

Job and Salary Negotiation

Salary is always based on the job and not necessarily on what you want or
feel you are worth. It's based on the current market value of the position.
Never discuss salary, except in general terms or in context of a range, until
the job responsibilities and reporting relationship have been agreed to.

I've noticed that handling salary negotiations is where most experienced
professionals blow it. Many people tend to fixate on a certain salary,
whether it is appropriate or not; they base their expectations on what they
were paid previously and on their experience. The irony is that the salary
you expect might be too low.

Understand that when an employer wants to interview you and make you
an offer, you have some power—and you can exercise your power to elevate
the amount you're offered. If you have a realistic ballpark figure in mind
going into the interview, then you can start the negotiations at a higher
point and work down if necessary. Network with associates and check
trade journals, associations, and other sources to find out an appropriate
salary range for the position. Also, remember that you are an experienced
individual, not a recent college graduate, so the salary will be dependent
on the job, its market value, and your experience rather than on a standard
rate that may be used for entry-level new hires.

On the other hand, if you quickly give up your power in the salary negotiations, you can easily reduce the amount the company is prepared to pay you. For example, poor image and lack of research may lead you to say to the employer something like, "I know I'll have to take less than I did on my last job." You certainly will now that you've mentioned it!

In some cases, however, it may be wise to accept a lower salary than your former position paid. For example, if your technical skills are not up to par or you're relocating to a geographic area that typically pays less, you'll need to take such factors into consideration when developing an appropriate salary range for yourself. Your primary consideration in these instances is that the job is one that will advance your career. Whatever the case, don't immediately advertise your willingness to accept a lower salary; let the employer be the first to take the negotiations in this direction.

The keys to successfully negotiating salary include the following:

- **Deciding what you want**—in terms of job responsibilities, salary, benefits, and other perks. Before salary negotiations begin, make a mental note of what you hope to get, the least you'd take, and where you might be willing to compromise.

- **Determining what reasons you should give for getting what you want**—what your discussion or argument will be—and then switching sides and looking at the picture from the employer's point of view—anticipating objections and planning a response to them.

- **Being prepared to compromise**—as long as the compromise does not affect your future career growth.

- **Not playing games**—with counteroffers after the top offer has been put on the table, which generally do not work out well. If the employer feels pushed into a corner because he has an immediate need for your services, he may accept the counteroffer, but your future may not be too bright at the company— if you're even retained beyond his immediate need. Even worse, if he feels like you're playing games or being too pushy, he may very well reconsider the job offer.

Be Ready to Step Up to the Plate in Your New Job

Unlike the novice whose value must be proved, you will start at a new company as a confident, experienced professional in possession of your career and your work skills. Start your new job with a clear vision of who you are, what skills you bring to the table, and where you see yourself going within the company. And you should feel comfortable sharing that vision with management and peers. It's all right to let it be known that you have your sights on developing in a specific area or that you aspire to a certain job or want to take on more responsibilities. Look for opportunities to open up and then volunteer for them; such initiative and commitment are two of the traits that lead to further success. As a matter of fact, this type of behavior is expected from professionals—and the higher your job level, the more it is expected of you.

MY BOTTOM LINE | Change can be frightening, but regardless, it's inevitable. It's a lot easier when you initiate the change that will impact your career. When a work situation has reached a point where it no longer supports your goals, accept that it is time to make a change and do it.

Resume Examples

The following resume examples reflect experienced applicants as opposed to the resume examples in Chapter 5. The key differences are the placement of education information, the amount of experience shown, and where the information about work experience is placed in the resume. People with more than 5 years of experience in their fields should show education at the end of the resume instead of the beginning as a novice would. Additionally, you only need to show 10 years of experience; if you have more than 10 years of relevant experience, you should use a functional resume format. The functional format would then focus on the experience itself and not when it was obtained.

A Chronological Resume

THOMAS MATSON
33243 Main Road
Kansas City, Kansas 66664
Phone: (301) 555-7743   Fax: (301) 555-7744   Email: tmatson@aol.com

SUMMARY

Contracts Manager with over 10 years of experience in complex business transaction, contracts, negotiations, software/hardware licensing agreements, procurement, and project management. Significant legal and business experience with an excellent record of sound business judgment. A teacher and communicator who can build a solid, highly motivated team.

PROFESSIONAL HISTORY

World Plus Instruments Company   1997 - Present
Manager, Contracts

Provided business support, contract management, and procurement of supplies and services for the Information Engineering Facility with $700M in annual sales. Principal negotiator with the authority to bind the corporation. Supervise contract administration, program planning, and financial management for multi-year contracts. Develop and review proposal data for major programs. Resolve contractual and audit disputes.

- Negotiated 15 corporate software licensing agreements with Fortune 500 companies.
- Developed business practice and contracts that grew in annual sales of sofware and services from $700K to $500K.
- Negotiated a $650M proposal with EDS to support the Department of Defense.
- Received "Top Performer" Award 1998.

ABC Defense Company   1995 - 1997
Manager, Finance

Handled contract administration, financial management, and pricing functions for 10 large contracts. Managed operating trends by preparing and analyzing financial reports involving revenue, expense, and schedule variations.

Supervisor, Contract Administration   1993 - 1995

Supervised contract administration function, proposals, and change orders for two large government contracts. Promoted to Manager, Finance, after 18 months.

Blue Space Technology Inc.   1989 - 1993
Attorney, NASA Contracts

Handled contract compliance, change orders, and modification for a large NASA contract with an Award Fee and Incentive Fee structure.

EDUCATION

Juris Doctorate, 1988 - Kansas City School of Law
Master of English, 1982 - Webster University
Bachelor of Arts, 1979 - Sinclair University

ASSOCIATIONS

American Bar Association
Federal Bar Association
Kansas State Bar Association
National Contract Managers Association

A Functional Resume

ANNA BULTEK
704 Armstead Avenue #300
Denver, Colorado 99393

Phone: (723) 555-9395
Fax: (723) 555-9396
Email: anabul@aol.com

SUMMARY

A seasoned professional with 11 years of experience in the management and administration of operations in branch offices and administrative support units for a major organization. Major strengths in workflow production, research and problem solving, heavy customer service interactions, staffing, personnel administration, and team building. A well-organized planner with a successful track record in loss prevention, customer satisfaction, and retention.

ACCOMPLISHMENTS

Workflow Production

- Developed and implemented operating procedures for the Benefits Plans Administration Unit, eliminating over $700,000 in overtime expense annually.
- Created and developed accounting and control procedures for the collection, remittance, balancing, and year-end reporting of tax withholding to the federal and state agencies.
- Increased productivity over 40% by formulating and administering the operational and audit criteria for an automated disbursement function and on-line file system.

Research/Problem Solving and Loss Prevention

- Recovered 3.5MM in potential losses, and set up control procedures to avoid recurrence.
- Alerted to unusual activity, uncovered and investigated fraudulent activity involving forgeries saving the bank over $850,000 in losses.
- Researched, investigated, and administered all year-end IRA reporting correction within a 60-day period (meeting IRS deadlines) from over 550 banking officers - totaling over 750 corrections.

Customer Service

- Achieved a 90% improvement in teller line "grid lock" by implementing new check cashing procedures on paydays.
- Won consistent recognition for the banking offices in accelerating quality customer service by resolving customer disputes and discrepancies in an expedient time frame.

Personnel Administration/Team Building

- Initiated monthly staff meetings and Employee of the Month Awards, increasing staff morale, performance, and involvement.
- Received Outstanding Service Award for establishing and communicating expected standards of performance, reviewing actual performance, counseling, coaching, and taking corrective action where necessary resulting in a cohesive department that delivered service effectively.

WORK HISTORY

American National Bank	VP, Operations Retirement Plans Administration
Englewood National Bank	VP, Operations
Southfork National Bank	VP, Operations
	AVP Operations, AVP Loans
Denver National Bank	Assistant Manager

EDUCATION

Diploma, Convent High School, Denver, Colorado
Business courses: Englewood City College, Denver City College, Colorado Springs Community College

A Scannable Resume

SAM JONES
5345 Wincrest Drive
Los Angeles, CA 99501

Home: (310) 555-4432
Email: sjones@aol.com
Office: (310) 555-3341
Fax: (310) 555-4433

Professional Profile

Accomplished business executive with extensive experience in domestic and international management and law. Proactively identifies, engages, and captures business opportunities. Skilled at project management and implementing best practices. Achieves business goals by collaborative style and participating as strategic business partner of the senior management team.

Career Highlights

Closed more than $3.2 million in commercial transactions inclusive of transactions in 3 states and 4 foreign countries.

Restructured 2 corporations and established and integrated a marketing division in each. Part of a team that successfully initiated and integrated mergers, acquisitions, marketing ventures, alliances, divestitures, exchanges, rollups, finance, and tax structures.

Implemented value adding programs relating to procurement, budgeting, training, risk assessment, environmental, human resource, corporate secretary, and general corporate matters.

Professional History

Associate General Counsel 1996 - 2000
Big Giant Oil, Inc., Los Angeles, CA

Managed functions relating to the acquisition and divestiture of oil and gas properties, litigation, corporate secretary, insurance, and property administration.

Negotiated and established $30 million marketing company synchronizing supply and transmission systems.

Implemented litigation and risk assessment programs that recovered $213 million in damages while eliminating $363 million in liability.

Division Attorney, Southwest, and International Divisions 1991 - 1996
The Blue Flash Oil Company, Dallas, TX

Negotiated and closed more than $100 million in acquisition and development of oil and gas properties in the United States, United Kingdom, Australia, Canada, Papua New Guinea, Peru, Israel, Norway, Netherlands, Dominican Republic, Egypt, and Indonesia. Conducted litigation before United States courts and foreign tribunals.

Education – Law Admissions – Military Service

Juris Doctor Degree, Los Angeles University School of Law, Los Angeles, CA
Bachelor of Science degree, University of Washington, Kennewick, Washington, Economics
Supreme Courts – United States, California, and Texas

Community Participation

Director, LaDera Heights Municipal Utility District
Director, Child Advocates of Los Angeles County

PART FOUR

What Next, After Success?

What comes now? Now that you've been successful working within "the system?" Now that you know you can set tough goals and achieve them? Now that you know the only limitations that truly exist are the ones you place on yourself?

At this stage, you might find yourself asking some new questions about your career. Should you work on changing your job so you can focus on the parts you like? Would a less stressful job be the answer—doing some part of the work you enjoy but leaving a lot more free time and energy for other pursuits? Or should you expand your career in some way, even take on new challenges? Is this the time to make that significant career change you've dreamed of making for years? Or to work more independently? Should you consider contracting or consulting or working part-time—or even starting your own business?

This part of the book looks at the issues and concerns you might face as you re-assess your work and career and the role you want them to play in your life now. It's at this stage that you will most likely develop and live your own version of the American dream.

CHAPTER 11

Changing Career Goals, Changing Life Goals

In stage one, the "exploration" stage of your career, you may have had a dream that you wondered whether it was possible to attain. Then you may have received support that enabled you to pursue the dream, or maybe you simply said to yourself "What the heck. Why not give it a try?" Thus you made a plan and moved into stage two, the "pursuit" phase. During this period you tested, expanded, or maybe modified the original goal. Your focus became very clear. By stage three, the "formative" stage of your career, you were in full gear, and you made the full commitment necessary to accomplish your goal at the level that felt comfortable for you, given your other commitments. Now you're at the fourth stage of your career; you've succeeded.

After attainment of your goal, your career may now assume a significantly different value in the overall scheme of things. It may become less of a priority, or it may take on an expanded, richer role in your life. This shift may occur quickly and dramatically—for example, as the result of a major event such as a serious illness or the loss of a loved one. Or it may be less dramatic; perhaps turning 50 or 60 or reaching a certain milestone in your life or career causes a subtle and gradual realization that a change is in order.

A friend described his change to me this way: "The alarm clock went off one morning, and I rolled over, looked at it for a moment, and wondered why it was ringing. At that point, I knew it was time to restructure my life. I had just returned from a month at my cabin in the country, working at my other business, and had absolutely no desire to return to my corporate job."

Whatever the catalyst for change is for you, when the time comes you will have a sense of it within yourself. It may even happen at a high point in your career, when you find yourself feeling that something is missing or that there's a new interest developing in your life.

This process of restructuring and refocusing is much like what you did in the first and second stages of your career; the difference now is that you have more options because you bring more to the table. Having already proven yourself, you're in the enviable position of being able to shape your career on your own terms.

Golden Harvest or Dust Bowl?

First, you need to consider where you are at this point in time and how much leverage and choice you actually have. If you've developed a career based on what you truly enjoy doing and you've successfully passed through the early and mid stages of your career, then you'll probably be well-positioned to take on and achieve whatever you choose to do at this point in your life. If, on the other hand, the first stages didn't go as well as you would have liked—or they did, but you didn't plan or organize the other aspects of your life well—you may have to struggle through and scramble to set your career on track now. At a time in your life when other priorities and psychological needs may demand that you redistribute your energy and devote less time to your career, you may find yourself still having to operate at the high energy level and with the same financial concerns of the early stages of your professional life.

Case 1: When the Cash Cow Dies

Because of poor planning or bad circumstances, I've known people to arrive at stage three, after years of working at a successful and lucrative career, with no real financial stability or savings to speak of. Katherine is one of them. A contractor who commanded high fees handling very difficult issues for a branch of the city's housing authority, Katherine was well-respected and her services were in demand. She enjoyed an affluent, even extravagant lifestyle, wearing fashionable clothes and buying a new luxury car every two years.

Katherine's comfortable lifestyle came to an abrupt halt, however, when a change in the department's policy forced management not to renew her contract. Katherine had not planned at all for this possibility. She had no financial reserves and had not developed or explored any other avenues for marketing her skills to maintain her lifestyle. Not surprisingly, at 47, she had neither the drive nor the time to begin again, to develop a new career that could support the lifestyle she'd been accustomed to. Eventually, she was able to find another job through networking contacts, but the pay was considerably less than what she'd gotten in the past. Poor planning had left Katherine ill-prepared for the future.

Case 2: A Well-Crafted Safety Net

Like Katherine, Hank had a successful career, but unlike her, he prepared and planned well for his future. As a result, he found his later years to be the best time of his life. At 62, when failing health necessitated a change in lifestyle, Hank restructured his tax preparation and financial-planning business so that he could work only four months a year. He had prepared ahead of time for this eventuality by bringing on and developing other talented people so that they could manage the major responsibilities of his business. Hank had also invested in property rentals that gave him a regular income without many demands on his time. He'd managed career stages one and two and his own finances so well that stage three turned out to be for him what it should be for everyone—a time of golden harvest.

 MY BOTTOM LINE Readiness includes being willing to make room for something new. Making room for change, even a good change, can be a little frightening. But it is easier if you step into the change by choice rather than getting pulled in.

New Priorities, Changing Interests

You don't have to spend your entire career preparing to accommodate a future change you might want to make. Often just a little advance planning is enough to refocus and ready yourself. For Louise, the catalyst for reassessing her priorities came when some family members were diagnosed with life-threatening illnesses. As she struggled to cope, supervisors at the high-tech firm where she worked asked her to take on the more responsible position of senior consultant. Faced with the decision to accept or decline the challenge in order to move forward in management, Louise realized that her next move would determine the quality of the rest of her life. She got subtle pressure from her peer group to take the new job, but Louise had reached the point where the opinions and judgment of others carried little weight. She decided that the need to have less stress in her life and spend more time saying "I love you" to the people she cared for had become her top priority.

Preparation Is Everything

Once she made the decision, Louise set about organizing things to accommodate this shift in priorities. She began by cutting her spending, eliminating anything she could do without. Then she set a goal to continue working full-time for 18 months to pay off bills and to prepare herself to live with less income. After those 18 months she left her job and got a part-time position that allowed her to use some of her skills. She knew that to satisfy her long-term financial needs, she would have to continue working, if only part-time, for at least another 10 years and, possibly, until after age 65. Because of this, she included in her new plan a strategy for staying competitive in her field; it involved setting aside time and money to regularly update her skills through school and professional courses.

Checking Your Readiness

Clearly Louise was ready to advance to the third stage of her career and was prepared for it. Are you ready? The following table should help clarify things for you; place a checkmark in the box for each statement that applies to you.

YOU'RE READY IF...	YOU'RE NOT READY IF...
☐ You've established a career that you've thoroughly enjoyed and that has provided for you financially so you're at a comfortable level.	☐ You've only recently begun a career, or the work you do does not support your financial needs.
☐ You're experiencing less desire and motivation to continue doing the work you've been doing.	☐ You're still thriving in your career, waking up each morning excited and raring to go to work, and positioning yourself for more responsibilities. (You're still working in stage two.)
☐ Other interests constantly conflict with career demands for your time.	☐ Your current career is still the number-one priority in your life, and you still get much of your identity from your work.

Know the Motives for Your Decision

If your answers in the preceding table reveal that you need to continue on your current career path, or at least maintain the present level of commitment to your career, you may need to make other changes in your life to gain a greater sense of balance, freedom, or whatever it is you seek at this point in your life.

If your answers indicate that you are ready to seek a different level of commitment to your career, you can help plan the right move by determining what you're seeking in a new career—and what positive things in your current career you may want to "carry over." You need to analyze your career and clearly identify the aspects of your work you enjoy most so that you can use that information to establish a new career direction or goal.

This analysis is very personal, so go through the process before you seek input from your colleagues or friends and risk being influenced by their feedback. If you've developed a good reputation that's based on certain pronounced traits or skills, people are likely to encourage you to go in a direction that uses them, but this might not be what you really want. For instance, if you have been very effective in a leadership role at your company or as part of community efforts, colleagues may advise you to continue doing that, even though you may be getting a sense that you're ready to shift your focus.

Take the following steps to arrive at the set of positive motivators you want to use now:

- Make a list of the most significant accomplishments you've made in the past decade (10 accomplishments would be good; that's 1 per year).

- Ask yourself what led you to your accepting the task. Were you pushed into it? Did you volunteer? If so, why? Next to each accomplishment indicate whether your motivation came from external sources (such as everyone thought you ought to) or internal ones.

- Ask yourself what felt good about accomplishing the activity. These are the positive factors that came after completion of the tasks.

- If you had a chance to do these things all over again, would you? If so, how would you do them differently?

- Now, choose the top three most significant accomplishments on the list, and write down why each of these made the top three.

- Finally, do the same for your number-one accomplishment. Writing out your reasons for these choices will be very helpful in determining career direction.

Your analysis will help you more clearly identify your motivators, whether you are influenced by external factors or an internal drive (either is all right as long as you know what it is), and the psychological needs that you should give priority to in setting a new goal for yourself.

Case 3: Finding Positive Motivators

When Trent's priorities changed, he had the freedom to make choices because he had planned well financially. A systems engineer who worked full-time while running his own consulting practice, Trent felt happy and productive. However, when he was laid off from his full-time job during a company restructuring, he found that at 67, he needed to re-evaluate his goals. He soon realized that he actually did not need to work for the money; in fact, at this point in his life, money had no motivational value for him at all. For him, true enjoyment and professional satisfaction came from intellectual stimulation and the sense of being valued for his knowledge and contribution.

When a technical professional group asked him to serve on its board, he knew that it was something he wanted to do. The position came with no salary, but in every other way the many responsibilities of the position satisfied Trent's work needs for stage three in his career. Not only that, members of the professional group often passed on information about short-term project assignments that enabled Trent to continue to participate in his field, stay challenged, and get paid. The following analysis of his accomplishments helped him to identify the psychological factors important to him and be receptive to fulfilling them in a new way.

ACCOMPLISHMENT	THE POSITIVE MOTIVATOR(S)
Technical director of a start-up company. Developed processes and a line of successful industrial products.	Feeling needed as a result of role as a key contributor. Creative challenge.
Electro-optical engineering and technical management of various projects for military systems, automotive displays, data communications, and sensor systems.	Variety of assignments. Expansion of experience. Expansion of personal network.
Developed complex laser instrumentation systems for industrial processes, the military, and consumer instruments.	Creative challenge. Variety of assignments.
Member of the editorial board of applied optics, patents' section. Eight patents and publications.	Recognition as expert Creative challenge. Developing something of value.

Future Outlook—Present Action

Naturally, the lifestyle you expect to enjoy in the coming years will greatly influence your career goals at this stage in your life. Now, perhaps more than ever before, you will have to weigh your choices carefully to ensure that you will be able to support for the long-term the lifestyle you desire. Begin by determining how much income you'll need to meet your responsibilities and maintain your lifestyle, as well as how little you can live on and still be content.

Analyzing your finances can be a little tricky at this stage. Often, career phase four coincides with significant personal changes that greatly impact in both positive and negative ways your financial picture. For example, you may be financing the education of college-age children or have just finished paying those bills, you may still be struggling to build up your retirement fund, you may have your heart set on buying that vacation home you've always dreamed of, or you may have finally achieved financial security, with enough money saved so that you don't have to worry about working to earn a living.

Case 4: Two Transitional Solutions

In Colleen's case, a significant decrease in her financial responsibilities allowed her to let go of a high-paying stressful job and spend some time just living. With her daughter finishing her last year of college, Colleen realized that she no longer needed to provide extra money in her budget for education. Set free of this huge responsibility, she had the opportunity to make a career decision based solely on her own needs.

This, however, proved to be something of a dilemma because Colleen had never based a career decision simply on her own needs. All she knew was that she no longer needed to drive herself to maintain the six-figure income she earned as an account executive. Ultimately, she decided to switch to an administrative position within the same company and take some time to reassess her career and her goals. The transition was easy because Colleen already knew the company culture, products, and services, and the new position provided her with enough of an income to support herself while she pursued outside interests and decided on her next step.

Like Colleen, Ted also wanted to cut back on his work. Although his executive-level position with a car manufacturer provided a lucrative income, it left him little time to spend with his family. As he made the psychological transition to middle age, he realized he wanted to spend more time with his adult children, his grandchildren, and his parents. He decided he needed a new job with fewer responsibilities and fewer demands on his time. His solution was to relocate his immediate family from the East Coast to his small hometown in the Midwest and work with his brother in the family store.

Take a Good Look at Your Situation

As Ted's and Colleen's examples show, it's important to be flexible, open to new ideas, and as aware as possible of factors, especially the financial ones, that will affect your life during stage three. Your responses to the following questions might help get you thinking:

- Do I still have school-age children or children who are or will soon be in college or living on their own? If so, what impact will this have on my time, money, or resources?

- Do I have a working spouse who wants to retire or wants to expand his or her career? How would his or her decision impact my career plans?

- Have I had a complete physical recently? Am I in good health? Are there any limitations I need to consider?

- What are the majority of my friends or peers doing? How do I feel about the changes, if any, in my social circle? How do they impact my decision?

- Do I have a stable financial plan that allows me to entertain a variety of career options, or do I need to put finances first in my decision?

- Are my parents well provided for? If they need help, would they have to rely on me?

- Do I have a stable marriage? If not, how would a divorce or breakup impact my career?

- Do I have enough leisure time in my life now?

- Am I willing to relocate?

- Do I need to get additional education or training to follow a new career path, and if so, will I be able to do this financially?

- Have I planned for my retirement? Do I have enough money saved to comfortably stop working at the time I hope to retire?

- Do I need to generate an income, and if so, how much? Do I have enough money in the bank today to stop working tomorrow?

It's Your Turn Now

In the beginning of stage three, it's not unusual for career choices to be motivated by a wish to provide security for family; often, your need for security will take priority over your need to be challenged and creative. But toward the end of the third stage, as you enter stage four and your financial responsibilities decrease, you finally have the opportunity to put your needs and desires above everything.

Surprisingly, this can cause some initial discomfort or negative feelings if you're not accustomed to putting yourself first. Making a good choice with so much freedom can be difficult at any age. But if you approach the decision making with the sure knowledge that it is your time to enjoy and fulfill any unmet dreams, you'll likely soar with this freedom rather than be weighed down by it.

New Goals for the Peak Period of Your Career

Give yourself some quiet time and space away from others to assess your situation and arrive at new goals. If you've been on a fast-paced treadmill, you may find yourself still in "go" for awhile, even though you are trying to gear down so that you have time to reflect.

Start by asking yourself what kind of work activities you enjoy and can visualize doing in the future. Don't feel pressured to come up with an immediate answer. (That's a need that reflects the "go" mode you will still be operating in for a while.) Write the question down on a pad, and jot down ideas that come to you over a period of several days.

After that, consider how the activities you enjoy are different from or similar to what you have been doing. Does anything stand out as a significant addition? For instance, you may enjoy providing individual help to people in your department rather than attending a strategy meeting focusing on the company's new direction; or you may prefer being a contributing member on committees rather than the head of them. If either is true, you may be a person who wants to get back to the rewards of being directly involved in the action (the implementation) rather than in the planning (the conceptualization).

You might want to estimate how much time you would like to devote to certain activities or interests: how much time you'd allot, say, to research, writing, leading workshops, or marketing. Start keeping a daily journal listing your activities and the time devoted to each so you get a sense of how you are actually prioritizing your time—and whether you are doing it in a way that satisfies you.

You can make this process even more worthwhile if you set priorities the night before, and then the following night compare this list to what you actually did. A significant departure from what you planned to do (especially on a consistent basis) should help show you your real priorities. In evaluating any departure, consider if what you actually did was more enjoyable than what you planned and why you changed your plans. Maybe you think you should be doing one thing, but deep down you're really more satisfied doing something else. If so, you'll want to factor that into your planning.

Make the process of this self-evaluation and goal-setting fun. Don't think of it as a task that you're pressured to complete. It will not only help you get the most out of the next phase, but it will also enable you to give to each area of your life the priority it deserves.

Once you have pinpointed your career priority, you can begin to look at your options for making it happen. The following chapters will review options and present strategies for realigning your career.

MY BOTTOM LINE Regardless of your age, or the obstacles you've had to overcome to reach this stage of your career, you've arrived. You're a success and you've got choices. Not everyone in life reaches this pinnacle. Success is not a gift. You've earned it. Enjoy.

CHAPTER 12

Re-Engineer Your Career and Keep the Best Parts

Has your life become increasingly filled with stress? Do the days seem too short and the responsibilities so burdensome that the overwhelming routine of your life and career leave you no time to stop and smell the roses? Maybe you need to make changes in your lifestyle or change how you work.

After careful consideration, if you are ready to change how you work, you might not have to look too hard for ways to make it happen. In fact, the opportunity to accomplish your new goal may be right under your nose—in your current job. Today, more than ever before, increasing numbers of people are renegotiating their jobs. These people cross all occupations. They include accountants, attorneys, career counselors, computer specialists, engineers, healthcare providers, lobbyists, public relations specialists, secretaries, and word processors, just to name a few.

Interesting? You bet.

The simple truth is that progressive companies recognize that they need to be more flexible in defining work schedules and work roles, and this is creating opportunities for new ways of working for many of us. If you're already working in a company you like and in a job that brings you some satisfaction, renegotiating your position may be a better way to make a career goal change than changing to another job or company. What does renegotiating involve? It depends on what you want. It can mean downsizing your current job (working fewer hours or days) so that you have more time to pursue other interests; realigning your responsibilities so that you take care of only those duties you enjoy; or taking on different responsibility (either in your current job or a new position) so that your work becomes more stimulating and meaningful.

Before You Begin: Assess the Stress

Before proposing a change to a job you enjoy or making a decision work in a different way, you can make the change easier if you do some work beforehand. First, get your family's support by discussing with them how they will be affected in both positive and negative ways. Second, take time to fully understand all the ramifications of the change you're considering so that you will know what to expect. If you prepare yourself in both areas of your life, the change can be positive right away.

When you have your family's support, it's time to determine which aspects of your career you want to change—and which you might want to keep. These pointers may help:

- Consider the non-job-related factors in your life that may be causing you stress and determine whether changing any of them will remedy the situation. For instance, could you get help for ailing parents, join a gym to develop better health, or better prioritize your activities to include more "rose-smelling time?" You may find that it's not your job that needs changing after all.

- Analyze the situation surrounding your work. Could your stress be reduced by changing from the culture that you're in or the activities that you have felt compelled to be involved with to support your job? For instance, could you eliminate golf, association meetings, or conferences that take you away from your family?

■ Consider taking a leave from your current job to try out a new goal before making a commitment to it.

■ If you're thinking about taking a lesser position, consider the factors that may surround a job with reduced responsibility and how easily you'll be able to adapt to them. For instance, the change may require you to work with a more youthful group, possibly doing routine tasks with little challenge. Is this going to add to your stress or reduce it?

■ Write down the advantages and disadvantages of taking a less stressful position—and consider a change only if your evaluation shows the advantages outweighing the disadvantages.

Prioritize Your Needs and Let Them Be Your Guide

Rather than chuck it all and quit, think about how you might be able to rework your job to solve your biggest problems. Sometimes we want it all. And we usually can have it all—just not all at once or not without some compromise.

The analysis of your current career that you developed in the last chapter should have helped you determine your new psychological needs. Let these needs help guide you in determining your new career direction and priorities.

Whether you want to enhance your position or realign or reduce your responsibilities, understand that you have to make it happen. You'll need to choose the option, develop the proposal, and convince your management that it fits the needs of the department. Don't expect anyone else to figure it out for you. You have a powerful advantage if you've developed a good track record at your company; the powers that be will at least listen to you when you have a proposal. Take the time to think it through and present a well-thought-out idea (both orally and in writing) as enthusiastically as you can to your higher-ups.

Does Your Job Lend Itself to Restructuring?

Before you approach management, you need to figure out whether it's even possible to restructure your job in the way you envision. If your position could not feasibly be handled a different way, then you'd be wasting your time trying to restructure it:

■ If you supervise very delicate processes in a research laboratory or on a production line, your job may have little flexibility built into it.

■ If you work in a capacity that requires a lot of personal appearances and community involvement, you probably could not get away with working only 9 to 5.

If neither of these situations is the case, you need to now analyze how the responsibilities of your current job can be transferred or handled differently if your job is restructured. Get out a pencil and paper, and get ready to create some more lists! Then, consider the following questions and follow the instructions to write your responses:

■ How would your responsibilities effectively be handled in a new structure? Remember that managers are always going to be primarily concerned with what is best for the company, and this means that you and your change proposal will have to add to— not take away from—the effectiveness of the department. On paper, categorize your job into major areas of responsibility, with each category containing a column listing the primary responsibilities. How are the various responsibilities are being handled now? Could any of them be dealt with differently? For instance, if you have a staff of 15 direct reports who handle a variety of functions, could the group be organized in three sections with a lead person for each?

■ In a management function, could you meet with the group on a weekly basis and be available by phone for serious problems? Add that as a solution, where appropriate.

■ How would the people and processes be affected by your change? Are there meetings you are required to attend? People you need to maintain regular contact with? Are serious decisions made in informal situations—lunch, coffee breaks, in the hallway outside someone's door—where you may no longer be available? If so, add a column to your list of responsibilities and write out the impact your change will have on people and processes. Start a third column next to that showing how you will address these issues or, if you cannot, how it will hinder your effectiveness.

How would a job restructuring affect your benefits or other perks? On another sheet of paper, list things you might have to give up if you redesign your job. Are you driving a company car? Do you have retirement or other benefit plans that are tied to full-time hours or a specific salary level? Would a shortened week affect any benefits that are important to you?

After you've analyzed each of your major responsibilities and how a change might affect them, review the information you've gathered and decide where you have some flexibility for restructuring and where you don't. If you think that you could effectively redesign your job, then read on for ideas on how to do so.

MY BOTTOM LINE | Carefully evaluate your lifestyle and job before making a move that may be reactionary. Don't let a possible mid-life crisis destroy everything you have worked for up to this point. If you're feeling stressed, you may simply be overworked and need a vacation.

New Ways to Work for Your Company

For many people at this stage, renegotiating their jobs often means cutting back on their working hours. If this is true for you, look at some of the ways to accomplish this so that you can still be effective on the job.

Flex Hours

Let's say you're considering flexible working hours because you need more time to run errands and take care of family matters or because you want more time for a hobby or new project. What are your options? Would

taking off early every Friday or Monday give you the time you're looking for? Or would you do just as well committing to four days, without
designating which four? If you're in a job that has work you can control
somewhat and often has downtime, this might work for you and cut costs
for the company (although that might mean a lower salary for you).

Jason, a counselor at a social services agency and a single parent, found
he was much more productive in a four-day week than in a five-day week.
Not working on Wednesdays gave him the boost he needed to be more
productive on the job and the extra energy to handle the responsibilities
connected with the children. By managing his caseload differently, he got
all the work done and saved the company a day's pay.

Job Sharing

Job sharing as an option is a little more complicated than some of the others because it involves two part-time employees sharing the responsibilities
and working hours of one job. Job sharing is a unique type of teamwork,
sometimes difficult to set up and maintain. The key is to find a compatible
partner who has similar goals and skills. If working this way interests you,
you will most likely need to locate your own partner and decide how you
will work together before proposing the arrangement to your employer.

Some, but not all, companies are amenable to job sharing. The obvious
advantage to employers is that the company, in effect, gains the mind
power of two people for the price of one. The advantage to the job sharers
is flexibility and part-time work. The disadvantages include the possibility
of working with someone who does not pull his or her share of the load or
the burden of having to find yourself a new partner if yours quits or you
find you're not compatible. Each person in a job share usually negotiates
her salary and benefits independently with the company. Each typically
receives a limited benefit package similar to the one offered to part-time
employees, which in most instances is substantially less than that offered
to full-time workers.

If you think job sharing might be a good work option for you, here are
some tips that can help make it happen:

■ For sources for a partner: Check with your human resources
  department to see whether someone has expressed a similar

desire, run an ad, check with placement agencies, and network with colleagues. Women just coming off of maternity are good candidates for this option.

▨ Set up an interview with your potential job-share partner to determine whether you can work together and whether you have similar goals for the job and the job-sharing arrangement. There is no need to commit to working with someone who sees it only as a short-term transitional job if you plan to make it a permanent way of working. During the interview, check for skills, motivation, chemistry, and strengths and weaknesses. Even though you will be at the job at different times, you'll be communicating and working together behind the scenes to be most effective, so you'll need to know how you fit as a team.

▨ Work up an agreement about how you want to divide the hours, days, work responsibilities, time off, emergencies, and vacation coverage. Try to think of all possible situations that might arise and how you would handle them now, before you have to deal with them on the job.

▨ Agree on a salary range and benefits for the job. Although you will be paid separately, you should be in agreement about the pay range before you begin negotiating with your employer. Because you will be doing similar work, you'll probably be receiving similar pay and benefits.

Temping

When we think of a temp, we usually envision someone in a clerical or blue-collar job. Although most temporary openings do, indeed, occur in such jobs, today a temp can be almost anyone, in almost any type of job. For many professionals, temping has become a very good, very legitimate way of working; it often offers a good deal of flexibility and variety without the stress and responsibility of managing a career and marketing one's skills. You may have two options as a temp with your company. You can work through an agency the company will direct you to or work as a company temp. If you work through an agency and it's a good one, it intercedes to negotiate salary and deal with any problems that arise. For Naomi, temping proved to be the perfect work option for stage three of her career. She wanted a low-stress job that would allow her to work three or four days a week and leave the cares of the job at the company when she went home each night. She was such an asset that the company negotiated with the temp agency to let Naomi work flexible hours (six-hour shifts four days a week), and it raised no objections when the agency asked for a higher hourly rate for Naomi's time.

Independent but Still Connected: Contracting

Unlike temping, contracting as a way of work involves providing services independently and for a specified period of time to a company, either on- or off-site. Generally, contractors perform their services for a pre-established fee and are not on the company's full-time payroll. Many corporations consider contracting an efficient and cost-effective means of quickly getting work done without having to make a commitment to the worker. It is becoming an increasingly viable and lucrative way of working that offers flexibility, independence, and variety.

Case 1: A Creative Way to Downsize

When her youngest son married, Joy decided that she wanted to work less so that she would have time to travel. Because the demands of her human resources position barely allowed her to take regular vacations, she could not foresee much flexibility in being able to take the time off that she wanted. Her first thought was to leave the company and get a part-time job that would be less demanding on her time and give her the flexibility she wanted. But one of her peers suggested she try working as a contractor for the company instead. The company had been using quite a few contractors for recruiting and training, and Joy had experience in both these areas.

She proposed to her manager that she leave the company as a permanent employee and join the contractors' pool, which would allow her to work on an as-needed basis providing support both in recruiting and training. (See the section "Is Contracting for You?") Fortunately, Joy had developed an excellent performance track record with the company and, because of this, got management's support when she proposed a new working relationship.

Case 2: The "Cons" of Contracting

After working as a contractor for 15 years, my friend Jerry still prefers the flexibility that contracting offers him, as well as the fact that he can remain on the sidelines of company politics. Even so, he readily admits that contracting, like temping, has its downsides. For example, he says some companies tend to misuse contractors. They often expect them to work ceaselessly and they dump a lot of work on them that they can't get their regular staff to do. Companies often expect contractors to work odd hours, handle rush assignments, or perform their services at an undesirable location.

Jerry has found that sometimes it's the contractors who give contracting a bad name. He's worked with some whose bad habits, such as alcoholism or difficulty getting along with people, made it impossible for them to maintain regular employment. Bad experiences with a few contractors make some companies reluctant to continue to contract work out, and this, in the long run, reduces the number of contracting opportunities available. It can also lower the pay scale for contractors because they're perceived as less-valued workers.

Is Contracting for You?

When deciding whether contracting is a good option for your career change, make sure to consider all of the "realities" this work-style choice entails. Although contracting offers the semi-security of fixed-length periods of steady work, it also demands that you take on the responsibility of "being" your business. Contractors are self-employed businesspeople who must handle their own taxes and market their services to companies. Successful contractors stay current on new market trends and budget for financial ebbs and flows.

You might not need to market yourself for each new assignment if you work under contract with a consulting firm that uses contractors; you join the firm's regular pool of contractors and are sent on assignments as they become available. You negotiate a per diem or per hour fee, sometimes with benefits, and you are paid at the completion of an assignment or at regular intervals throughout the course of the work (usually at the same time as the regular employees) for the amount accrued during that period. An excellent source for identifying consulting organizations in your field is the *Consultants and Consulting Organizations Directory,* which is available in the reference section of the library.

The best source for contract work may be your former employer. Not uncommonly, an employer will downsize a group within the company and then offer some of the individuals in that group the opportunity to come back as contractors. You may find that your hourly rate as a contractor is higher than it was when you were on staff, but you no longer enjoy such benefits as life and medical insurance and may need to pay your own income and Social Security taxes.

Tax Implications of Contracting

Because there are tax advantages to being self-employed, and because contractors can be in a position that seems very much like being an employee, the IRS issued a ruling in 1987 that established a 20-point guideline for determining whether someone is an employee or a contractor. The distinction between independent contractor and employee has to do with whether the organization you work for has control over when, where, and how you do your work. A good tax consultant can advise you about your particular situation.

Some Additional Help

Talk with people about the options they see being used at their companies. A professional group such as the Association of Part-Time Professionals (APTP), a national organization that promotes flexible work options to both employers and individuals, might be able to help you examine your options and suggest strategies for implementing them.

When you've established a good track record with a company, you are in an excellent position to renegotiate how you can continue to make a contribution.

Realigning Your Responsibilities

You may have no interest in cutting back your work time but only in letting go of responsibilities that have grown unpleasant and unrewarding. You might want to restructure your job simply to get rid of certain administrative or managerial responsibilities so that you have more time and focus to do the work you truly enjoy.

If you've decided you want to restructure your job so that you can focus on using the skills you find most rewarding, you'll have to figure out how your other responsibilities can be effectively handled. Is there someone else in your department who could take them on? Or could they be divided among several people? What would be the impact of dividing the work, and how would you then interact with these people? Maybe it would be best to leave your position but continue working with the company on a consulting basis. Try to determine whether there are portions of the work that could be done by a consultant or contractor. How is your type of work handled in other companies? Do they provide examples you could use?

Case 3: Escaping "Administrivia"

When Sharon got married, she closed down her consulting business and relocated to another state with her husband. With 25 years of experience in business systems consulting, she had no problem getting a position with a management consulting firm. She worked for six years as one of the company's most valued consultants and, for a time, enjoyed her position. At a certain point, however, she became increasingly overwhelmed by the "administrivia" of the job. She made up her mind to quit and return to consulting so that she could use her working time more constructively. She wanted to use her creative skills while freeing herself from administration duties so that her job would be more satisfying. She also wanted to reduce her hours somewhat to pursue leisure activities with her husband.

Just as Sharon started to develop her plan for moving on, however, the company's leadership announced a new strategic direction that coincided perfectly with her career goals and the skills she enjoyed using. They proposed a new service that would use consulting partners who would have the flexibility to work from home part of the time. A junior partner training with each partner would handle the administrative tasks.

Sharon saw an opportunity here to use her creative skills to help develop a new product for the company, and by participating in its development, she could minimize her involvement in the administrative work she disliked. She submitted a proposal to her manager outlining a new area of responsibility for herself and, after getting his buy-in, worked with him to structure a new job for herself. Because she had, like Joy, established such a high level of credibility within the company, the next two levels of approval were relatively easy to obtain. After negotiating a revised compensation package, Sharon had a new job and had let go of the day-to-day duties that had grown so tedious after 30 years.

"Upsizing" Your Position

Is your desire for change motivated by a need for more fulfilling work and, perhaps, increased responsibility? Quality assignments? More autonomy? Increased creativity? Project assignments that permit bringing closure to an activity rather than an ongoing management responsibility? Look at areas in your department or company that appeal to you and see whether there might be room for you to contribute—either by changing your job altogether or by enhancing your current position to include more challenge.

The best way to find these growth opportunities is to be on the lookout for changes in the company or for departments that are not effectively accomplishing their goals. The following scenarios will give you some places to look for opportunities to enhance your responsibilities so you can upsize your job:

- **The company moves in a new strategic direction.** A new business strategy usually opens up opportunities for meeting new corporate needs. Talk with people connected with the new plan to determine whether there might be a niche for the skills you enjoy using.

- **Company merger.** When a merger occurs, new opportunities always exist. The keys to maneuvering for a good job fit during this time is to be very good at what you do; to be flexible about whom you are willing to do it for; to align yourself with the acquiring company; and to let it be known to all that you see the change as a great opportunity. As the dust settles, stay in touch with the internal network so that you'll hear about new opportunities for developing work around those skills you enjoy using.

Change in leadership. Be alert to the subtle (and sometimes not so subtle) messages from a new department, division, or company leader. For instance: "I'm not so sure that we're going in the right direction"; "That new plan doesn't seem to be working out as we expected"; or "The competition is doing something that seems to be working more effectively than what we're doing." These messages could signal impending changes. Sometimes a little brainstorming (maybe around the water cooler) with peers will uncover a niche for your skills in these anticipated changes.

Global changes within the industry. Typically, when one company in an industry comes out with a new bell or whistle, other companies in the industry follow suit. Stay current on industry trends by reading trade magazines, attending professional meetings, and subscribing to relevant online news groups. If you're quick enough, you might find an opportunity for a new job as part of the group or department that will be helping your company align with the industry trend.

Functional problems. Wherever chaos exists, so does opportunity. When a functional area (such as accounting, engineering, public affairs, or human resources) is not effectively providing the service it should, it's usually a strong indication that certain needs are not being met. These voids may provide a niche that you can fill by using the skills you enjoy, either as an employee, consultant, or contractor.

People problems. This is possibly the greatest of all areas for the use of expanded skills. When the people in a department are not working together effectively as a team to meet departmental objectives, it's usually because of one of several things: an ineffective organizational structure, politics, or deficits in the skills of the people or the existing leadership. These situations provide an opportunity to solve problems and come up with creative solutions. Evaluate them to determine whether the skills you enjoy using can be developed into a job here.

■ **Money problems.** A company is in business to make a profit, which it cannot do if revenues do not significantly exceed costs. You're sure to have a winning proposal if you can identify profit issues and then come up with a solution to decrease costs or increase revenue.

Develop a Proposal for Re-Engineering Your Job

Once you've decided on an approach for changing your job—whether it is to realign your responsibilities or to increase your responsibilities—you'll need to develop a proposal for doing so and present it to your management. Here are my tips for developing a strong proposal:

■ **Clearly identify the problem.** As explained earlier, it is important to focus on a situation that a number of people agree is a problem. It should be something that is not being handled well through the established processes and that is apparent to people whose work has been impaired because of it.

■ **Gather support.** It is very important to get the support of those who would be impacted by your new job and who could influence the acceptance of your idea. They may be people who are concerned about turf issues and who need to see that what you propose will help them perform their jobs better. Getting input from these people and addressing any issues or objections they have will help you lay a proper foundation for succeeding with those at the management level, who will have to give final approval to your proposal.

■ **Put your proposal in writing.** You'll probably make your proposal in person, but the process of writing it out will force you to bring clarity to your thoughts; also it will usually be necessary to have the idea in writing for those who will have to take it to the next levels for approval. Your proposal should include the problem, quantified by statistics, costs, or situations; how it can be addressed by the new job you propose; your qualifications for the new job; and how the excess responsibilities of your current job could be handled.

■ **Consider the personality of the decision maker.** Proposals are not sold in writing, they are sold in person—to another person. You can increase your chance for success tremendously by gearing your presentation to the personality and values of the decision maker. For example, if you know the person likes to talk ideas through thoroughly before making a decision, allow plenty of time for that. For a more analytic type, make sure you have all your facts straight and that your presentation is organized, logical, and systematic. If you are pitching it to a very warm and personable manager, then you can probably present your proposal somewhat informally. Finally, for the really action-oriented manager, your presentation should be concise, with the bottom line expressed first, and a clear outline of your plan for action.

■ **Go for the win/win solution.** Your proposal may be accepted verbatim, but don't be surprised or disappointed if it is not. At every level, expect input that could alter your ideas. If you want to be successful, you'll need to listen nondefensively to any and all suggestions and either incorporate those ideas into your proposal or demonstrate how you will address any objections.

Constructing the Proposal

Look at the following hypothetical scenario to get a sense of how to go about putting together a proposal to enhance your job or to change the way you work.

Step 1: State the problem.

As the manager of a customer service function, I am responsible for supporting three product lines and overseeing a staff of 65, spread out over three offices within a large region. When I accepted the job 10 years ago, it had a staff of 15. My boss is a demanding, action-oriented taskmaster who looks for immediate results. Whenever there is a problem, he expects me to stop whatever I'm doing to handle it. I've reached a point where I would like time to use my creative skills to develop systems to make the operation more efficient, but I cannot do this while handling all the day-to-day staff problems and acting as a troubleshooter.

Step 2: Develop options for handling the problem.
Option 1: Keep my job as it is (essentially supervising and fighting fires). I need to make clear to the boss that this option has the potential of forcing me into inefficiency and therefore not able to provide the level of productivity desired by the boss.

BENEFITS	PROBLEMS
Boss has high level of confidence in my ability to handle all situations.	I'm getting burned out trying to handle all facets of the operation independently.
I have complete control of the operation.	No backup systems in place to manage any portion of the operation if I'm not available.
	No time to be proactive in developing systems for increased efficiency.
	I'm concerned that I really don't have a handle on everything the way I'd like.

Option 2: Restructure my job into a consultant position (to provide supervision, troubleshooting, and cross-training).

BENEFITS	POSSIBLE PROBLEMS
Give me more time to develop new ideas and make the operation more efficient.	Boss would be insecure about working with new, inexperienced people.
Opportunity to implement backup systems.	Some inefficiency during the learning curve of the transition.

Step 3: Choose the option that best supports the needs of the organization and your objective and develop a response to potential objections.
I want to address this problem by restructuring my job so that I will be relieved of the day-to-day supervision of the staff as well as the troubleshooting responsibility and promote two staff members to group

leaders to handle the day-to-day supervision and troubleshooting responsibility. This way, I can focus on using my creative skills in designing new systems to make the overall function more efficient. To accomplish this, I want to make the transition from a managerial role to consultant role.

My boss's objections would be addressed as follows:

- My boss has come to rely on me as the source for answers and would not know to whom to go if I were not in the role. Response: I would help the new group leaders to transition into their responsibilities so there would be no break in quality or productivity. I would be available as a consultant and by pager for an agreed-upon time until the transition has been made successfully.

- No one on my staff has the overall knowledge to troubleshoot all the problems the way I do. Response: I would be available by pager until the learning curve has been reduced.

- No one could step into the manager's role and handle supervision and staff problems while keeping the operation running smoothly. Response: Training will be provided for the group leaders. After a predetermined transition time, duing which they will be supported by me through meetings, conference calls, and availability by pager, there would in effect be increased management available.

Step 4: Put your proposal in writing.

I suggest the following steps and language for the written proposal:

> Dear _____
> Following is a proposal to realign the responsibilities of my current position from Manager to Consultant.
>
> **The Problem**
> I started my present job as manager with a staff of 15; it has grown to 65 with no change in how the function is handled. The job requires that all my time be devoted to day-to-day supervision of the staff and troubleshooting problems. This leaves me no time to work on developing a more efficient cost-effective operation, provide advancement opportunities for the staff, or set up processes for cross-training. The current arrangement is no longer efficient and is beginning to affect the quality of service delivered.

Proposed Solution

I propose that my position be restructured from a manager's role into that of consultant. Along with that, I propose that the departmental staff be realigned to include a group leader at each of our locations and that I work to make this a smooth transition within the next few months.

These changes would:

- Allow me to concentrate on assessing the needs of the department, evaluating the feasibility of new processes and equipment, and developing new systems to make our service more efficient.

- Place the primary supervisory responsibility within each unit, thereby increasing operational efficiency and creating a backup system of management support.

- Supervise the transition of the responsibilities to the group leaders so there is no break in quality of service and to allow all team members to be comfortable with the transition.

- Provide an opportunity to develop potential candidates for vacancies as they occur within the department and establish a logical and natural avenue for upward mobility for the staff.

Recommended Implementation Plan

I am the only person in the department who handles the immediate staff problems and troubleshoots service areas. I realize that people count on me to perform these duties and that it will take time to transfer these responsibilities to others.

I appreciate the need for this transition to occur smoothly, so I suggest making the change over a 90-day period, during which time the group leaders would be selected, trained, and given an opportunity to function within their new roles while still under my direct guidance. This would provide you and the department with three qualified people who could be relied on for troubleshooting problems and supervising the staff after I assume the consultant responsibility.

I look forward to a favorable review of the proposed change.

Presenting the Proposal

The next step is to review the written proposal with a mentor and with others who would be impacted by the change. Then set an appointment time with your boss and present the proposal orally, leaving the written proposal for review and discussion. In communicating the proposal to your manager, the specific technique for saying it right depends on your nature, your boss's nature, and the strength of your relationship. If possible, before making your proposal, talk with someone who has had a proposal accepted by your boss (or other company manager) to get an idea of what is likely to work best.

If your boss is open to new ideas, you may be able to be very direct in communicating your proposal. If, however, he or she is more closed and needs to be involved in every aspect of a decision, you might be better off outlining the problems, offering several options for addressing them, and suggesting to your boss that you work together to develop the best solution.

With an action-oriented boss, take the direct approach. Be sure to stress the benefits of the change, while recognizing and minimizing any resistance. Make sure that the benefits that are currently being received will continue, but make the strong point that if the change is not made, definite problems will get worse. Also, be sure to suggest a timetable for making the transition that would allow time for everyone to be trained before final implementation. End your discussion by presenting the written proposal and then setting a time you can get back together to review and revise it prior to forwarding it to the next level for approval.

MY BOTTOM LINE You may very well find that you can use the professional skills you've acquired over the years and apply them to part-time or more flexible work. Don't be limited by the obvious methods of working or by what others have done before. Think out of the box in designing the "ideal" way of work for you. Making the choice to work in a new way allows you to adopt a slightly different "business mindset," one that you'll probably find more comfortable. In fact, redefining your work can be the most rewarding time of your career—personally and, perhaps, financially, too—because you get to work on your own terms, not someone else's.

CHAPTER 13

It's Never Too Late to Try Something New

The other day, I listened to a report on TV about a 79-year-old man, married to a 37-year-old woman, who had just climbed a mountain. Now he is looking for a new challenge. He is part of that special group of people who will always have the energy and drive for another difficult challenge. For this type of person, making dramatic career changes is a lifestyle. For the rest of the population, a career change will be more gradual. Most people do not make dramatic career changes; rather, they develop and build on their skills until certain ones become strengths, and then they gradually take on challenges in new areas of interest. Those who do may seem to make extreme changes—for example, from bartender to doctor, personnel clerk to veterinarian, personal trainer to record producer—but generally they have been working toward that second career for a long time before they eventually make the final transition.

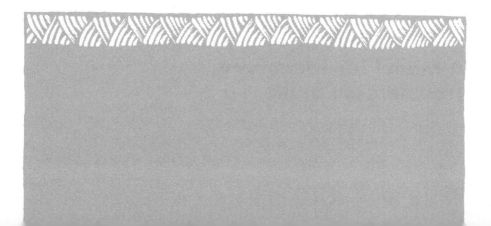

When You Sense It's Time for a Change

It is not unusual to know for years in advance that you want to make a career change. You may have commented to others about what you plan to do "when the kids finish college," "when the major bills are paid off," or "when I finish school." Knowing what you want to do at some point in the future can give you plenty of time to plan and build the necessary foundation while you continue in your current career. In fact, if you plan your career change while working in another job, you may discover that you can draw on company resources and contacts to help make the transition to your new career easier.

A personal trainer I know learned the value of working at one career while laying the foundation for his move into record production. He networked among his clients and met professionals in the entertainment business who helped him. As a trainer he was an entrepreneur; he was self-disciplined, accustomed to working independently, and skilled at developing and implementing a plan to accomplish his goal. He could transfer these skills to his new career, making the change less difficult than it might otherwise have been.

It takes drive, energy, and focus to successfully make the leap from one career to a totally different one, and for those who do, the result can be quite rewarding. Most people who make a change mid-life typically choose to move into a less demanding job using some of the skills they enjoy. But others choose to start their own business, consult, or even explore the challenge of something entirely different. If you're up to the challenge of the change, whether a bigger job or a lesser job, it will usually involve taking the skills you already have and combining them with new interests, setting a new or modified goal that is a better reflection of your self-knowledge, and then deciding where to market the skills.

A Model for Identifying Transferable Skills

Regardless of how the desire for a career change comes about, once it does, you need to identify a new goal. If you've been in the workforce for several years, you can usually do this by analyzing the pattern of your past accomplishments to determine the direction in which your skills are now pointing. After that, it's a matter of honing in on the assets you want to market.

Start by putting together a list of your accomplishments, as described in Chapter 10. (Also revisit the list you made in Chapter 11 for another review of your important accomplishments.) Most likely the accomplishments you've achieved in the last 10 years or so will be fine, but use a longer time span if necessary. Highlight relevant accomplishments from both work and outside activities. Concentrate on identifying accomplishments you made while involved in activities you truly enjoyed. Then analyze them for the skills and traits you developed as a result of each. As you do this, you will likely note the following:

- Significant accomplishments led to bigger accomplishments and thus involved the use of additional skills.

- Overall patterns of skills and traits run throughout all or most of your accomplishments.

Those skills that appear often are probably your dominant ones and the ones that you will want to transfer to another career.

To get an idea of how to identify transferable skills, read the interview with Ed Chapman ("Burned Out and Renewed") and then look at the table in "Case 1: Ed's Analysis of His Accomplishments and Career Options," later in this chapter.

Combining Skills and Interests into New Career Options

After identifying your strongest skills, your next step is to identify those you most enjoy using and consider what types of work would allow you to use them. Just as important, you need to determine the functions that, over the course of your career, you've come to find uninteresting, unpleasant, or uncomfortable to perform. All of this requires an honest self-analysis of the activities you do and do not enjoy. Essentially, your aim is to ensure that your new career options reflect the inner you that has surfaced since you set your original career goal years ago.

Matching Your Skills to Your Interests

Carolyn, an accounting supervisor, made a careful self-analysis when she grew dissatisfied in her position. By determining what she didn't want to do, she was able to make a smooth and personally rewarding career switch. Looking back on her work history, she realized that although she had significant experience as a supervisor, she disliked managing people. She had originally accepted a supervisory role simply because it offered a significant increase in pay.

Now ready for a change, she evaluated her skills, along with her likes and dislikes, and incorporated them into a new focus. Knowing that she wanted to stay in accounting, Carolyn decided to move into a role where she would tackle work assignments as part of a team but where she would not directly supervise, give performance reviews, or handle the grievances of others. Her new job, as a member of the finance team with a management consulting firm, allowed her to do just that.

If you can identify the skills you enjoy using most, while taking into account the ones you're sure you no longer want to use, you have a good basis for developing options for a career change. The following steps will help with the process.

- On a sheet of paper, write a list of the skills you enjoy using. Try to express each in one word or two-word phrases; avoid listing skills in broad categories. For instance, instead of using the broad term *leadership*, break it down into specifics: *communicating information, convincing others, writing letters, conducting meetings, supervising others.*

- On another sheet of paper, make a column for each job that interests you. Three jobs is a manageable number. (Reread Chapter 2 if you need help with this step.)

- For each job, do research to find the required skills. The reference or career librarian at your local library will be able to direct you to books that describe most occupations. But the best way to determine what real-life skills are necessary for a job is to ask a person already employed in that occupation. If you don't have a direct contact, ask your friends and peers to help you locate such a person. In questioning these contacts, ask them to give you examples of how the skills are used so that you get a clear idea of what is required. Come up with a list of five to seven primary skills and then write them in the columns below each job heading.

■ Now compare the skills you most enjoy with the skills required for each of the jobs you listed. The job that best matches your skills is probably your best bet for a new career.

Take steps to explore that option. But plan to research the other two options as well. You may find as you explore your first option that it is not feasible for any number of reasons (money, timing, or educational requirements). If so, you can focus on your next strongest option.

Burned Out and Renewed

The opportunity to create a new career for yourself will come when you're ready for a change, whether you immediately realize you're ready or not. Often you can anticipate coming changes and new areas for growth and opportunity when you see existing situations begin to deteriorate or come to an end.

Ed managed a consulting group at Digital Equipment Corporation for seven years before making his first career change. He realized after a heated discussion with his boss that he had outgrown his job and was ready to move on. An offer to stay with the company and start a new division selling software solutions allowed him to use his technical knowledge while he developed new skills in marketing and sales. Working at this position for another seven years, he helped to build up a $12 million business. Then an industry downturn forced the company to downsize, and Ed, finding himself dealing daily with office politics in order to survive, decided to accept the company's buyout package.

"I was going to find another job but discovered it wasn't that easy at my age [50] to get a job as a middle manager. And after a long time in middle management, I had lost many of my technical skills, making it hard to find another job. Also corporations were flattening and moving to high-performance teams, so there were fewer positions available like the one I'd had."

A visit to his uncle in the Caribbean, where Ed went to do some consulting work, inspired him to start his own business. "My 75-year-old uncle was a tremendous motivating force for me," Ed explains. "I was trying to figure out what I wanted to do and was fearful of starting my own business. I had an opportunity to interact with him and observe what can be done when one has no fear of failure. Here was a man who had constructed a 12-unit villa at 70 years of age. He had been motivated to do so by a promise he'd made to himself years ago; at the young age of 7 he looked up to the mountain and said, 'I will have a villa up there someday.'"

Ed spent some time evaluating his career path and looking back on his experience writing business plans in a corporate environment. In doing so, he realized that nearly all his significant positions involved starting up new ventures within the company. So it was natural for him to begin a new business venture of his own—his current consulting practice.

"If you want to make a career change, make sure you have a clear motivation and objective; you'll need this focus to give you the steam to reach your goal. While in the Caribbean, I realized I was adept at working with people; now I know that my enjoyment comes from working with people, not with technology. That's what drives me."

> **Ed Chapman**
> Black entrepreneur
> President, Business Development Concepts,
> Laguna Niguel, California
> Business: New business development, business plans
> for start-up and expansion

Case 1: Ed's Analysis of His Accomplishments and Career Options

Ed Chapman created the following list of his accomplishments and the skills and traits he used in achieving them. Take a look at his example, to get a better idea of how you can create an accomplishment analysis of your own.

ACCOMPLISHMENT	RESULT	SKILLS AND TRAITS
Played in a band to finance college education.	Declined music scholarship because of dislike of lifestyle and, instead, chose to finish business school.	Creativity, resourcefulness, self-knowledge.
Excelled in college: graduated in upper 2 percent of class in computer information systems.	Led to job developing new systems and applying innovative computer skills to the company.	Analytical ability, perseverance, concentration.
Developed an automated evaluation and compensation system allowing people to be placed in their jobs at an equitable pay scale.	Leadership skills surfaced; successfully engendered support and cooperation from others.	Negotiation, influencing upper management.
Promoted to upper management position with staff of 60.	Discovered people skills.	Selling, influencing, proposing, tracking, managing, working well with people.
Set up a new business for software development within a major company.	Established and implemented a business plan.	Business startup, ability to secure financing, initiative, vision, resourcefulness, product development, marketing, consulting.

The preceding table identifies certain patterns in Ed's career, including a progression from using analytical skills to using people skills, a transition from managing to visionary leadership and then to consulting, and a successful history of handling start-up operations or projects. For Ed, recognizing this pattern helped him get a clear picture of the skills he enjoyed using most. This information, listed in the left column of that table, represents a group of skills that he used most often and against which he evaluated his options. As a result of that analysis, Ed determined that the skills he most enjoyed using were management skills, leadership, consulting start-up activities, and technical knowledge.

Next, Ed put together a list of career options that he felt would incorporate the most important and fulfilling of his skills. Ed's options and the results of his pursuit of each of those options appear in the following table:

CAREER OPTION	RESULT
1. Job with another company.	Couldn't find job at desired salary and location. Wasn't motivated.
2. Work outside of corporate America in hotel management in Caribbean.	Discovered skills were transferable, but location was not desirable for long-term.
3. Consulting business writing and expansion.	Best choice. Able to transfer skills developing business plans for start-up and maintain options.

In the second table, a further evaluation of Ed's background demonstrates how he combined skills and interests into new career options and then through a process of elimination chose the best one. He developed option 1 because he assumed the next logical step for him was to get a job at another company doing the same thing he had done. During the process of trying to find that type of job, however, he discovered he wasn't really motivated to continue doing the same job elsewhere. Option 2 came from his uncle in the Caribbean, who had asked Ed to help with the family business for a while. After exploring this second possibility, Ed decided he was not interested in pursuing it either. He then decided to start his own consulting business using the skills he was comfortable with. This turned out to be his best option, even though it was not his first choice.

When you have settled on a new career option, be sure to compare it to your list of skills to be certain that it will not eventually lead to using many of the skills you want to avoid. Finally, evaluate the feasibility of your interest options against the information you've discovered about yourself. You may discover, as Ed did, that the process is essentially one of elimination.

MY BOTTOM LINE	During the first part of your career, it was more difficult to decide on a direction because your experience was so limited. You'll find that at this juncture the process is a lot more fun, and you'll likely have several enticing options to choose from. Allow room to change your mind if necessary until you arrive at the very best one for you at this time.

Evaluating Factors That Could Impact the Goal

In an ideal world, your strengths would align perfectly with one of your options and you could just go for it. But the world, as we all know, isn't perfect. And it may actually be "less perfect" for you than it was 10 years ago because family, new responsibilities, and other social and economic factors have made it more complicated. More than likely, you probably now have issues and considerations that you didn't face when first starting out. The following list should help you identify the realities that apply to your current situation. These are the concerns you may need to consider as you pinpoint your career options and develop the objectives to reach your goal.

How High Should the Goal Be?

You need to think about developing a goal for which you'll have the time, energy, and drive to support. Be realistic; don't set yourself up for failure by developing a goal you know you can't reach. Of course, if you are an exceptional person—like Ed's uncle, who fulfilled a dream at the age of 70—then age is truly just a number. But many people find their drive diminishes, at least temporarily, around middle age.

Lifestyle Change

One action, like embarking on a new career, can cause a ripple effect that can change your whole life. You may find that some friends drift away; you may find yourself interacting with new and different professional groups and business associates. You might have less personal time to spend with friends and family if you have to go to school a couple of nights a week. You might have to accept a lower salary. How do you think you'll handle the adjustment? What about your family?

Family Support

It's a good idea to talk over your plans with your spouse (and children). Involvement produces commitment. If they're involved in your decision, you'll have their support and understanding. This will be especially important if you plan to start a business or make a career move that means re-education, a new work schedule, or a reduction in income.

Time—Is It Worth It?

Even if the learning curve is relatively short and the transition smooth, a career change requires time for you to adjust to a new role and then come up to speed. You may have to return to school for additional training or spend extra hours in the evening boning up on required information. Obviously, if you start at a lower position than you've normally held, it will take time to move up to the level you're accustomed to. How much time are you willing to commit to a career switch?

Culture Shock

Consider the impact of possibly working with younger, more experienced people. You may have to adjust to being the oldest person in the group.

Of course that can have its advantages in certain professions—real estate or financial planning, for example—where your age can work to your advantage by making you seem more experienced and wiser and, thus, enhancing your credibility.

Starting at the Bottom

If you're accustomed to having a secretary and staff, starting over without these may seem like a real handicap, especially if you're lacking in organizational and administrative skills. It could be particularly problematic if you're starting your own business because there will be no more company supplies or services at your disposal.

What If It Doesn't Work?

It's always wise to have an alternate route to your goal, as well as a backup plan. You can gain valuable insight into what to expect in the new career if you take the time to research it beforehand—for example, by talking with people who do what you want to do. In exploring your alternatives, make sure you choose ones that allow you to use the same skills—for example, coaching at a university or coaching at a junior college, with a backup plan for earning a living if coaching does not work out at all. Go through the same process for developing backup options that you used for developing your original career goal. The more thoroughly informed you are about what to expect, the more assured you can be about your decision.

Maintaining Your Own Business

A very frequent cry from those who are seeking a change is "I want to start my own business because I'm tired of working for someone else." I'll get right to the point here. Having your own business is three times harder than working for someone else. Ask any businessperson, and he will verify this fact. One business owner told me he works 24 hours a day, 8 days a week. No, that was not a typo. Working for yourself involves not just doing the work you've been hired to do or simply selling the product; it also involves taking on the management and administrative duties associated with maintaining a business. You'll be responsible for everything from answering the telephone to negotiating fees and paying taxes. Some people find it very stressful making the transition from working in an office with structure and support to being an independent entrepreneur with no fixed workday or office environment. Handling all the administrative and clerical details can add to the stress, especially if you dislike such tasks. Before considering this option seriously, observe and talk with someone who has the kind of business you want to start. It is definitely the biggest challenge if you're planning on a career change.

Don't Just Do It

"There is risk in being an entrepreneur," says industrial designer William Barlett. "It's not for everybody. Even with careful planning, you still have to be comfortable with not knowing just what to expect next."

After 20 years as a consultant, Bill doesn't mind taking risks, and he still loves his work. The hard part, he says, is managing the business and dealing with the responsibility involved. "The actual work is the fun part of being an entrepreneur, but managing the business is another thing all together," he says. "Anyone thinking of being a consultant or pursuing his own business needs to do some serious planning and have reasonable financial resources.

"Most people think only about the excitement and freedom of being their own boss without considering the downsides. For instance, there are the tax implications, such as double FICA and a higher tax rate than salaried employees. Medical and life insurance are not completely tax deductible. Then there's the matter of vacations; when you're your own business, you don't get paid when you don't work. I didn't take a vacation for more than 10 years. Also working alone, with no support or camaraderie, can be difficult. You can't rely on anyone to back you up when you need help. One thing that has been helpful is having a supportive spouse. She is an entrepreneur also, so that makes it easier for me."

Still Bill willingly takes on the risks and management of his business activities. He admits that his entrepreneurial drive comes sometimes from his confidence in his ability and sometimes from the simple need to make money. Over the long run, both have paid off. His business successes include attaining a copyright for new computer software, several patents, and numerous international design awards.

Like most entrepreneurs, Bill is driven to accomplish his goals and needs, which he describes as creativity/design satisfaction, variety, personal responsibility, and financial reward. When the business demands it, he takes night classes to upgrade his skills or learn new ones. "It's always necessary to maintain state-of-the-art knowledge in your field. Anyone who wants to be a consultant has to make a commitment to do this in order to stay in business," Bill advises. "But the most important thing is to have a well-thought-out business plan and keep working toward your goals.

> **William L. Barlett**
> Hispanic-American consultant
> Barlett Design Associates, Inc. Santa Barbara, California
> Business: Industrial design

Consulting

Webster describes a consultant as "one who gives professional advice or services." This can mean many types of professionals: artists, writers, editors, trainers, marketing consultants, managers, engineers, computer experts…you name it. This is typically the option chosen by people who want to make a career change and have a lot of expertise in their field. As a consultant, you will have truly moved beyond working for someone; you've assumed all the responsibilities, risks—and rewards—of having your own business. You are marketing yourself—your skills, your expertise, and the results you can produce for clients. To do this well, you need to have highly marketable skills and expertise and the motivation to succeed. A consultant is different from a contractor. Companies look to contractors to produce repeatable ongoing tasks, not give advice. They expect consultants to be experts in their fields and to have enough influence that others are willing to listen to them and follow their advice.

For instance, if a company asks a consultant to perform a certain function, the consultant should have the knowledge and expertise to view the function in context so that she can advise company managers about what they may need in addition to—or in place of—the requested service. Managing this process requires proven expertise and experience, as well as strong interpersonal and communication skills that can be used to overcome resistance and influence clients to change their current policies, practices, or systems.

If you've decided to be a consultant because you want more time and freedom, you may have chosen the wrong work option. In switching from the role of employee to entrepreneur, you'll likely find that consulting can be an intensive, all-encompassing profession, requiring a greater commitment of time, resources, and energy than you anticipated.

Is Consulting for You?

To help you decide whether consulting would suit you, take a look at this list of personal traits and priorities found in many successful consultants and see how many describe you:

- **Control and freedom.** You feel more comfortable trusting your future to yourself than being dependent on a company.

- **Self-confidence.** You believe in yourself and your ability.

- **Resilience.** You are emotionally stable and are not overcome by disappointments.

- **Money.** A good income is one of your career motivators.

- **Sales skills.** You're a good networker and have the ability to market yourself.

▧ **Good interpersonal skills.** You have the ability to get along well with all kinds of people.

▧ **Good communication skills.** You have strong oral and written communication skills.

▧ **Skills.** Your research has shown that you have the right combination of skills and experience to meet current market needs.

Doing Your Homework

If you've worked in the field before, you probably have a good sense of what these needs are. To be sure, you might want to do some research. You can start by talking with colleagues and then expand to members of professional associations. If you don't belong to such an association, this is the time to join! Look up the association that represents your area of expertise (check the *Encyclopedia of Associations* at the library) or check web sites and other online sources for information about consulting; then contact a local chapter, attend one of its meetings, and talk with the participants about the skills and experience needed in your field. Also, check with department heads at your company (before you leave) and ask what kind of skills they look for in the people they use as consultants. Because contracting and consulting can be closely connected, talking with a representative at an executive placement firm who specializes in your field might also provide good information.

You can identify how your skills and experience should be packaged and presented in the market as well as to whom they should be presented. In other words, you can determine who benefits most from your expertise and is willing to pay for it. Then evaluate how you stack up against the competition (that is, what you have that they may be lacking). You might want to take this additional skill and make it one of your specialties. For instance, if you're a competent leadership trainer but know that there are already plenty of trainers selling their services, identify something that makes you unique. Let's say you're bilingual. You can either work directly with a company that has a multicultural employee base or work in conjunction with other trainers servicing a contract that involves bilingual work.

A Job Change at Your Company

You may decide that making a career change in your current company is your best option. Two of the biggest advantages of staying with your company are credibility and money. If you have established a good reputation and your philosophy is in line with that of the company, you will likely be given serious consideration when you propose a career change. Because you've already proven yourself, management will have faith in you and assume you'll perform well in a new job. Also, many companies, especially large ones, will keep job changers at their current salary although they move into positions that would normally pay less.

But not everyone finds it easy to make a career change at their present company. I know a number of people who found it difficult to make a lateral or a downward move; the stigma of not moving up when they had the opportunity took a long time to wear off. If you do move up, you may find that your new salary is not as much of an increase as you expected because you came into the job with a low pay basis. If you are considering a job change within your company, refer to Chapters 8 and 12 for more discussion of these issues and all of the essential factors you need to consider in making a career change there.

Moving to Another Company

Maybe the best change option involves moving to another company. You might find that moving to another company and making a career change simultaneously is more challenging than making a change within your current company. You will probably start out at a lower salary and in a lesser role and then have to work your way back up both the economic and corporate ladder. When making a simultaneous career and company change, you can increase your chances of success by incorporating the following factors into the process. Chapter 10 offers a complete discussion of the how, why, and when of moving to another company.

Making the Decision to Take a Less Stressful Job

You may arrive at the fourth stage of your career with no interest in renegotiating your job or realigning your career but rather with an eye toward reducing your focus on your work and the stress that goes with it. You may have good reason for wanting to jump off the corporate ladder. Usually, the upward climb is very difficult and quite stressful. The balancing act between work and home can take such a toll on all parts of your life that the signal that it's time to make a change often comes as welcome relief.

Less Can Be a Challenge Too

Taking a lesser job is initially stressful for anyone because it requires making lifestyle and career adjustments. You may have the added stress of dealing with the subtle but pervasive message that says, "You should be grateful you have such a good job; how dare you think about giving it up?" You've had to work hard to achieve your success and status, so be prepared for people to ask you whether you've lost your mind when you tell them you want to give it up or take a lesser job. Expect some to believe that you just couldn't cut the mustard. Understand that when people express these attitudes, they are operating from their own value system and are not considering your needs.

When I left my corporate job, a white peer flatly told me that I was going to starve to death, and an older black friend asked me if I were nuts. In a sense, I felt they were both communicating the same thing: How dare you (a black person) leave when a good job is so hard for black people to get? Their message to me, I believe, was that a person of color doesn't have a right to make this change and that we should always value a job above any other consideration.

This kind of attitude can stop you from making a change if you let it. You have to remember that you have achieved what you have because you did not let negative attitudes such as these stop you before, and you shouldn't let them interfere now with your new decision. In America we have the freedom to come full circle in our careers and give ourselves the option of taking a lesser job if it's better for our overall life-career plan.

A Lesser Job Will Affect Your Whole Life

Before you make a drastic change, however, realize that although changing to a lesser job will probably reduce your work stress, improve your health, and allow you more time to spend with your family and to do other things you enjoy, making the transition will bring new stress to other areas of your life. You will be adjusting to a new routine, different responsibilities, and a different level of authority—or no authority at all. If you're starting out on a new path (rather than "downsizing" into a less stressful job in your current career area), expect the transitional stress to be even greater and to last for a longer period of time. Transferring your skills into a new profession or starting over in a new career will bring on the additional stress of a culture change and probably a different work location. Plus you may have to get more training to bring your skill level up for the new job, even though it's at a level lower than your former job. Be prepared for the change to be a little bumpy at first, as every area under your life-career umbrella adjusts.

For starters, you'll be earning less money, which means you'll probably have to make changes in your lifestyle. Perhaps you'll be dining out less, taking fewer vacations, keeping your car longer, or moving to a smaller, more affordable house or apartment. You may also find that your circle of friends will change to realign with your new values and priorities. Don't be surprised if, for a while, you feel pulled between the new friends and the old, as well as between the activities of the old lifestyle and the new. Family members may be happy that you have more available time but can also take a while to accept that the change will affect the things they can do or have, too.

Taking a Lesser Job Within Your Profession

Some of the most successful transitions I've seen involved individuals taking jobs in the same or a related profession but at a less responsible level. Usually, you can accomplish this more easily by changing companies, because you, as well as your colleagues, might find it difficult to adjust to your change within the company. Typically, when you change jobs at your company, you will find that others are not making the adjustment as quickly as you are; they're still coming to you for the information and support you gave them in your previous position.

Either way, whether you change to a lesser position within your company or move to another company, you'll be an asset in the job. You'll be able to carry over some aspects of the former work that you enjoyed, while bringing added value to the function. For instance, if you step down as a human resources director with several functional areas reporting to you and move to a position of recruiter, you will better appreciate your manager's need for receiving timely staffing reports. You could also be an asset to your colleagues, willing to share information and support their efforts because you're not competing with them to move up a ladder you've just descended.

For John, the career transition in stage three presented less stress because he stayed within a field that he knew and loved. As director for a community program in a major city for 20 years, his high-profile role demanded he be in the public eye a great deal and attend a lot of social events. He relished his many responsibilities but decided to change jobs when they began to consume the better part of his waking hours, including weekends.

Two factors contributed to John's decision to make a change. His father, whom he considered his best friend, was diagnosed with cancer and needed a lot of his son's attention. Around the same time, John developed diabetes. It became clear to him that his job was one of the things he could alter to relieve stress and leave more time to spend with his family. In deciding what he could do next, John asked himself a few questions, some of which are listed here.

If you can answer yes to the following questions, then taking a lesser job in your field, either at your present company or at another company, could be a good move for you:

■ Would your stress be reduced by eliminating some of the secondary functions in your job, or is the stress caused by the major responsibilities?

■ Is it feasible to move to a lesser position in your profession, continue to use the skills you enjoy, and still reduce your stress?

■ Will you be accepted by your peers and management in a lesser role in your profession and be expected only to make a contribution at that level?

■ Is it really feasible to move to a more flexible job without feeling awkward about it—or without feeling pressure to carry out some of your previous responsibilities?

■ Can you let go of the power and influence of the higher level position and adjust psychologically to having less influence, especially if you remain in your present company?

■ Can you deal with the possibility that others may perceive you as not as competent as before if you accept a lesser position in your profession?

Developing the Right Marketing Tools for Your Job Change

Whether you go after a different job in your current field or one in a different field, you'll need a new résumé to go along with your new career goal. In revising your résumé, keep in mind that you will be seeking a position that is different or less than what you have done in the past. A chronological (the standard type) résumé that lists your full work history and accomplishments might make you feel good but probably won't help you land a job that is different from what you've held.

As a staffing professional for a Fortune 100 company, I had an opportunity to assess résumés and compile a list of promising candidates for managers to review for their openings. I remember once feeling quite satisfied with the a list of candidates I submitted for an opening and then feeling extremely disappointed when most of them were rejected—without being interviewed. I had mistakenly thought the manager would be pleased to see the most qualified applicants available. As the manager discarded most of the people on my list, he jokingly commented, "Some of these people are more qualified than I am, and their skills do not line up with the job. What do you want me to do, lose my job?"

Employers seek the best fit for their openings, which is not necessarily the most experienced or most impressive person who applies. Most believe that if they hire an overqualified person, they'll end up with a disgruntled, hard-to-manage employee who is only using the position as a stop-gap measure until he gets something he really wants. Most managers consider hiring an overqualified person a bad investment for the long term.

In spite of these obstacles, changing to a lesser or different position can be done successfully with some forethought and planning. The information outlined here will guide you in developing a résumé that will help you get consideration as a viable candidate. This résumé will also set the stage for a good interview.

Developing Your Career Change Résumé

Your old résumé absolutely will not do. Develop a new résumé rather than use an edited version of your old one. (Refer to Chapters 5 and 10 for tips on résumé writing.) Follow these steps:

- Use a functional résumé format. The traditional chronological résumé, which typically reveals your age, years of service, titles, and levels of responsibility, may wind up being your kiss of death. Employers looking at it may think you're overqualified or feel that your last job doesn't qualify you for the position you're seeking. Eliminate dates and group accomplishments by function to fit your new job target.

- Develop a résumé targeted to the goal. At the top of the paper, write down the job you want to get—for example, "product representative." Then test all the information you put in the rest of the résumé against this objective. If you prefer not to include an objective on your résumé, you can delete it after you have developed the résumé and done your test.

- Develop a summary statement at the top of the résumé. After the objective, in five to seven lines summarize the skills, traits (the way you work), experience, and knowledge that you would bring to this position. Refer back to the information that people gave you when you talked with them about this type of work. Emphasize the skills, traits, knowledge, and experience they told you were needed. Include skills that you used in your old job only when they fit the new job, and at the same time, use only the portion of those skills and traits that will transfer to the new job.

■ Provide examples of accomplishments in your résumé that support the information in the summary. Word them so they fit the needs of the job emphasizing skills that relate to the job.

■ Describe your previous jobs in the most generic terms possible to avoid any issue of being overqualified.

■ Have someone review your résumé. Find someone who does the kind of work you want to do or is at least knowledgeable about that field.

Presenting Your Case: Some Career Change Resume "Do's and Don'ts"

When you're creating a resume for "downsizing" your career, it's important that you present your skills, background, and experiences in way that won't give the impression that you're overqualified for the type of work you're seeking. If you're entering an entirely new field, you want to make sure that your résumé highlights what you're capable of doing, not the specifics of the tasks you performed in your former career.

For example, imagine that a newscaster is looking for a new job as a product representative in sales or customer service, and consider how his skills and experience might be used in his new résumé. The following information on the left is appropriate; that on the right is not. Although the right-hand information is indicative of what most newscasters would be inclined to include in their résumés and is impressive, it does not align as well with the new job requirements as the information on the left. Rather, it underscores what a high-achieving go-getter the job applicant is and would create doubt in the prospective employer's mind about the newscaster's ability to be happy as a customer service representative.

DO'S	DON'TS
Objective: A position as a product representative where I can apply my experience in influencing others to make positive decisions.	**Objective:** A responsible position in a progressive organization where I can make a contribution.
Summary: A seasoned professional with more than 10 years' experience developing and communicating information. Excellent analytical and problem-solving skills. Easy to talk with. Projects corporate image. Politically savvy. A resourceful self-starter who can work independently or as part of a team.	**Summary:** More than 20 years' experience as a newscaster for three major stations. Knowledgeable director and producer. Traveled extensively in China, Caribbean, Germany, Switzerland, and Thailand. Considerable experience handling investigative and on-the-spot news stories. Fluent in Chinese and Spanish.
Selected Accomplishments: Developed, sold to upper management, and implemented a proposal that expanded company's service by 10 percent. Independently handled all functions of a satellite location for 11 months. Worked with division within a client company to identify and resolve resistance to a major access station.	**Selected Accomplishments:** Received a national award for top investigative story in 1991. Special commendation for work with Chinese businessmen to establish a positive link with US television stations. Part of team that developed KPPC proposal, which resulted in $350,000 in revenues.
Professional History: KNWC News, News Department; ACCX NEWS, Community Relations Department; VMES News, Media Division. (Note: No titles given, just departments.)	**Professional History:** News Anchor, KNWC; News Producer, Community Relations, ACCX News; Media Director, VMES News.

To see the career change résumé in action, take a look at the two résumé examples, "Before" and "After," that demonstrate how a professional resume might be altered to be an effective tool for marketing yourself for a career change. In this example, Frank Wales, who is established in his career in customer service, has adapted his résumé to help him in his pursuit of a career in human resources.

The "Before" Résumé

This is a chronological format with a customer service focus.

FRANK WALES
2300 Park Avenue
New York, New York 20023
(212) 555-1223

SUMMARY

As a customer services professional for eight years, I have managed groups supporting retail, product, and services industries. Strengths include strong organizational ability and team-building development of systems for efficient processing of information, complemented by effective management and interpersonal skills.

WORK EXPERIENCE

MANAGER, CUSTOMER SERVICE
Hi Tech Computer Company
1995-present

Hired and supervised a staff of fifty people to service the needs of the highest revenue commercial accounts. Assumed responsibility for managing a remote location of fifteen people for nine months while that supervisor was on medical leave.

Held quarterly "Your Best" training programs for entire staff, which kept quality at the forefront and helped maintain an account retention percentage of 99 percent.

Kept revenue loss through credits to less than 1%.

CUSTOMER SERVICE—TELEMARKETING MANAGER
Excel Communications—Northwest Service Center
1990-1995

Hired and developed a staff of sixty customer service-telemarketing representatives and supervisors.

Managed heavy workload of inbound and outbound call activities.

Resolved a major conflict with another department, which prevented a serious work stoppage.

CUSTOMER SERVICE SUPERVISOR
Cirro Retail Outlet
1987-1990

Supervised division customer service site and provided support to the sales force and sales management.

Promoted from Customer Service Representative after three months.

EDUCATION

1995, M.B.A., University of New York
1984, B.S. Marketing, Syracuse University

The "After" Résumé

This is a functional format, changed from a customer service focus to a human resources focus.

FRANK WALES
2300 Park Avenue
New York, New York 20023
(212) 555-1223

SUMMARY

An experienced manager who has successfully influenced direct and indirect reports to provide quality service within retail, manufacturing, and service environments. Effective interpersonal skills have been an asset in training, counseling, and arbitrating conflicts. Strong analytical skills help with planning and project management. M.B.A. degree and professional strengths would enhance time quality of a human resources function. Computer literate.

SELECTED ACCOMPLISHMENTS

Communication/Interpersonal
- Trained seventy new hires in five classes within thirty days. Productivity increased by 13 percent within ninety days.
- Advised upper management on major hiring decisions after a division reorganization.
- Counseled a difficult employee who was abusing alcohol to independently sign up for an employee assistance program.
- Convinced upper management to establish a special awards program to recognize top performers.

Project Management
- Part of a team that reviewed and developed new benefit programs, which were offered to all employees.
- Hired and supervised a staff of fifty people to service the needs of company's highest revenue commercial accounts.
- Assumed responsibility for managing a remote location of fifteen people for nine months while that supervisor was on medical leave.

Problem Resolution
- Established a system to handle an unexpected heavy workload involving large volumes of paper.
- Resolved a major conflict with another division and prevented a serious work stoppage.
- Scheduled maintenance of fields, gym set-ups, and cleanups.
- Determined player eligibility.

PROFESSIONAL HISTORY

High Tech Computer Company, Manager of Customer Service 1995-present
Excel Communications, Customer Service—Telemarketing Manager 1990-1995
Cirro Retail Outlet, Customer Service Supervisor 1987-1990

EDUCATION

1995, M.B.A, University of New York
1984, B.S. in Marketing, Syracuse University

Finding New Positions

You should certainly use ads and agencies to find new positions outside your company, but networking will probably be the best method for finding the new job. This is not the time to restrict your search to a small circle of close friends. You should talk with everyone of both genders and all races. Sometimes we are closed about wanting to make a career change (don't let that old pride gets in the way) because we don't want anyone to think that we couldn't handle the last job. But interestingly, if we discuss it with other people, especially people in our age group, they will probably relate, no matter what their race, because they may have some similar feelings themselves about changing their priorities.

For John, whom I spoke about earlier in this chapter, networking proved to be an excellent avenue for his job change. Because he was known for strong performance, all his contacts considered him an asset. Before talking with anyone about a change, John evaluated what he could do next so he would be able to discuss with his contacts the skills and activities he enjoyed. He decided to look for work placing people in jobs and to minimize his involvement in the social and administrative part of the work.

John used his networking contacts to help him land a new position as a job development counselor with a citywide job training program. He worked flexible hours, had one major responsibility instead of several, and was still involved in the kind of work he enjoyed. In his new role, he reported to a director, someone at the level John was at in his former job. This didn't bother John because he had willingly given up the old position and was not at all envious of the demands that went with the director's role. Rather, John's experience enabled him to serve as a valuable resource to the director; he could help ensure the program's success without having the responsibility and stress of being held accountable for it.

Interviewing for a Career Change Position

It is pointless to spend time researching the position you want and tailoring a résumé for it—just to get to the interview and blow the opportunity to show them how right you are for the job. Unfortunately, this is exactly what can happen if you don't come to the interview well-prepared. Your past successes and experience have probably left you feeling quite confident in your abilities, but this heightened confidence can be a drawback in an interview situation. If you've been working at a very responsible job, you probably have the authoritative attitude that goes along with it. The new position might not call for all that strength and poise, so it's wise to adjust your interviewing style in advance.

Case 2: Do You Need to Check the Attitude?

For Ken, an ulcer, concern over ailing parents, and intense company politics forced him to give up his position as program manager for a high-tech supplier of defense parts. Years of leading a team of professionals and winning contracts worth millions of dollars had made him into a confident individual with a commanding presence.

To help him with his job search, Ken signed on with a permanent place-ment agency. The staffing consultant assigned to his case pegged Ken as a professional who would be an asset to a number of companies. After interviewing him for about 45 minutes, however, the search consultant had some other feedback for Ken that caught him by surprise. He told Ken that his attitude was almost too authoritative for the positions for which he would be applying. He pointed out that Ken had taken control of their interview and seemed impatient with answering the types of questions that would probably be asked on a job interview. The consultant warned him that some of the interviewers might be younger than Ken and that they could well feel intimidated by his manner; he advised him to work on being more relaxed and less intimidating. Fortunately Ken took this advice to heart and adjusted his interview style; he ended up being offered and accepting a systems engineering position with a small company, where he clicked well with the executives.

Be Prepared for a New Interview Process

If you haven't interviewed in years, you can expect a different process than you remember from 10 or 20 years ago. Much work now is project-oriented and handled by teams. You may be interviewed by several people, either in a group interview or individually, to determine whether you will fit with the "team." And don't be surprised if the selection process takes six to eight weeks.

Because most companies tend to follow the current market patterns, the interview process at your current company should reflect what you can expect at another company. You can get a sense of this process by talking informally with someone in your human resources department. If you're not currently working or are working at a small company with no human resources department, join forces with a reputable search consultant. He or she will be able to give you an idea of what to expect in the interview, as well as offer feedback and tips on your interview style.

Know About the Company and the Interviewer

You can get general information on most publicly held companies at the public library or by calling the firm's public relations or public affairs department and requesting it. But the unpublished information you can get through networking sources will be the most valuable. Use your contacts to find out as much as you can about the interviewer, the department, company culture, and major projects underway in the functional area for which you'll be interviewing.

The better your understanding of the backgrounds and motivations of the decision makers, the better your chances of selling yourself in the interview. For instance, if you discover that the decision maker believes that everyone has to prove himself before taking on prize projects, then it will be to your advantage to approach the interview ready to express your willingness to do just that—even if you already have experience handling similar projects.

Look and Act the Part

I've learned through experience that a job candidate should always dress and behave according to the level of the position for which he or she is interviewing. If you usually dress well—in expensive, designer clothes— you might have to tone down your look a bit. You don't have to look drab or bargain basement, but a Pierre Cardin suit for an engineering position may be overdoing it. The standard middle-of-the-road blue or gray suit always works—and leave off the expensive watch or ring.

On the other hand, if you have never made your appearance a priority, your image may need to be updated. Dressing out of style can be just as bad as overdressing because it could signal to a potential employer that if your wardrobe is out of step, your thinking might be as well. If this applies to you, update your whole appearance before starting the interview process. Get your hair styled and buy a good new suit and a pair of new shoes. No need to be trendy—go for a conservative look consistent with the current styles.

Be sure not to be condescending or patronizing in the interview. Have an air of respect for the process and the interviewer (even if the person is your son or daughter's age). Be open, flexible, and friendly. Let the interviewer lead the session and don't make any references to him or her sharing some similarity in style or experience to your children. Before going to the interview, you might want to practice interviewing with someone about the same age as your prospective employer.

During the process, remember to consider the point of view of the employer, who may be concerned that you are a deadbeat or couldn't cut it in your former position. Because of this, your entire approach should be upbeat, open, and positive to convince him or her of your interest in the position and your value to the company. (Also see Chapters 5 and 10 for more information on interviewing.)

Prepare for Key Questions

Here are some sample questions often asked at interviews. Be prepared by having good answers worked out ahead of time:

- **Tell me about yourself.** Keep your answer short and relevant to the job. This is not the time to expound on all your accomplishments (just those that are relevant to the position). Use the same approach in the interview that you used for the résumé: Give an overview of your career, using generic terms as much as possible; only highlight those skills and characteristics that support this lesser position. I recommend something like, "I've been in the industry for a number of years. I've had an opportunity to work with ABC Company, Universal Defense, and High-Tech Incorporated. I've enjoyed my job most when I've been able to use my creative and technical skills, which is why I'm very interested in your opening. I believe it's one where I would be fulfilled and where I could add value."

- **Why do you want this job?** It's important that you have an enthusiastic, convincing answer here, or the interviewer is liable to think that the only reason you're making a change is because you became deadwood in your former position. Something along the lines of the following answer might effectively sum up your thoughts and give a positive impression: "I have reached a point in my life and my career where I want to concentrate on doing just those things I enjoy. I found my former position to be very challenging and am proud of what I accomplished in that job. Now I'd like to return to using my creative skills and believe I can bring that expertise to this job."

- **Why did you leave your last company?** The prior answer will work well for this question, too.

- **What kind of salary do you expect?** Do not expect to receive a salary consistent with your last job; remember, this is a lesser position. Be sure to know what a fair range is if you have to suggest a salary and begin with something like this: "I would expect to receive a fair salary consistent with the market and the skills I will be using in the job. I'm sure that if we agree on me for the position, we'll be able to work out a fair salary."

Follow Up

Sending a thank-you letter is still in style. It makes a very positive point, shows that you follow through, and may be the deciding factor that gets you the job. In the letter, mention something that seemed important to the interviewer to let him or her know that you were listening to what was said. Also, be clear that you would like to have the job, if that's the case.

MY BOTTOM LINE Making a career change can be even more challenging than starting the original career, because typically you don't have the same level of energy and motivation. But if done right, the new choice will be even more rewarding in most ways than the first career.

CHAPTER 14

Giving Back: Completing the Cycle of Success

There is hardly a greater joy than being able to give to someone and see them advance because of the help you've been blessed to share. Most successful people I've spoken with see having this capacity to share as the pinnacle of success.

In establishing my own success pattern, I set some goals (and was pushed into others) and worked to achieve them. Gradually, in my small way, I began to be viewed as a success, and, by some, as a role model. I overheard people I knew comparing me to others. "She's an 'Ollie'" or "She's not an 'Ollie,'" they sometimes said. How does one get to this place called success? How does one get to experience the joy of giving back?

For me, it has simply been a matter of being motivated to set a goal, accomplishing it by whatever honorable means possible, and then using that as a step up to my next goal—and accomplishing that new goal by whatever honorable means possible. Out of curiosity, I began to look at the careers of highly visible, very successful people and those of others I know personally who have achieved success. I found there to be certain qualities that all successful people share:

- They are moved by the spirit of love of something or someone. They are motivated by something beyond money and, usually, beyond themselves. Great athletic performances, unbelievable acts of courage, and other extraordinary achievements usually stem from a desire to do something for someone the person cares for deeply or for something (often an ideal) that inspires her passion. Carol Maninger, a social worker at Redwood Coast Regional Center in Clearlake Park, California, is such a person. For more than 20 years, she has dedicated her life to working to ensure that developmentally disabled people would have the chance to live a quality life and be able to live in their own homes instead of being institutionalized. "My challenge is to try to figure out a way to substitute negative behavior so that the people can be successful in the community. Success for me is seeing a person develop new, positive behavior."

- They have charted a path and stay on it to reach their goal. These highly motivated and self-directed people haven't copped out, taken a job just to get by, or been persuaded to follow someone else's path. Rather, fueled by a passion or a mission, they have allowed themselves to be divinely guided to use the gifts that they have been given for the highest good of all. Johnnie Savoy, executive director of College Bound in Cerritos, California, is such a person. She founded the organization with her husband to help African Americans, Hispanic Americans, and Native Americans get into college. "You don't take on something like this unless you have the heart for it," she says. "You have to have a real commitment to the cause and the kids. When I look into their faces, I can't give up. One of the greatest rewards I get is when I see them make it and become successful. When I see something in a kid and that kid passes my expectation, or when someone beats the odds by being accepted into the school of their choice—when they didn't think they would make it—my fulfillment is in seeing their joy." In helping others beat the odds, Johnnie, like all successful people, knows that her success comes from a strong desire—in her case to help young people get the education they need. If your desire is strong enough, you can achieve the same kind of success, too.

■ People who achieve success ultimately speak a similar language, which evolves from the spiritual strength and character they've developed by achieving a tough goal. And they project their faith by behaving in a way that shows they believe in their ability to accomplish their goals. This is why when successful people say "Yes, you can!" with such certainty, it's because they have accomplished their goals in spite of insurmountable obstacles.

■ People who achieve success go through a similar process in achieving that success. They are challenged to overcome road-blocks that seem to appear out of nowhere. Remember Kerry Strugs, the Olympic gymnast who hurt her leg in the 1996 Summer Olympics just before her final jump but jumped any-way? And took the gold medal? Clearly, a roadblock is just another challenge to a success-oriented person—something that causes her to stretch in one or more skill areas and go beyond what she thought she was capable of.

■ Successful people do not limit themselves, nor do they limit others. They know the process is ageless, timeless, nongender-specific, and colorblind—and that, fueled by a belief in their vision, enables them to set a goal at any time or any age and accomplish it.

Anyone who has accomplished a difficult goal needed the motivation to do so. Although this motivation may be different for each person, it is always something more than money. You know that you are on a plateau of success when you are motivated by your commitment and belief rather than money or glory, and you allow this motivation to take you where you want to go.

You should go as high as your motivation will carry you. And you will know how high that is by how you respond to the challenges or opportunities that will be presented to you at each step along the way. At the point that challenges become burdens and new opportunities no longer interest you, you will know that you have reached your pinnacle.

Maybe the challenges will never become burdensome, and new opportunities will always be exciting; if so, there is no limit to how high you can go.

The Responsibility at the Top

So far, I've stressed the importance of acquiring skills, developing effective networks, creating opportunities, drawing on your motivation—in short, doing all the things necessary to grasp the golden ring of success. Having reached the pinnacle of success, should you then just set yet another goal and climb higher? Should anything be different after you're there? Surely, new dimensions of your life will have opened up—a new home, cars, clothes, investments, maybe a boat or a vacation home. But still—is that all? Will all these luxuries that come with success give you true satisfaction?

I think not.

True success, with all its satisfaction and fulfillment, comes when we complete the cycle of our success by giving back to others who are struggling to reach their own goals. Actually, the higher you go, the more opportunity you will have to give back to the universe and to help others. And when it is time to give that help, you will know because people will come to you for advice. You may be asked to give on an individual basis (personally mentoring or coaching someone) or to join others in movements for social change. To continue evolving, you will have to willingly give more of yourself.

Does this mean that you are responsible for giving indiscriminately to anyone who asks for a handout? No. You are not in the business of giving handouts. It is your responsibility to give a hand—a word of encouragement, an introduction, a tip on how to do something, but not to do it for them—not to get in the way of their growth. You should be there to support their effort.

Mentoring: A Networking Nudge

As you move to increasingly higher levels, you will find yourself serving as a mentor for others. Effective mentoring is a positive way to help others—but it's serious business, says George Fraser in *Success Runs in Our Race* (published by William Morrow & Co., Inc., 1994). "As young people receive the benefits of mentoring, they grow and achieve. Their roots go deep into the community and, once established, they give back," Fraser writes.

Being a good mentor means that you endeavor to bring out the best in those you focus on. Here are seven important keys to successful mentoring, reprinted with permission of William Morrow & Co., Inc. from *Success Runs in Our Race*:

- Be attentive and listen. Once you have committed to mentoring someone, you must accept that your attentions have to be focused during mentoring sessions.

- Keep your word. Chances are, disappointment has been a big part of the lives of those you are mentoring. You must not add to those disappointments.

- Bring something to the party. Have a story to tell, an experience to relate, something intriguing to impart.

- Nurture the spirit as well as the mind. Mentor the spirit, too. Uplift the person you're mentoring.

- Put yourself in their shoes; try to understand the particular mindset of the age group and background of those whom you mentor.

- Cheerlead, encourage, praise, salute. Generally, those who seek mentors have been deprived of positive feedback. One of your biggest jobs is to give that to them.

- Don't always assume that those whom you are mentoring will get the point. Make sure they understand or see the value in what you are telling and showing them.

Let Your Help Be Color-Blind

When I attend conferences and professional meetings, I am often approached by both white people and people of color for guidance in their careers. These are the people who have had a chord struck in them by something I have said or done that provides the encouragement they need. I don't let myself be inhibited by their color or gender or by sticking to some preconceived plan that I have for helping others; I just simply respond.

Recently, I attended a community support group, looking for a way to use my services to help support its program (whose target population was mostly people of color). I made a presentation outlining the kind of service that I could provide. A young white woman in the all black group came up to me after the presentation and asked me if I would give her private counseling to help her with her career. She told me all the things she had already done and how she was stuck. She had done her homework and was not expecting something for nothing or for someone to do it for her. She simply wanted guidance, and my message had struck a chord in her; she felt that I could—and would—help her.

It is not unusual for me to be approached by a white person after a lecture or seminar, but in a presentation that was directed specifically to people of color and given to an audience that was 99 percent black, I was surprised that the message most strongly reached a white person.

It shouldn't have surprised me really, because the simple truth is that the universe is color-blind. No doubt, you've been helped along the way by white people as well as by people of color. You, in turn, must do the same. When you are led to give that help, give the person what she needs, not what you think she needs. (See "What Do You Mean by What You Say?")

Also, keep in mind that helping others does not mean that you no longer need help in accomplishing your goals—because you do. Not only will you need help, but you will also have to reach out to people who are different from you, both to ask for help and to offer your help. Part of the process of expanding, progressing, and succeeding involves learning about and interacting effectively with others.

What Do You Mean by What You Say?

To succeed, we've got to be involved with other people; we cannot do it alone. Those of us who desire to accomplish a goal need to acquire as part of our mix of skills the ability to deal successfully with others; it is our responsibility to learn how to do that.

As a diversity consultant, Roberta has wise advice about interacting with others: "I believe in the platinum rule, which is to do unto others as they would have done unto themselves. Everyone does not want to be treated the way that you want to be treated. For instance, not everyone in the corporate world would consider it a reward to be the focus of a big lunch; some cultures consider that kind of glory embarrassing. Or a Hispanic man who's offered a promotion that takes him away from his family might not see that promotion as a benefit at all, although a white male probably won't understand why the Hispanic male doesn't appreciate it. Neither one of them is wrong; it's just a case of different values and a need for communication on both sides to gain understanding."

Roberta, quoting Workforce 2000, a study conducted by the Hudson Institute,* points out that 75 percent of new entrants into the workforce in the future will be people of color, immigrants, and women. "Obviously, we cannot concentrate on just dealing effectively with the white race. We have to learn to deal with each other. We have to learn to be cognizant of what is going on and not be exclusionary. We need to understand that people in all cultures simply express themselves in ways that are comfortable for them and which may be different from the culture we know. We all need to learn to value each other and respect our differences."

"The 1992 riots in Los Angeles showed what happens when we don't reach out and try to understand one another. Blacks and Koreans were in a conflict that may have been avoided if there had been better communication between them; then perhaps the Koreans would have learned how blacks feel about their not making eye contact, and blacks would have learned that the Koreans mean no disrespect by that."

Clearly, to advance, we all need to increase our self-awareness by taking time to find out where the other person is coming from. The ability to live and work in harmony with others comes from an understanding heart.

Roberta Youtan Kay
Caucasian-American
Corporate trainer, Camarillo, California
Specialty: Cultural diversity, team building, and communications

*The Hudson Institute, an Indianapolis, Indiana, think tank, worked with the U.S. Bureau of Labor Statistics to develop Workforce 2000, a 1987 study that predicted what the workforce would look like in 2000.

MY BOTTOM LINE Reach forward with one hand to receive the new, reach back with the other hand to share what you have received. Be open always to receiving and giving that which is good.

PART FIVE
Food for Thought

Included in this section are books I have found to be helpful to me or to others I've known who are on the path of success. Some of the references I've listed here elaborate on some of the central themes in *Career Success Is Color-Blind*; others bring in totally fresh perspectives or explore areas I was only able to touch on in this book. I've arranged the resources by topic; within each topic, listings appear in alphabetic order by title, and in most cases, I provide a brief description of the listings to help you locate information quickly.

Also included in this section are a number of career web sites that I strongly encourage you to visit. These sites provide valuable guidance in creating a resume, finding job opportunities, researching specific careers, tracking the growth and development of industries in regions throughout the country (and the world), finding sources for continuing education and career development, and much, much more. Use this list as a starting point for exploring web resources. You'll find a world of information that will help advance your career.

RESOURCES

Finding Motivation

Don't Sweat the Small Stuff at Work by Richard Carson, Ph.D. (Hyperion, 1998). An easy-to-read book that provides simple ways to minimize stress and conflict while bringing out the best in yourself and others. Some contents: Dare to Be Happy; Make the Best of Boring Meetings; Don't Sweat the Bureaucracy; Home; Some "No Phone" Time at Work; and Get it Over With (my personal favorite).

Latino Success: Insights from 100 of America's Most Powerful Latino Business Professionals by Augusto Failde and William Doyle (Simon & Schuster, 1996). Gives a unique perspective on what it takes for a Hispanic person to succeed in the American business environment. The concepts in the book are universal and will be motivational to anyone. Includes information that is especially good for addressing some cultural limitations and how to overcome them.

Personal Approach: A Game Plan for Unlimited Success by Johnnie Johnson (Dove Books, 1996). Written by a former Los Angeles Rams superstar, this book offers a game plan for unlimited success. While stressing preparation and self-control, it focuses on unlocking your potential.

Choosing a Career

Do What You Are—Discover the Perfect Career for You Through the Secrets of Personality Type by Paul D. Tieger and Barbara Barron-Tieger (Little Brown, 1995). This material uses the Myers-Briggs model for determining personality type—a model used by many companies for career development. This book is especially good for people with very pronounced personality traits, traits that can be detrimental in the wrong job or environment. After taking you through a process to determine your personality type, this book offers suggested careers for a number of personality-type groups.

What Color Is Your Parachute? by Richard Nelson Bolles (Ten Speed Press, updated annually). Deals with the comprehensive process of finding a first job, as well as making a career change and finding alternative ways to work when you can't find a traditional job. Provides a process for identifying and deciding where you want to use the skills you most enjoy.

Career Sourcebooks

The American Almanac of Jobs and Salaries, 2000–2001, by John W. Wright (Avon Books). Includes information on salaries for a variety of professions and directs readers to online resources for more information. This is just one source for obtaining salary information. Because salaries fluctuate so dramatically from area to area, I suggest checking with networking contacts at three companies in your area of interest as well as with several staffing agencies. The agencies are very much up-to-date on salaries in the local area for professions they handle.

The Career Guide: Dun's Employment Opportunities Directory, Dun's Marketing Services, Dun & Bradstreet Corporation, 49 Old Bloomfield Road, Mountain Lakes, NJ 07046 (published annually in November). Lists more than 5,000 companies—with 1,000 or more employees—that may offer job opportunities in sales, marketing, management, engineering, life and physical sciences, computer science, mathematics, statistics planning, accounting and finance, liberal arts fields, and other technical and professional areas. Also lists personnel consultants and some government employers.

Dictionary of Occupational Titles, Volume 1, Fourth Edition developed by U.S. Department of Labor Employment and Training Administration (JIST Works, 1991). This is the recognized source for standardized occupational information. It provides descriptions of thousands of jobs, including such vital information as tasks performed, skills required, job locations, related careers, and working conditions.

Occupational Outlook Handbook, 2000–2001 Edition, JIST Works, (updated every two years). This standard reference includes narrative descriptions of more than 250 occupations. For each occupation, you learn about the nature of the work, the working conditions, employment opportunities, required training, advancement potential, earnings, and more.

101 Careers: A Guide to the Fastest Growing Opportunities, 2nd ed., by Michael Harkavy (John Wiley & Sons, Inc., 1998). Based on the 1997 research of the Bureau of Labor Statistics, this guide provides information on the most promising high-level jobs in today's market, while discussing tomorrow's growing job markets, as well. This is a good source of information on training requirements, working conditions, salary, regional trends, and advancement opportunities.

The Princeton Review Guide to Your Career, 3rd ed., by Alan B. Bernstein, CSW, PC, and Nicholas R. Schaffzin (Random House, 1998). A very helpful book that gives a good overview of what is required and what to expect for more than 180 professions. It highlights job requirements and salary ranges and provides self-assessment profile information for helping you identify your potential. It deals with "a day in the life" of each career, "paying your dues," and related careers. Lists major associations and employers, what to read, and the types of clients and other professionals you'll encounter.

Avenues to Education

The College Directory of Cooperative Education, edited by Stewart B. Collins (Drexel University). An excellent reference source for cooperative education programs in the United States and Canada.

Distance Learning 2000 (Peterson's, 1999). A complete sourcebook of accredited educational programs delivered electronically. The book includes a full range of degree and non-degree programs available from more than 700 American and Canadian colleges and universities. Information includes how distance education compares to more traditional programs, how programs are assessed to ensure quality, selecting the right program, the nuts and bolts of applying and registering, taking exams, transferring credits, interacting with professors and classmates, and how to locate financial aid.

Peterson's 2000 Internships The Largest Source of Internships Available (Peterson's, 1999). This excellent resource lists more than 50,000 opportunities (paid and unpaid, national and abroad) for internships in the United States and abroad. Lists hard-to-find positions from organizations such as Procter & Gamble and Amnesty International to stints with BMW of North America. Listings are conveniently organized by subject areas and include descriptions of each organization, type and number of positions available, salary (if a paid internship), eligibility, and contact information.

Virtual College by Pam Dixon (Peterson's, 1996). A concise guide to what distance education is all about, the equipment and technology know-how you'll need, time commitment and costs, what it's like being a student without a classroom, and more. A good book to read before you look at the course directories or sign up for a class.

Best Companies to Work for

The Best Companies for Minorities: Employers Across America Who Recruit, Train and Promote Minorities by Lawrence Otis Graham (Plume, 1993). This excellent resource provides a listing of companies that offer tuition reimbursement programs, and it includes guidance for evaluating a company's commitment to its employees.

The 100 Best Companies to Work for in America by Robert Levering & Milton Moskowitz (Plume, 1994). This book will help you understand the culture of many companies. The 100 companies profiled in this book are ranked by pay and benefits, opportunities, job security, pride in work and company, openness and fairness, and camaraderie and friendliness. Also noted are the biggest plus and the biggest minus of each organization. Companies tend to be competitive within their industry, so even though the company you're interested in might not be listed, it's worthwhile to note what other companies in the industry are doing.

Job Search

Best Jobs for the 21st Century by J. Michael Farr and LaVerne L. Ludden, Ed.D (JIST Works, 2000). This book rates nearly 700 jobs in America's fastest growing industries. It also includes lists of the best jobs, grouped by category, and it describes training and education requirements of careers in major industries.

Career Choice, Change & Challenge: 125 Strategies from the Experts at careerjournal.com by Deb Koen and Tony Lee (JIST Works, 2000). Get authoritative career guidance from real-life questions and answers on all aspects of job searching and career management. This book provides vital information from the online Careers Q&A column at careerjournal.com, a site used by professionals and executives worldwide for thoughtful career advice. In addition to the Q&A, features such as topic overviews and helpful checklists give you insights into tackling career-transition issues. You'll gain practical, specific ideas for applying the information to your situation.

The Complete Guide to Finding the Hottest Internet Jobs, by John Kador (McGraw Hill, 2000). This book guides you to your best fit in the Internet world and provides job descriptions, salaries, and all the information needed to access the field. Offers a web site as well for additional information.

The Directory of Executive Recruiters 2000 (Kennedy Publications, 1999). An excellent source for agencies that handle permanent placement. The information is organized both alphabetically and functionally. The directory has a listing of more than 4,100 offices nationwide, representing almost 3,000 contingency and retainer search firms.

The Directory of Executive Temporary Placement Firms (Kennedy Publications). One of the newer and more valuable employment directories, which lists more than 225 firms that place executives in short-term positions.

Job Offer! A How-To Negotiation Guide by Maryanne L. Wegerbauer (JIST Works, 2000). Designed to guide both the hiring manager and the successful job applicant through the final, critical pre-employment step—

negotiating the conditions of the job offer. Will help stimulate communication between potential employees and employers by exploring the many facets of the conditions to employment, including job design, pay, benefits to education, training, community involvement, and social programs.

Job Search Handbook for People with Disabilities, by Daniel J. Ryan, Ph.D. (JIST Works, 2000). This guide offers sound advice for finding the right career field, negotiating for special accommodations, continuing education, networking, finding a mentor, and self-promotion.

101 Great Answers to the Toughest Job Search Problems by Ollie Stevenson (Career Press, 1995). There are times when you will follow all the proper steps in your job search and nothing seems to work—because you have a unique situation or problem. I wrote this book to help with those problems in any area of the job search. It addresses such dilemmas as age, qualifications, race, gender, salary, relocation, handicaps, and so on.

303 Off-the-Wall Ways to Get a Job by Brandon Toropov (Career Press, 1995). When you cannot seem to get to the right job no matter how much you try with traditional methods, then it's time to be creative. This book offers real methods used by real people who've obtained real results by using all kinds of methods to get that right job—from cornering decision makers during plane flights to making a name for themselves in the organization by working for free. One approach I liked was to find out who got the job you went after and ask that person about the leads they didn't follow through on. Obviously, the innovative approach you try has to be something that fits your personality, but the book may give you some ideas.

Where the Jobs Are: The Hottest Careers for the 21st Century, by Joyce Hadley (Career Press, 2000). This book provides information on salary levels, skills, and education required, as well as the largest employers in the field and advancement opportunities.

Networking

Networking for Everyone! Connecting with People for Career and Job Success by Michelle Tullier, Ph.D. (JIST Works, 1998). This book provides valuable information about how to find and cultivate a personal career support network. Case studies let you learn from real examples of people who've built successful career networks. It also includes extensive lists of

books, web sites, career and business advisors, and professional organizations that will help you build your own networking skills.

Power Networking, by Marc Kramer (VGM Career Horizons, 1998). This book is about using the contacts you don't even know you have to succeed in the job you want. It includes keys to being a great networker, networking to find a job, networking at different corporate levels, maintaining networking relationships, networking through the Internet, and much more.

Résumés and Cover Letters

101 Best Résumés, by Jay A. Block & Michael Betrus (McGraw Hill, 1999). Addresses skills assessment and provides a variety of résumé styles. Outlines a five-step process for résumé writing and provides good guidelines for cover letters and broadcast letters. Includes sample résumés in 70 categories, from students to general managers, in a variety of industries. This book discusses how to create effective electronic and online résumés, and it shows how to capitalize on military experience, networking, and salary negotiations.

Gallery of Best Cover Letters by David F. Noble, Ph.D. (JIST Works, 2000). Step-by-step instructions on how to build an effective cover letter and pair it with the right résumé. Contains samples from the country's best professional résumé writers!

The Quick Résumé and Cover Letter Book, 2nd edition, by J. Michael Farr (JIST Works, 2000). Friendly, easy-to-follow advice for creating effective résumés and cover letters and more than 60 professionally written sample résumés. Learn how to write a résumé and cover letter in less time!

Résumés for College Students and Recent Graduates with Sample Cover Letters the by Editors of VGM Career Horizons (VGM Career Horizons).

Résumé Magic by Susan Britton Whitcomb (JIST Works, 1999). Packed with before-and-after examples, this books shows you how to take an average résumé and turn it into a masterpiece. Reveals how to create résumés that attract top companies. Almost 600 pages of expert advice!

The Wall Street Journal's National Business Employment Weekly on Résumés by Taunee S. Besson (John Wiley & Sons). A variety of excellent examples of résumés for all levels of job seeker.

Interviewing Skills

Get It Together by 30...and Be Set for the Rest of Your Life by Richard D. Thau and Jay S. Heflin (AMACOM, 1997). Includes how to interview for internships, tips on networking, temping, résumés, cover letters, interviewing, rules for the office, and the art of self-promotion.

Interview Power: Selling Yourself Face to Face by Tom Washington (Mount Vernon Press, 2000). This book lists 101 tough interview questions and the best answers; it also provides good suggestions for salary negotiation.

60 Seconds & You're Hired by Robin Ryan (Penguin USA, 2000). This book suggests answers plus employers' reasoning behind 70 of the toughest questions that could be asked during the interview. It also includes tough questions for college students and new grads and gives examples of illegal questions.

The Wall Street Journal's National Employment Weekly on Interviewing, 3rd ed., by Arlene S. Hirsch (John Wiley & Sons, 1999). A compilation of superb tips for the interviewing process.

Interpersonal Skills Development

How to Say It at Work by Jack Griffin (Prentice Hall Press, 1998). This book will help you avoid the common verbal and nonverbal pitfalls that can derail your career. You will learn to overcome hostility, unfairness, and indifference...yours and others. This book may provide insight about why you've been stuck at your company or unable to move forward. Good help for communicating with subordinates, peers, and superiors.

Mentoring: The Tao of Giving and Receiving Wisdom by Chungliang A. Huang and Jerry Lynch (HarperCollins, 1995). This book outlines easy-to-understand principles that incorporate the Taoist teachings of self-reflection, simplicity, openness to others, and sharing to have mutually beneficial relationships. This is a great book that leaves the spirit feeling grounded and assured. It is perfect as a guide for developing characteristics that support the cooperation and team building necessary to move ahead in the new business world of self-directed work teams.

Personal Job Power: Discover Your Own Power Style for Work Satisfaction and Success by Clay Carr and Valorie Beer (Peterson's, 1996). This book explores seven different power styles you'll find at work and explains how to use them to enrich your own potential. It also shows you how to recognize the power style of others so that you can work with them more effectively.

Personality Types: Using the Eneagram for Self-Discovery by Don Richard Riso (Houghton Mifflin Company, 1995). The technique put forward in this book breaks personality types into nine categories and helps you understand your strengths and weaknesses and the impact of your personality. This material will help you make adjustments, if necessary, to get along better with others. It offers good information in a format that's easy to follow.

We've Got to Start Meeting Like This! by Roger K. Mosvick & Robert B. Nelson, (JIST Works, 1996). This book emphasizes upgrading your leadership skills so you can hold better meetings and get better results. A good look at effective ways to plan and conduct meetings.

Life and Career Change

Build Your Own Rainbow—A Workbook for Career and Life Management by Barrie Hopson and Mike Scally (Pfeiffer & Company, 1995). This book guides you through a personal inventory to determine your present level of satisfaction and shows you how to achieve and maintain a sense of fulfillment throughout your life.

The End of Work: The Decline of the Global Labor Force and the Dawn of the Post-Market Era by Jeremy Rifkin (Tarcher/Putnam, 1995). This book provides help in directing your thinking when creating your new job. It deals with the reality of the changing business arena, new technology, and how we fit into all this. Because everything is becoming more productive, it encourages people to get on top of the new technology or be left behind.

Finding Your Perfect Work: The New Career Guide to Making a Living, Creating a Life by Paul and Sarah Edwards (J.P. Tarcher, 1996). If making a career change means working on your own, this book can show you how to blend your personal goals and dreams with the practical realities of having your own business. Intertwined in the book are the essential points you need to decide upon and factor in to any good business plan. Includes real-life examples of people who successfully implemented a plan for their own businesses.

Going to Plan B—How You Can Cope, Regroup and Start Your Life on a New Path by Nancy K. Schlossberg and Susan Porter Robinson (Fireside, 1996). This book shows what to do when nothing happens but everything changes. Deals with how to recast your career goals to accommodate today's radically changed workplace and how to reconcile an unrealistic self-image and find inner peace. Also deals with letting go of old ideas and dreams and reshaping the dream.

Survive & Profit from a Mid-Career Change by Daniel Moreau (Random House, 1996). Geared specifically toward people working in companies that are downsized, this book provides a good model for examining yourself, your job, and your career before making a change.

Quality of Life, How to Get it, How to Keep It, by Shauna Ries and Genna Murphy (Eagle Brook, 1999). Wonderful book for a person seeking to change her life. Good reading for those in a job that's eating away at their passion and aliveness. This book will help you evaluate where you are in life and how to make changes to enjoy life more. Great for getting out of a rut.

Where Do I Go from Here? An Inspirational Guide to Making Authentic Career & Life Choices by Kenneth C. Ruge (McGraw-Hill, 1998). A good book for those contemplating a major life change and those who are feeling they are not living the life they are truly meant to lead or not using the gifts and talents they were given. This book will help you let go of limiting beliefs, conquer fear, listen to your own inner voice, and learn to translate your insights into a more satisfying and life-affirming path.

Women in Career & Life Transitions by Sandy Anderson (JIST Works, 2000). A nuts-and-bolts guide specially designed to help women define and pursue a desirable work/life path. Steers women through the obstacle courses encountered during major life changes. Helps women define where they are now—and how to get where they want to be. Anecdotes, real-life stories, and exercises advance readers step by step through strategies for overcoming personal obstacles and achieving personal goals.

Workforce 2000: The Revolution Reshaping American Business by Joseph H. Boyett and Henry P. Conn (Dutton, 1992). An excellent book to help you understand the changes in business and better determine how you can fit in. It offers valuable personal guidance and charts the education, skills, and attitudes that positions in the new workplace will demand.

Help for a Stalled Career

Women Breaking Through: Overcoming the Final 10 Obstacles at Work by Deborah J. Swiss (Peterson's/Pacesetter Books, 1996). This book provides advice for any woman who has ever felt her career stalled just because she was born female. Swiss outlines strategies for overcoming the remaining obstacles to fair treatment and equal opportunity at work. It contains good advice for both genders.

Renegotiating and Advancing Your Career

How to Become CEO, The Rules for Rising to the Top of Any Organization by Jeffrey J. Fox (Hyperion, 1998). Seventy-five simply written and to-the-point rules for advancing within a corporation. Some of these rules are excellent.

How to Manage Your Boss by Roger Fritz and Kristie Kennard (Career Press, 1994). This book provides tips on working with your boss to get the support for the things you want to do. An excellent aid for the person who wants to make a pitch to renegotiate a current job.

Rites of Passage at $100,000+: The Insider's Lifetime Guide to Executive Job-Changing and Faster Career Progress in the 21st Century, by John Lucht (Holt & Co., 2000). This is a very upscale approach to the job search. Covers everything from clothes to the style of pen you should carry—and why. A great guide for that executive who has grown beyond the job and needs to make a change but doesn't know how—and may not even realize that he or she needs to make a change. (Lucht also has a comprehensive workbook of the same title supporting this book, which includes information on taxes, outplacement, and negotiating an ideal employment contract.)

Internet Job Search

Cyberspace Job Search Kit by Fred Jandt and Mary Nemnich (JIST Works, updated annually). Descriptions of thousands of Internet sites make it easy for users to decide which sites best suit their needs. Up-to-date information on electronic résumé preparation, including how to incorporate photographs and audio with a résumé.

Cyberspace Resume Kit by Fred Jandt and Mary Nemnich (JIST Works, updated annually). Includes easy steps for converting paper résumés into technically sound electronic files; explains multimedia attributes, including graphics, sound, and interactivity. Includes real-life examples!

The Quick Internet Guide to Career and Education Information, updated annually, by Anne Wolfinger (JIST Works, 2000). The author has reviewed thousands of job search and career-related Internet sites and in this book provides you with 350 of the best she's found. This book is helpful for both beginners and experienced Internet users, with good information on finding the best job-related web sites and exploring career alternatives, instructional programs, temporary employment, and volunteer opportunities online.

Job Search Web Sites

America's Job Bank (maintained by the U.S. Department of Labor)
http://www.ajb.dni.us

The Black Collegian Job Assistance Selection Service
http://www.black-collegian.com

Business/Employment Department of Labor
http://www.careers.org/

CareerBuilder
http://www.careerbuilder.com
Jobs all over the place. Just started a cooperative network with 16 other sources to give you a one-stop entry to all these sources.

CareerExpress
http://www.careerexpress.com
Distributes your résumé to thousands of employers and recruiters.

CareerMosaic
http://www.careermosaic.com

CareerPath
http://www.careerpath.com
Newspaper ads from many major cities in the United States.

CareerWeb
http://www.careerweb.com

DICE
http://www.dice.com
High-tech jobs for computer specialists.

Future Step
http://www.futurestep.com
Korn/Ferry International, a leading executive search firm, working with
Wall Street Journal Interactive. Executive search service for management
professionals.

Headhunters
http://www.headhunters.com
All kinds of jobs in all fields. No listing is more than 45 days old. Use the
form to set your search parameters, but you can leave keywords, salary, and
location boxes empty.

Leaders Online
http://www.leadersonline.com
Complete end-to-end online recruiting solution. Integrates proactive sourc-
ing, candidate tracking, workflow, and background verifications.

Careers.Org
http://www.careers.org
A meta-list of online job-services

Monster.com
http://www.monster.com
Where some of the hottest companies are advertising right now.

My Job Search
http://www.myjobsearch.com
Organizes the entire online employment sphere for the convenience of job
seekers. It links to human resource departments at Fortune 500 companies,
all the major recruiting firms grouped into 45 different fields, and all newspaper classified ad sections available in the United States.

Recruiters Online
http://www.recruitersonline.com
Executive recruiters and search firms. Hot Jobs list open searches being
conducted.

The Riley Guide—Directory of employment resources
http://www.jobtrak.com

6 Figure Jobs
http://www.6figurejobs.com
Provides experienced professionals the opportunity to confidentially seek
and be considered for some of the most prestigious jobs in the country.

Yahoo Careers
http://www.yahoo.com
Yahoo Careers—For a job search, enter the city, state, or ZIP code you are
targeting. You then see a form targeted to this location, allowing you to do
a more specific search. The target will be the metro region. Yahoo
Company Job Listings has direct links to company career and job pages.

Reference Material

Available at libraries and career centers. You can access some material
online by using standard call letters and the title of the reference.

> *The American Almanac of Jobs and Salaries*
> *The Career Guide: Dun's Employment Opportunities Directory*
> *Directory of Industry Data Sources*
> *Directory of U.S. Labor Organizations*
> *Dun & Bradstreet's Reference Book of Corporate Management*
> *Dun & Bradstreet's Million Dollar Directory*
> *Encyclopedia of Associations*
> *Encyclopedia of Career and Vocational Guidance*
> *Moody's Manuals*
> *National Trade and Professional Associations of the United States*
> *Occupational Outlook Handbook*
> *Standard and Poor's Register of Corporations, Directors, and
> Executives*
> *Thomas Register*
> *U.S. Industrial Directory*

FINAL THOUGHTS

The true beauty of career success is that it's what you define it to be. And how you get there will be uniquely your journey. Here are some clues to whether you're going in the right direction: You know you have chosen the right career if...

- You truly are enjoying every aspect of the journey.
- You have not been deterred in the pursuit of your career by race, culture, gender, or disability.
- You are so inspired that obstacles seem only like opportunities to excel.
- When others look at what is before you and say "How can you?," you say "How can I not?"

You might know this level of commitment a step at a time, a job at a time. For some, the whole goal will be clear and always in sight. We are all different; therefore there will always be many variations on the theme of success. That's part of the beauty of getting there. So take no one's absolute word as the only way to go. Take information in and add it to the pot of your own imagination and creativity. And always, always trust your instincts and the spirit that guides you. Good Luck!

INDEX